D1519653

Feminism in Search of an Identity

Feminism in Search of an Identity

The Indian Context

Edited by

Meena Kelkar

Deepti Gangavane

RAWAT PUBLICATIONS

Jaipur and New Delhi

ISBN 81-7033-759-3
© Contributors, 2003

No part of this book may be reproduced or transmitted in any form or by any means, electronic or mechanical, including photocopying, recording or by any information storage and retrieval system, without permission in writing from the publishers.

Published by
Prem Rawat for *Rawat Publications*
Satyam Apts., Sector 3, Jain Temple Road, Jawahar Nagar, Jaipur - 4 (India)
Phone: 0141 265 1748 / 7006 Fax: 0141 265 1748
E-mail : info@rawatbooks.com
Website: rawatbooks.com

Delhi Office
G-4, 4832/24, Ansari Road, Daryaganj, New Delhi 110 002
Phone: 011-23263290

Typeset by Rawat Computers, Jaipur
Printed at Chaman Enterprises, New Delhi

Contents

Foreword

This volume is an outcome of a research project undertaken initially by Dr. Meena Kelkar and carried further by Dr. Deepti Gangavane of the Department of Philosophy, University of Pune. About twelve years ago the University Grants Commission honoured the department by according the status of Departmental Special Assistance (DSA). Under its first phase the department undertook various research projects. Towards the end of the first phase some faculty members began taking active interest in the newly emerging feminist studies. This process was further facilitated by the late Professor R. Sundara Rajan, the then Head of Department, by way of informal discussions with the faculty as well as by way of giving formal lectures on suitable occasions. Accordingly, in the second phase of the DSA programme a research project titled *Feminism in Search of an Identity: The Indian Context* was undertaken by Dr. Meena Kelkar. At a later stage Dr. Deepti Gangavane joined it as co-investigator. The project is devoted to a dialogue with the Indian tradition in its manifold appearance with the objective of searching for theoretical possibilities available within the tradition itself that may serve as a new vantage point in the struggle for the empowerment of women.

With this objective in mind, Dr. Kelkar and Dr. Gangavane have structured the project around various themes, perspectives and concerns in terms of which the issue of the identity of women and Indian tradition appears and reappears itself. The various contributions in this volume are arranged, outwardly chronologically, but thematically from within, by way of tracing and critiquing the development and dynamism which the tradition allegedly seeks to offer. The historical and the critical understanding of tradition must be dialogical in character. The editors of this volume are well aware that theirs is neither the first nor the last instance of such a dialogue. It, as they rightly observe, is an ongoing process and it is in and through such a process that any tradition remains a living source for knowledge and inspiration. The editors also believe that the dialectic of criticism and appreciation provides a wide spectrum for the creation of a new sensibility to understand feminism. I hope that the volume receives the critical notice of scholars and readers interested in feminist studies.

Prof. Sharad Deshpande
Co-ordinator, DSA Programme
Department of Philosophy
University of Pune

Acknowledgements

The present volume has evolved from a study of the Indian tradition from the gender perspective. This study was carried out in the second phase of the Departmental Special Assistance Programme of the Department of Philosophy, University of Pune. As this volume is a result of team work it is our privilege to thank all the scholars who have contributed to it. Without their active participation, it would not have been possible for us to bring out this volume in its present form. Our special thanks are due to the late Professor R. Sundara Rajan, the then Head of Department of Philosophy, for initiating discussions in feminist theory. Many of us in the department were benefited by his insightful lectures. We are equally grateful to the present co-ordinator of the Departmental Special Assistance Programme, Prof. Sharad Deshpande for incorporating this project into the second phase of the programme and for his cooperation, encouragement and keen interest in the completion and publication of this project. We take this opportunity to thank all our colleagues in the department for being very helpful throughout the tenure of the project. We also thank the non-teaching staff of the department for their assistance at various stages of the project.

Meena Kelkar
Deepti Gangavane

Introduction

The question of identity presupposes an awareness of one's own existence as a person having positive self-image and the ability to think. When raised with reference to women, the question acquires many new dimensions. Empowerment becomes an important issue because women lack power. Many times it is said that women lack physical power and this is justified by biological theories. The lack of power at the socio-political, intellectual, moral and spiritual level is justified by referring to many theories in the respective areas of knowledge. The question becomes critical because at the existential level women do not have a right to be born and consequently a right to live. Their having any kind of right presupposes the basic right to live. The denial of this right is the result of the acceptance of cultural normative values that form and regulate the individual and social life. Empowerment of women thus centers around the search for those belief-systems, doctrines and presuppositions, which have provided foundation to our form of life. It is concerned with both the theoretical and practical aspects of human inquiry. Both the aspects are interdependent. Sometimes the struggle for empowerment at the level of practice leads to the modification or even overthrow of a theory. For example, the struggle of Indian women for equal treatment has made them sensitive to modern theories that endorse the inferior status of women. It has given them an opportunity to deconstruct all those theories and has created a possibility of evolving new theories. Similarly, struggle for freedom on the part of women in the West has opened new ways of understanding epistemology, ethics and politics. They have questioned the standard definition of human being in terms of rationality and have explored the hidden logic behind distinctions of nature/culture, rationality/emotion, universal/particular, mind/matter and such others.

On the other hand, development of theory also has influenced the practical aspects of life. The theory that woman has equal rights and a right over her body and mind has made women aware of the exploitation they had to experience and it has at least evoked a possibility of awakening their minds. Similarly, the radical feminist theories also have brought considerable changes in the lives of Western women.

If we grant that theory and practice are so interdependent, then we can understand the necessity of bridging a gap between the means of empowerment and the justificatory theories that provide foundation to all such attempts. At this stage, it is necessary to acknowledge the contributions by activists all over the world to the cause of liberation of women vis-à-vis the empowerment of women. However, as noted earlier, the removal of obstructive socio-political conditions should be supplemented by adequate re-understanding or even by overthrowing of the present theoretical frameworks. All such attempts to theorize presuppose and depend on understanding the nature of the world and ourselves. In other words, unless there is a definite perspective towards the world in general, theorizing has no meaning. Evolving the horizons of meaning where women perform the function of giving meaning becomes the primary need for feminism. For this, empowerment at the level of thought becomes indispensable.

There is an awareness in the Indian feminist discourse regarding the limitations of approaches that try to impose non-indigenous concepts and frameworks on the studies of problems of empowerment of women in India. If these problems are the outcome of the Indian historical conditions, perhaps their solutions will also emerge from a reconsideration of those conditions. It would be definitely unwise to turn our back to tradition considering it as a dead weight, without investigating it properly and thoroughly.

What follows in the pages to come, is the humble beginning of a dialogue with tradition with the objective of searching for theoretical possibilities available within the tradition that may serve as new vantage points in the struggle for empowerment.

We are well aware of the fact that this is neither the first nor the last instance of a dialogue with tradition. Such a dialogue is an ongoing process and it is in fact in and through such a process that any tradition remains a living source for knowledge and inspiration. There are moments in history when a need for reappraising the tradition is strongly felt. We believe that we are witnessing such a moment right now.

Such a need was also experienced during the period of British colonization of India. The Indian renaissance movement was obviously not ignorant about women's problems and its connections with the socio-cultural history of India. In fact significant achievements regarding re-evaluation as well as re-appropriation of tradition coupled with actual attempts to rid women of miserable conditions are to be found in this period. Feminist discourse in India cannot afford to neglect the contributions of eminent personalities like Mahatma Phule, Raja Ram Mohan Roy, Agarkar, Mahatma Gandhi and Babasaheb Ambedkar in this regard. We must confess, that a major lacuna in this book is an absence of any discussion of the views of these thinkers. However, we are happy to have once again initiated the dialogue and hope that it will be continued by all of us in various ways.

The first article in this collection is co-authored by Meena Kelkar and Deepti Gangavane. It addresses itself to the concepts of identity and empowerment, pointing out the connections between the two. It underlines the importance of freedom and discusses various senses of the term. Finally, it suggests that in ancient Indian thought, the question of identity is never treated in individualistic terms. The basic objective of this article is to provide some theoretical reflections regarding feminist discourse with special reference to India. With the same objective in mind the scholars who have contributed to this project discuss various systems of thought within the Indian tradition. Their contributions are arranged in a chronological manner. Starting with the image of woman in the Vedic period, tracing the development and dynamism within the tradition during the Middle Ages, the dialogue momentarily culminates into an analysis of the portrayal of woman in popular culture, viz. contemporary Hindi cinema.

In her article Sucheta Paranjape states how the exalted position of woman was characteristic to Rgvedic period. She argues that in this period, the description of the female body was within the limits of decency but these limits were transgressed in later literary works. She points out that the high status and position of woman slowly became less important and the Vedic insights were totally ignored.

Nirmala Kulkarni shows how the complimentary role of woman in Vedic rituals was rejected in the period of *Satpatha Brahmana*. She explains this with special reference to the *pravargya* ritual. Both these articles highlight the fact that the primitive, simple form of life that was nearer to nature did not contain any derogatory references to womanhood but along with the ritualistic pattern of life, the degrading forces came into existence and that resulted in the lowering of the status of woman.

Mangala Athalye attempts the examination of some images of woman. She states that the ideal and exemplary image of Draupadi has another side to it. She also describes the images of Amba, Suvarchala, Panchchuda and Sulbha, which are deviant, neglected images, and yet are significant from the modern point of view.

Meena Kelkar argues that the model of *Beeja-Ksetra* is at the back of male-domination. This model was treated as if it was a scientific truth and later on it percolated into literature, customs and practices. In her article on man-woman relationship she suggests that even within the male-dominated discourse there is a possibility of progressive transcendence in terms of a better attitude towards woman. The same discourse contains the *Brahma-Maya* model that denies any status to woman, the *Purusa-Prakriti* model that grants independent existence to woman and the *Siva-Sakti* model opens up a new form of life wherein woman is respected. Both the glorified and the denigrated versions highlight new areas of research.

Lata Chhatre handles the issue of empowerment of women from the Buddhist perspective. She argues that there is a gap between the theoretical and the practical aspects of empowerment due to what the Buddhists call the *klesavarana* and *jneyavarana*. She further suggests that for solving the problem of women's empowerment, it is necessary to transcend the dualistic model and to accept that each individual is an aggregation of *panchaskandha*.

Nirmala Kulkarni describes the concept of woman in the Jaina philosophy with special reference to Prabhacandra Suri. She traces the concept of identity of woman in Prabhacandra on the cultural-historical background of his time. She points out that the denial of woman's individuality and of her rights in the material and spiritual realms that we find here was continued for centuries.

Vaijayanti Arun Belsare brings out the nature and significance of gender perspective and uses it as a methodological tool to explore the presuppositions and principles underlying the doctrine of *purusartha*, which is supposed to be one of the basic doctrines that constitute the Indian ethos.

Radhika Seshan addresses herself to the question of identity and relates this question to the life and work of three medieval women saints -- Auvaiyyar, Akkamahadevi and Mirabai. She makes a significant conceptual distinction between 'being deviant' and 'being different' and suggests that the rebellious spirit of these saints was socially appropriated in such a manner that their dissent was subsumed within the tradition of *Bhakti* movement.

Vidyut Bhagwat deals with the understanding of womanhood in the writings of woman saints of Maharashtra. She concentrates on man-woman relationship in the writings of Janabai, Muktabai and other such women saints. She brings to light the marginalized literature, which has an emancipatory potential for feminism. Adopting the insider's point of view she presents the unique contributions of these women saints by quoting their own words along with her own views about it.

Shantishree Pandit in her contribution presents deliberations of a 19th century reformist movement in South India. She highlights Periyar's contribution in providing a non-western framework to gender identity from below. Periyar has brought out the connections between the hegemonic *Brahmanical* discourse on the one hand and patriarchy and caste system on the other hand. Shantishree suggests that Periyar's reconstruction of the feminine in the private and the public sphere is a useful framework for situating the women's movement in India.

The last article takes up a significant yet rather neglected issue of the role of media in constructing the image of a woman. We believe that in contemporary times, the audio-visual medium such as cinema plays an influential role in the formation of the identity of today's woman. Shyamala Vanarase provides a very illuminating analysis of the visual images and the ideological messages presented by popular cinema. She rightly insists on the need for having critical equipment in order to resist the tremendous force of what she calls the "Grand Reduction Sale".

All these attempts could be seen as exercises in the methodology of dialogue. The dialogic communication with tradition takes two forms. Sometimes it ends up in providing a focus on those areas which are neglected and marginalized. Sometimes the dialogue results in the new hermeneutics of the discourse. The critical and the explorative awareness initiate freedom from the restrictive forces which have captivated thousands of minds and it also encourages freedom to construct new images of womanhood. The question of identity thus is not a search for something that is already given but search for those pointers, which will allow us to establish a new relationship with our own tradition. The dialectic of criticism and appreciation will provide a wide spectrum for the creation of a new sensibility to understand feminism and will remove our prejudice to look at it as an imported, fanciful ideology borrowed from the West.

Meena Kelkar
Deepti Gangavane

1

Identity, Freedom, and Empowerment: Some Theoretical Reflections

Meena Kelkar and Deepti Gangavane

The issue of empowerment of women, which is a central concern for feminism, is conceptually interconnected with the concepts of identity and freedom. Unless and until the possibility of having a stable identity and freedom is assumed, all deliberations regarding empowerment become redundant. The concept of identity is crucially important as it provides a locus for freedom and fulfils a precondition of empowerment. Thus, the feminist discourse, in general, has to take up the question of identity. Moreover, when one deals with a localized feminist discourse the problem of localized, i.e., culture specific identities becomes relevant. The feminist discourse in India can be seen as such a localized discourse. However, it is not entirely bound by its cultural context and the potentialities of transcending this are inherently present in it. Nonetheless, one way to understand this discourse is to see the way in which the question of identity is discussed at both the theoretical and practical level.

However, raising the problem of identity of women, and that too within a particular context, may seem to be a regressive step in this era which is well aware of the postmodern criticism of essentialism. In raising it, are we not going back in search of essences and thus exposing ourselves to the tyranny of those rigid categories, all over again? In order to respond to such an objection, it needs to be seen whether accepting identity necessitates acceptance of essences. Further, it can also be asked whether it is desirable to give up the notion of identity altogether especially in a theoretical discourse such as the feminist discourse which originates from and leads to certain social practices.

It must be emphasized at the outset that the concept of identity that is being evolved here, is not essentialistic, because it is neither rigid nor static. A little reflection over the process of identification reveals the possibility of evolving such a concept. It is through the process of description, that a thing or a person is identified as having some peculiar characteristics, some relations with other things or persons. In principle, it is possible for any individual (thing or person) to have a fairly large number of characteristics and relations. In practice, only some of these are used for describing the identity of an individual and ascribing a name to it. This seemingly innocent process of description is transformed later on into a normative claim leading to a philosophical distinction between essential properties and accidental properties. The stipulated set of essential characteristics sets a standard for correct application of a given name to an identified individual.

Strictly speaking, descriptions are open ended in the sense of not presuming absolutely determinate boundaries of an individual. Every description involves evaluation in so far as it is a choice of one particular set of characteristics from among various possible sets. This choice is based on needs and interests of those who choose. Partially at least, then descriptions are conventional. When this point is lost sight of, the description tends to crystallize and what is conventional is seen as being natural in the process towards essentialization. Henceforward, differences from the so-called essential nature of individuals are seen as deviations, which need to be accounted for and possibly regulated.

The process towards essentialization is not without its own telos. The need to characterize an individual in one particular way rather than another is rooted in the prevailing interests, perceived problems and anticipated solutions. An entire structure of values, norms and standards is constructed to guard those interests. The internalization of these values through socialization at times appears so complete that the perception of one's identity from within matches totally with its artificial construction from without. Although a process of transition from neutral description to essentialization can be seen in all cultures, the particular form that the essentialization takes and the conceptual normative structure that underlies it, is culture specific. In other words, the process of essentialization, which uses the language of a 'true woman' or 'a real woman', is culture transcending, but the product, i.e., the actual content of this idea of 'true' or 'real' woman is culture specific. It is an outcome of a complex interaction among various social, political, economic and ideological forces and conditions peculiar to that culture. Thus, to understand the product is partially at least to understand the forces and conditions responsible for its emergence.

The critique of essentialism has made us aware of the need for being extremely cautious about any essentializing vocabulary. It is a very brisk step from the dissolution of essences that this critique invites to the dissolution of identities of any kind. It seems as if the death of the essences, is at the same time the death of identities as well. To accept such a view is to accept that there can be no identities, without essences. Such a claim has to face some serious difficulties. First of all, a total, complete dissolution of identities does not seems possible, for they are those indispensable elements of our language, thought and knowledge, that have meaning and use and unless and until we find something to replace them or else drastically change the structure of language and thought, no communication is possible.

Further, if the bond between identity and essences can be broken, it will be possible to have identities that are not essentialized. Obviously, the way in which this can be done, consists in understanding identities, basically as descriptions which are used conventionally as conceptual tools. It must be noted that, there is no need to fall back upon nominalism and invite the problems associated with it, in the attempt of escaping the problems of essentialism. For, though the descriptions are conventional, they are not totally arbitrary, but are based on resemblances and differences that exist among objects of description. If there is no such ontological base, either all descriptions and identities become purely arbitrary, or we are left with some kind of bare particulars, i.e., particulars stripped of all descriptions of their qualitative particularities and left possibly only with numerical identities.

The identities, seen as conventional descriptions based on ontological resemblances then do not become rigid and determinate like essences. They remain fluid, plastic, and capable of being moulded and remoulded in the changing contexts of needs, interests and purposes.

In the case of identity of women, the ontological resemblances are of course basically biological in nature. However, what is more significant for the feminist discourse is the gender identity which is fundamentally a social construct. It must be noted that what differentiates gender identity and racial identity from other types of identities in terms of religion, class, caste, nationality, etc., is the fact that the former have a biological base. Gender discrimination is basically rooted in this biological base. For example, the ways in which the role of women in reproduction is perceived, evaluated and manipulated for different purposes forms a major part of women subjugation. Although technological advancements have posed many challenges to the understanding of female contribution in reproduction and the associated practices, the basic biological division among male and female remains intact.

Thus, at the present stage of scientific and technological development at least, it seems that gender identity cannot be totally separated from the biological one. In fact, rejecting the latter is not required, what is required is the rejection of the all too evident hierarchy involved. If hierarchy is a social construct, it has to be countered at the social level itself.

The second question about the notion of identity that was posed in the beginning, i.e., the question regarding desirability of giving up the notion of identity can now be addressed more confidently and comfortably in the light of the preceding discussion. If the possibility of having identities without essentializing them is accepted, a major theoretical obstacle is removed for the feminist discourse, which basically is oriented towards the issue of women's empowerment. Any struggle for empowerment originates in the felt need to empower a particular group. Such a need obviously presupposes that there is a group which lacks power and the first step in the struggle for empowerment involves strategic attempts for removing the obstructive social, economic, political conditions and these conditions seem to be changing for different groups that lack power within a society. Naturally, the politics of empowerment has to be sensitive to the differences among these groups. The identity of a group to be empowered is defined in terms of the similarities and differences it has with other groups, both powerless as well as powerful.

In fact, the very logic of the concept of identity leads us not just to commonalties shared by all members of a group, but also to the differences that exist between them and the members of the other groups. This should not lead one to believe that any particular group is completely homogeneous. For the kind of interplay of similarities and differences that operates at the level of group, also operates at the level of the individuals. Coming specifically to the issue of empowerment of women and that of gender identity, it can be said that gender discrimination and subordination of women resulting from it is the basic characteristic with reference to which an identity is bestowed on women as a group to be empowered. The particular form and extent of discrimination and subordination may change not only from society to society, but also within a single society depending on various conditions. This form is something that can be identified through the concepts, values, norms, standards, institutes and practices in which it is manifested.

Over and above the assumption of identity of the group that lacks power, the theories and movements of empowerment rest on another assumption, i.e., assumption of freedom as an all important characteristic of human nature. Without such an assumption, we are thrown into the abyss of blind or semi-blind social forces interacting with each other, without any sense of directionality. If we shun from explicitly holding to the assumption regarding freedom, it is very difficult to assign any profound meaning or value to any struggle for empowerment or any attempt to change and improve the existing conditions.

The question of freedom or empowerment can be significantly discussed in the anthropocentric world. The anthropocentric world refers to reality that is constructed and built by human beings. At the basis of this world lies the human ability to know, act and enjoy. Unless human beings know, and act they cannot establish any relation or any contact with the world around. It is through the medium of knowledge and action that they relate to the world; while establishing contact with the world, they create a new world. The question which becomes important is: "Do women participate in making this world of culture by becoming knowers, actors and enjoyers?" If we look at the history, we find that these roles have been denied to them because the normative theory of human life which determines these roles, is at the basic level founded on social hierarchy. So one has to question the root cause of their being denied the right to know and act. For this, clarity at the level of thought is essential. Empowerment in this context is an achievement of the right to know. Knowledge does not mean information (or knowing what) or just theoretical knowledge, but that knowledge which makes them aware of their own existence as real human beings. It is that which liberates one from the old fetters of thoughts and provides wings to thoughts. At this level, it is essential to know what one is -- what is one's identity. Unless men and women are free they cannot achieve the right to know.

Freedom to know, act and enjoy is a basic postulate of the socio-cultural world. Freedom is usually understood as freedom from exploitation, injustice and such other evils. Sometimes it also signifies capacity to do something, to take independent decisions. The feminist theories have concentrated on these two senses of freedom and have related the issue of freedom to the notion of gendered identity. Hence, the issue of empowerment first and foremost initiates a search for one's identity on the part of women.

Both the senses of freedom -- "freedom from" and "freedom to" presuppose that freedom is something to be achieved, to be demanded or to be given. In order to attain freedom to live one's life the way one wants, empowerment at the basic level is always in terms of "freedom to" or "freedom from". Yet, there is one more way of understanding freedom. Freedom understood in this way, is not something that is constructed by culture. It is not a matter of 'having' but a matter of 'being'. It is the natural dimension of human existence. It is not a reaction to a stimulus because any reaction will lead to another reaction which will bring about another conformity, another form of domination. It is also not freedom to revolt against society, as this also is a reaction and has its own pattern. Freedom is a state of mind wherein one can doubt and question everything and therefore it is so intense, active and vigorous that it throws away every form of dependence, slavery and acceptance. Freedom in this sense, is not freedom from external things but freedom from our own internal prejudices that have created a bondage for us. It is freedom to dismantle even our thought structures. At this level it is not the realization of one's gendered identity but going beyond one's gendered identity as a male or female that becomes important.

In a way, it is/the process of mental deconditioning, leading towards the possibility of transcendence of the given categories of knowing. This transcendence will be available to anyone who is willing to share a new way of thinking. Freedom thus will not be a cathartic expression of dissatisfaction but an expression of an ability to transcend the given and thus have an emancipatory value. Over and above the external compulsions, social and cultural pressures in terms of customs, taboos and regulations there are inner compulsions, compulsions which are deep-rooted in the minds of thousands of women. It is necessary to look at oneself as a person and go beyond the various roles imposed by the society. Awareness of oneself as an independent person, as a free being will liberate a woman and she will not expect that others will free her. The real bondage is within and once that is thrown there is the sunrise of knowledge.

It is necessary at this juncture to understand a distinction between what is called 'culture' and 'tradition'. The term 'culture' refers to art, religion, literature and everything that is created by human beings. It is transmitted through various traditions which are handed down from generation to generation. By its very nature 'tradition' is a repetitive exercise of certain ways of thought and praxis. Our identity is basically shaped by following the tradition that represents and propagates that culture. Tradition acts as a vehicle of culture and concretizes something that is rich, complex and dynamic. In terms of modes of thought and action it symbolizes the exemplification of culture.

Tradition has two aspects. One aspect is oriented towards the past and hence to history. It refers to conscious or unconscious personal and social memories and also to the racial memories which have already made imprints on the psyche of men and women. The other aspect is oriented towards the future, the possible new ways of interpreting and reconstructing the tradition. Inquiry into the first aspect is usually expressed in search for deep-rooted thoughts. It consists in deconstructing the ideas, the images, the belief systems by peeling off different layers so that the deep structure becomes visible. This exercise follows the method of debate and results in what may be called a philosophical archaeology of concepts and ideas.

Most of the ancient Indian *darsanas* have adopted and used the method of debate. The method of debate includes criticizing the opposite view, demolishing it, stating one's own view and then justifying it logically. The motive behind debate is to have victory over the opponent.

The debate with the Indian tradition from the woman's point of view creates a robust, militant form of woman's philosophy which is expressed in criticism on the established ways of thinking and doing. This results in exploration of the metaphysical, epistemological and ethical presuppositions which have held us captive. For instance, there is a concept that a woman is a field. The field cannot create life but nourishes the seed. On the other hand, the male is the seed giver, has potency to generate new life. This theory is called *Beeja-Ksetra-Nyaya*. This theory provides a so-called scientific evidence for the claim that woman is an inferior being. This is again percolated to the level of creating an ethics based on hierarchy. For woman there is a code of conduct in terms of *streedharma*, giving her a subordinate status in personal and social life. Literature, art, law-making, rituals, practice of medicine, politics, in short, every activity echoes the basic prejudice that woman is a lesser being. The subtle ways of control and exploitation take the form of glorification of the prescribed and the condemnation of the unwanted and unexpected. Questioning such standardized ontological, epistemological and ethical presuppositions is the first step towards throwing away the burden of the tradition so that a new horizon comes into the foreground.

However, the method of debate itself has certain inherent limitations. The method is negative and destructive in the sense that it refuses to allow new possibilities. Any point of view that lies outside the circumference of the context is just left out. In a debate, the speaker and the listener operate at two entirely different planes. Sometimes unknowingly the debate is converted into a quarrel or a battle-like situation where aggressiveness takes the form of intellectual violence. In a debate, the discourse of language becomes a dead structure of grammar, a static picture of syntax, an impersonal and dry conversation. The dynamic live communicative activity of using language is reduced to the examination of arguments that are expressed in the strict logical form.

There is another form of communication which will overcome these limitations. This is the method of dialogue which is many times neglected and sometimes abused too. This would consist in establishing a dialogue with that aspect of the tradition which is oriented towards future and in exploring new ways of understanding and interpreting it. Such an inquiry would take the form of building new pathways by finding out gaps between what is stated and what is practised. The dialogic communication demands that one has respect and not hatred towards the other. It consists in providing a new context by enlarging the horizons of meaning by freeing the concepts by way of erasing the set boundaries. It consists in making a sketch of possible new structures. It is to visualize how concepts and theories can be seen differently so that new designs could be made. This exercise may result in what may be called a philosophical architecture. Application of this method of dialogue begins with the presupposition that there is no single, final point of view. It is to accept that there is always a counter argument to any argument and both the argument and its counter argument would be included under the wider context of discourse.

A philosophical foundation can be provided to the dialogic method by three doctrines of the Jaina philosophy. The Jaina philosophy describes the reality in terms of many substances. According to it, there are many substances in the world. Every substance has many qualities (*ananta dharma*). Their metaphysics allows manifoldness of the reals. At the level of knowledge, it is held that it is possible to know the object from many points of view. Each point of view is imperfect, incomplete and one-sided (*nayavada*). At the level of description there could be different descriptions of the same object so that the object can be described from seven different points of view. At the level of logic, the Jaina philosophy accepts the possibility of many logical systems and hence different logics.

The recognition that the dynamics of communication is very complex is grounded in the awareness of 'the other' or 'others' at the metaphysical, epistemological and logical level. Reality is vast and grand enough to allow any number of kaleidoscopic perceptions. This methodological stance opens up new ways of understanding the world that is given and also the world that is made by human beings. From this stance it is logically wrong to study any social reality from any one single point of view because such a procedure would always give us a partial knowledge. Thus, any inquiry that centres round or begins with anything like caste, class, religion, gender, person, race etc. cannot in principle give the knowledge of the entire society and is bound to be incomplete. If this is so, then the question about the validity or adequacy of feminism becomes problematic and this will be true in the case of every other point of view, stated above. Every philosophical theory in social sciences will be considered as imperfect. At the most one can talk about a certain point of view or a standpoint and not about any theory in the strict sense of the term.

As pointed out earlier, reality can be understood from various perspectives or *Nayas*. Every perspective has its own claim to authenticity, and yet is inherently limited. It is not possible to transcend all such perspectives at any given moment and to adopt a God's eye view. Similarly, it is rather simplistic to assume that by taking into account the findings of various perspectives, it may be possible to know the totality at some point of time. Firstly, in principle, there can be innumerable possible perspectives. Secondly, and more importantly, such an assumption tacitly leads one to the belief in a rigid, fixed social reality and changes are then seen as merely transitory, superficial appearances of the basic underlying reality.

The question of identity then can be discussed: (1) with reference to the gender point of view in the context of other points of view; (2) with reference to different formulations of the gender point of view; and (3) with reference to the identity of the individual woman.

In the first context, gender point of view could be considered as one of the points of view and it cannot remain isolated from the other theoretical positions. The feminist theoreticians have tried to relate their theories to psychoanalysis, Marxism, liberalism, biological deterministic theories and anthropological theories also. In order to understand the gender point of view one has to accept the basic presuppositions and postulates that are taken for granted by feminism in general in its interaction with the other theories. At the same time, it cannot remain rigid with reference to other theories and claim universal validity and application. Same will be the situation with other theories. As a result every theory has to consider the possibility of transcendence of its own categories so as to reach the total complex of knowledge. So in the long run we have a totality of different theories acting and interacting with one another and yet maintaining their own identity.

In the case of formulations of feminism various feminist theories across history would have their place in the network of criss-cross interrelationships that invoke newer and newer interpretations. At a certain point, one can relate oneself to any formulation of feminism that might belong to the past, present and future. Feminist discourse in India or any particular discourse may begin with the context bound interpretation but there is no ultimate limit or boundary because we do share a distinctively human form of life that includes infinite actual and possible manifestations.

In the case of the identity of individual women the issue becomes more complex. In a sense, the ascription of identity presupposes the acceptance of individuality. It is to have the right over one's own body and mind. This presupposes a certain conception of society. The society is built by individuals. It is a collection of individuals who are free, independent and who willingly come together to form a society. In such a society every individual has certain rights which are protected and respected by the political institution of that society. The identity of a person is determined by reference to other equally free and independent beings. It follows the logic which is based on the difference between 'I' and 'you'. 'I' is excluded and separated from 'you'. The gap between the self and the other is widened to such an extent that it cannot be bridged easily. In this logic the individual is at the centre and society is at the periphery. This perspective is consistent with the right-centred ethics where the values of liberty, equality and brotherhood become important. The question that is normally raised is: "Did Indian women have or do they have this kind of identity?" It is argued that women were not treated as individuals and hence they did not have identity of this kind. However, men also did not have this kind of identity because they too were not individuals who had independent existence. The *varna* and *asrama* system was an institution in a society which was not a collection of individuals but a whole made up of tiny wholes so to say. It was like an organic system of small organic structures. The individuals were dependent for their existence on the society and had an identity which could be derived from the identity of a society. The society consisted of individuals who shared already set customs, traditions and a value framework. It was the question of maintaining the identity of a society and not that of an individual. The so-called identity was determined by the status of the individual in a social structure.

Varna and *asrama* were the two social institutions that provided the mechanisms of bestowing the identity. At the microlevel, every individual was supposed to be an individual not in the sense of being an independent free person, but being an integrated and balanced person, who is not separated from others. Such a procedure follows the logic of 'I' and 'we' where the emphasis is on similarity rather than difference. The gap between the self and the other is almost reduced to a minimum. In this logic society is at the centre and the individual is at the periphery. This perspective is consistent with the duty-centred ethics where values of obedience, commitment, willingness to sacrifice become important. The whole world with the animate and inanimate creatures provides a space for expansion of 'I'. The boundaries of identity go on enlarging so much so that one's identity is merged into the existence of the world of nature. Here identity itself becomes a product of alienating oneself from the world. Formation of an identity is something temporary, artificial and meaningless. What becomes important is the dissolution and not the formation of identity. Answer to the question 'who am I' does not lead to 'I am so and so' but initially leads to 'what I am not' and then ends up in the realization that I am a part of reality par excellence. Whether this reality is called *Brahman, God* or *Tathata* is a different question.

The ancient Indian discourse exhibits an awareness of this derived identity in the context of merging of social reality into the metaphysical realm. The same awareness is reflected in a different kind of language. It never uses the language of rights but the language of privileges. In a duty-centred ethics a person who had fulfilled her/his obligations towards family and society could have only certain privileges. He or she did not have rights which could be demanded but privileges which could be conferred on persons who were eligible.

Who were the eligible persons? Those who could transcend the narrow limits of human nature and see the world as a whole, perfect and complete in itself or see the world as a totality of everchanging phenomena leading to impermanent, momentary existence. The context for the discussion of identity thus takes us to the possible wide spectrum provided by different metaphysical systems.

It is not very much the question whether reality is one or many that is significant over here, but it is the question of the relationship between me and the world, 'I' and 'It' that becomes important. If 'I' am somebody separate from the 'world' then 'I' look upon 'It' as something 'other' and then 'I' also use the expression like 'you' for somebody other than 'me'. The distinction between 'I' and 'you' gives me a sense of identity. If on the other hand 'I' am a part of 'It' then I look upon 'It' as something like myself extended to infinity. It is myself discovering reality and reality manifesting itself to me. 'I' is included in 'we' and 'we' includes both 'I' and 'you'. Hence the expression 'we' refers to every being and every thing that shares my relation to 'It'.

It is interesting to note that in most of the Indian systems of metaphysics, the relation of 'I' and 'we' and not the relation of 'I' and 'you' becomes important. Even though some systems accept dualism ultimately they end up either in pluralism or monism. The modern understanding of identity in terms of 'I' and 'you' does not seem to be significant in the ancient Indian discourse. The acceptance of identity either becomes unnecessary and hence unimportant or even the language of substantial existence of any object providing the locus for identity is seen as misleading. Identity is something which is constructed and not a part of the ontological world. This can be seen by referring to some Indian philosophies, the *Advaita Vedanta* of Sankaracharya, *Samkhya* philosophy and the early Buddhist philosophy.

Advaita Vedanta of Sankaracharya describes the world in terms of one single reality called *Brahman*. It is the cause of generation, growth and decay of the whole world. *Brahman* is pure existence, existence par excellence, dynamic and full of energy. It is the ground existence of things. Whatever exists in the world is the expression of *Brahman*. A human being is a mode of existence. Metaphysically, a human being has a self and a body. The body is perishable but the self is immortal. It is identical with *Brahman*. It is because of ignorance that the self identifies itself with the body and then there is a superimposition of the bodily qualities on the nature of self. The identification of the body with the self and its differentiation from another body as the other is the basis of the empirical world. The identification of the self with the body later on results in identification of oneself with one's family, community and then the whole world of name and form provides a context for different layers of identity that are false in the real sense of the term. At the transcendental level, to understand that self is *Brahman* and to get rid of false identity is called *moksa*. The transference from pseudo identity to the real identity is expressed in terms of dissolution of the false and merging with the real. Identity of self and *Brahman* is then described as the identity of waves and water. They are not separables but distinguishables, i.e., one can make a distinction between them by using two different words at the level of language but one cannot separate them in reality.

Thus, the two senses of identity become meaningful; the genuine and the pseudo. The pseudo identity in terms of 'I' and 'You' is the basis of everyday commonsense world but the real identity is the ground of self-realization where identity itself is ontologized. Here it is a relation between 'I' and 'It'.

At this level, identity in terms of either male or female becomes insignificant. At the level of common sense world, one's identity as male or female could become meaningful but from the transcendental point of view the question of gender identity simply becomes superficial. It has to be transcended and raised to the human level and again to the level of self. In these progressive layers of identity, the first two are illusory, only the third level becomes important; but it leads to the negation of the so-called identity. Thus, the problem of identity in the modern sense of the term has no place in the *Advaita Vedanta* philosophy.

The *Samkhya* philosophy does not believe in the existence of one single reality but in the existence of two realities – *Purusa* and *Prakriti*. Both are pure existents and cannot be directly perceived. *Purusa* is the seer and one who witnesses everything. He is not subject to the experience of pleasure and pain. He is neither the doer nor the enjoyer. He is above bondage and liberation, in the sense that he never falls into bondage or gets liberated. The experience of pleasure or pain is for the body-mind complex (*jiva*) and never for *Purusa*. The *Purusa* identifies itself with the body-mind complex and hence experiences sorrows. The moment he understands that he is totally different from the subtle body-mind complex, he is liberated. *Purusas* are many and because of their contact with the *Prakriti* they get the forms of subtle body-mind organisms. Thus there are many realities.

Prakriti is inert and wholly devoid of consciousness. She has to go through the cycle of birth and death. *Prakriti* is made up of three qualities, *Satva*, *Rajas* and *Tamas*. These three qualities act and interact with one another, sometimes helping one another, sometimes dominating one another. *Purusa* and *Prakriti* coexist and behave like man and woman. The mere existence of sentient neutral *Purusa* activates *Prakriti* and the equilibrium of three qualities is disturbed. The coming together of *Purusa* and *Prakriti* is like the coming together of a lame and a blind person. The whole world is produced through their contact.

Human beings are combinations of these two elements. There are different beings and they have different physical qualities. Each human being has an independent existence. Each one's identity is determined by the configuration of the physical and mental qualities, but consciousness is something that is common to all human beings. Realizing that one is not a body-mind complex but pure consciousness or sentience is the realization of identity. It is by negating one's misplaced identity as a body that the true identity is established. However, the essential precondition for identity is the presence of consciousness. The physical body which is made up of five gross elements does not have consciousness of its own and hence it cannot have an identity. Realization of oneself as the pure consciousness is a transition from one type of identity to another; from one's identification with gross body, then with the mind, then with the ego and finally with the self. The gender identity then reflects the difference of qualities that is biological and natural. This kind of identity is a temporary phase in the process of realizing the true identity. Even though there are two realities these are not on par with one another. The dualism of *Purusa* and *Prakriti* ultimately does end up in unity in diversity. The so-called diverse identities (*Purusa*) are in the long run reduced to a collection of identities. The identity is diffused as it were like the rays of the sun.

The early Buddhist philosophy does not accept any permanent reality which can be named and referred to as the reality par excellence. Everything is constantly changing and flowing and the so-called existence is momentary. One cannot talk of reality as one or many because it is not something that can be numerically named. The only thing that can be said is that there are states of existence occurring one after another; just as one cannot show waterdrops in flowing water and yet they are there for a moment, one cannot show any permanent entity existing in its own right. Similarly, there is nothing like self, a supersensible reality, the bearer of qualities. Everything is an aggregate of five *skandhas* (*rupa, samjnna, samskara, vedana, vijnana*). The aggregate is constantly changing and the so-called 'self' is only a name having no reference at all.

What is called as person is a name given to a constantly changing configuration of five *skandhas*. The language of identity or sameness is wrong. The very notion of identity is evaded because there is no permanent entity and hence the question of identity does not arise. Identity is a human construction and it is a fluid concept, having no precise definite meaning.

These insights of ancient Indian philosophies are at least points to be considered in the modern discussions of identity from various points of views. At the practical level it is not the relation between 'I' and 'It', but the one between 'I' and 'we' that becomes problematic. Either 'I' has to negate, deny itself or 'I' has to merge itself in 'we'. There is no third option like asserting 'I'. The depth grammar of Indian philosophical discourse does not encourage the language of identity, rather it encourages sublimation of identity in the form of consideration of all. The very process of making a search for 'the third I' becomes a challenge for modern thinkers.

2

Position and Role of Women in *Rgveda*

Sucheta Paranjape

Almost four thousand years ago, the Indo-Aryans branched off from their European and Iranian brothers and moved to the southeast. They crossed the Khyber pass and settled in the fertile basin of Indus and other rivers. During this process of colonization, the nomadic society changed its structure to a settled one and became socially stable and secure. With agriculture came steady economic growth and prosperity. All this culminated in a refined culture.

During this period, religion also took firm roots. Gods were created, praised and worshipped. Agni, Savitr, Usas, the rivers, the rain -- almost all the benevolent and miraculous powers in nature were defined. Hymns were composed to laud this pantheon. Rituals were designed to appease and pacify these Gods. These hymns were later on edited and compiled in a text called *Rgveda*.

It is very difficult to date the composition of the *Rgveda*. Scholars vary drastically in their estimation. However, now it is generally agreed upon that the *Rgveda*, as it is available to us today was compiled in this form by at least 1500 B.C. This means that the hymns were composed earlier to this. In other words, we have before us a literature that records and reflects the period, which is at least 4,000 years old.

Rgveda is the oldest recorded literature not only from India, but the world over. It depicts for us, through these prayers and lauds, the social conditions of the Vedic society. However, it must be borne in our mind that we have only this 'literary' source to draw upon. One wonders whether the text can be taken literally or only as an image of the society. If it is an image, we should remember that images can, at times, distort or enhance the actual picture. It is extremely difficult to construct a picture of the Vedic women in the context of the Vedic society from nothing but 'words'. One has to be cautious and careful. No tall claims can be made and no false colours added. However, considering the honest and transparent poetry of the Rgvedic hymns, one can depend on it to a large extent and get a fairly authentic picture of the Vedic society.

As already seen, the Vedic pantheon consisted mostly of powers from nature to which even war-heros like Indra were added. What strikes most to a student of religion is the large number of female deities like Usas, Ratri, Prithvi, Sarasvati, Kuhu, Raka, Sinivati and many others. The religion of a people reflects their own mental frame. If so, then a religion that respects and worships so many female deities is a clear image of a people who respect and honour the women -- a fact very strongly borne out by all the material gleaned through the hymns.

The position of the women in Rgvedic times is enviable! Right from her birth, the female child was treated almost on par with the male one. Continuous fights and battles did make the need for brave 'sons' very urgent, no doubt about this. Many hymns pray God for male progeny. But though sons were sought, after daughters were not exactly unwanted. In fact, they are praised and appreciated. While describing a happy household, a Vedic seer describes the couple as *putrinastah kumarinah* -- those with sons and daughters. Another seer describes earth and sky as "two sisters playing on the lap of their parents". Usas, one of the popular goddesses, is invariably referred to as *divo duhita* -- the daughter of the heaven. All such references collectively show that a daughter was treated with love and brought up with affection.

It must be pointed out that around the same time, in the hot deserts of Arabia, the birth of a female child was considered to be inauspicious and she was buried alive in the burning sand! Compared to this, the Rgvedic daughter was very fortunate. Even the later Vedic literature at times, shows total contempt and gloom at the birth of a female. *Atharvaveda*, which represents the religion of the masses, has numerous hymns to get a son and, the worse part of the story is that there are hymns to bring about a miscarriage of a female embryo. Domestic rituals like *pumsavanam* mirror a growing desire for sons. In one of the legends, *Aitareya Brahmana* praises a male child and shows discontent for a daughter, when it says: *Krpanam ha duhita, jyotirha putrah*.

Unlike all this, the Rgvedic daughter was born with good stars. She got all the love and affection that she deserved. She proved by her behaviour that she was a worthy daughter. She was a great help in the domestic chores. She got the name *duhita* because she milked the cows. She brought water in pitchers from the river -- a scene, which can be witnessed in rural India even today. These girls were expert at weaving garments, stitching them with an eyeless needle (*sucya acchidyamanaya*) and also embroidering them with golden threads.

These were young and beautiful maidens. They were conscious of their youth and beauty and spent time on decking up. They were always well-dressed (*supesah*) and had different hairstyles like four pleats (*catuskapardh*) etc. A number of garments like *adhivasa, drapi, sich*, etc. are referred to. The marriage hymns (*Rgveda* X.85) also talk about *samulya* which must have been a special bridal attire. In addition, they wore ornaments like necklaces (*niska*) and anklets made mainly of gold and studded with precious stones. Pearls (*krsana*) were also used. They always put unguent to their eyes and used perfumes on their body. Ladies from a noble family are described by Vasistha (*Rgveda* VII. 55) as *punya gandhah*.

The detailed description about cosmetics is not as important as the fact that the Vedic maiden had the right to use cosmetics, and that the Vedic society not only approved of this, but encouraged it. This is very striking as putting on make-up and using cosmetics was considered to be 'indecent' in India even in the 20th century. But the Vedic society approved of this and made the young girl look happy and so, more beautiful.

The shrewd maiden used this as a 'weapon' to attract a suitable bachelor into marrying her. There were fairs called *samana* where young men and damsels flocked together to find a suitable life partner. The *Rgveda* tells us that the *samanas* were held during night, were heavily attended by the young men and women and the crowd dispersed at the advent of dawn. The most striking feature of the *samana* is that it had parental encouragement and social sanction. Mothers took special care to deck up their daughters going to *samana*. This shows not only the freedom the girls enjoyed in choosing their husband but also the faith and trust of the parents and society in the young generation. Later on, the puritanical Hindu society could not tolerate this moral freedom to its youth and totally abolished this wonderful practice. The freedom which the matured -- both physically and emotionally -- Vedic maiden enjoyed in this manner will be a matter of envy even for a so-called highly educated girl of the twenty-first century who more often than not has to marry someone much against her wishes. But the *Rgveda* all the time talks of girls 'choosing' their husbands. The marriage hymns say the same about Surya – *yosa vrnita janya yuvam pati*. In another hymn (*Rgveda* X.27) the seer happily describes the great fortune of such a lady – *bhadra vadhurbhavati yatsupesah svayam sa mitram vanute jane cit*. In fact, the word *vara* meaning husband, can be derived from the root *vr* which means to choose; so, *vara* is the chosen one.

As the girl married someone of her own choice, she lived 'happily ever after'. As the maiden crossed the threshold of virginity and stepped into the nuptial life, she was transformed into the important roles of *jaya* and *grhini*.

As we read through the various hymns, we realise that marriage was a long established institution in the Vedic times. The famous marriage hymn offers ample evidence of this. When a society thinks of marriage as a religious sacrament (*samskara*) it actually transforms the primal male-female relationship into a social tie and an emotional bond. The society adds thereby an entirely different dimension to the image of a woman, who otherwise would have been reduced to nothing more than a sex-machine producing children. There is no denying the fact that these two are the two major motives behind marriage; but, the Vedic people gave a very tender form to this primitive relationship and thus, offered respect and honour to the Vedic woman. This status and position was well received by the woman and she was extra careful in performing her role as a wife.

At this juncture, we must have a clear understanding of words like 'position' and 'role'.

'Position' is accorded to a person by the society. It is a passive concept and one has to receive it, whether one likes it or not. 'Role', on the other hand, is something, which the person actively takes up and plays on his/her own and is responsible for that. In other words the 'position' of a person is -- or, at least, it should be -- directly dependent on and proportional to the 'role' the person plays. When there is a perfect balance between the position and the role, we can infer that the people have a strong sense of social justice. The position of the Vedic woman amply testifies to the fair and just society.

Whatever may be the personal and emotional effects of a marriage, socially it was essential for two reasons. First, marriage and subsequent family life give stability to a society, which in turn, goes on to give a secure foundation to the nation.

Secondly, to protect and enhance this nation, constant wars were common and for this the Vedic Aryans needed strong and brave young men. The main purpose of matrimony was to beget progeny. At one place, a seer says (*Rgveda* X.85) – *dasasyam putrana dhehi patimekadasam kuru* – meaning "May this wife have ten sons, the husband being the eleventh member". Children were always wished for – more the merrier. Indrani, the powerful consort of Indra, praises and appreciates (*Rgveda* X. 86) Parsu Manavi, "who gave birth to twenty children".

The mantras from the marriage hymns are very eloquent and throw light on the woman's role as a wife. She is asked to take care of the entire household – *samrajni bhava*, including the father-in-law, mother-in-law, brother-in-law and the sister-in-law. The list of these relations gives us a fair idea of the joint family system even in the Vedic times. In a joint family, the role of a woman is very decisive and matters the most. Though the society is patriarchal, the family seems to be headed by the woman (*samrajni*).

She was a loving wife to her husband. One *mantra* says: 'May the Visvedevas unite our hearts.' It is noteworthy that for the Vedic people, marriage was not merely a physical union, it was much deeper than that – it was a confluence of two hearts. When this happens, the wife feels honoured and content with a sense of fulfilment, she offers herself to her husband. The husband promises her to bring prosperity through progeny and doing things, which will be dear to her – *iha priyam prajaya te samrdhyatam*. This wife is not only his sex-mate, she becomes his friend as well. Surya is supposed to get married for being a wife and friend – *avam patitvam sakhyaya jagmusi*.

The wife in her role as woman of the house (*grhini*) looked after the entire household. Even a martial seer like Visvamitra admits that wife indeed is home – *jaya id astam* (*Rgveda* III. 53). Later on, when the poet laureate praises a woman, he says *grhini sacivah saki mithah....* The first thing he expects from a woman is the looking after of the house. It has always been a pleasurable duty for the women to transform the 'house' into a 'home'. The gambler's hymn (*Rgveda* X.34) also depicts this aspect. The gambler, a total loser because of his addiction to gambling and hence abandoned by his wife, peeps through the window of someone's house and sees *anyesam jayam shkrtam ca yonim* -- a well-kept house and the lady of the house. And then he realizes what he has missed by behaving badly with his wife and with a remorseful heart, resolves not to gamble again.

The role of a wife was so adorable that even the Gods are said to have wives. Indrani is so powerful an individual that she commands respect from everybody, including her husband. While praising Indra, one seer says: *kalyanih jaya suranam grham te* -- "Your wife is so good and what a comfortable home you have."

A *mantra* from the marriage hymn expresses a blessing to the newly-weds. Translated literally it says: "Oh the newly-weds, live together forever, may you not be separated. May you two enjoy your entire long life happily in this house of yours, playing with your children and grandchildren". This was the meaning of a happy married life. This would make the wife content. The culmination of womanhood was being a mother.

As a mother, the women asserts her creativity. As a mother, she is very powerful. She raised her children with conscious effort. For the Vedic people, the best facet of a woman was her motherhood. To felicitate someone, they would call that person mother. Earth (*prthivi*) is always referred to as *mata*. In the funeral rites described in the *Rgveda* (X.118), after cremation the bones of the dead are buried underground. While pouring a fistful of soil on that urn a request is made to the mother Earth to "lovingly and softly cover the person, just as a mother covers her baby under her upper garment" (*pallu*). Even the rivers are referred to as mothers, Sindhu being the *ambitama* -- the most motherly one.

The seers feel that the picture of a God will be incomplete without mentioning his mother. In the *Rgveda*, there are references to Indramata -- Indra's mother. Adityas get their name after their mother Aditi. Even the demons' mothers are loving and kind: Danu lay weeping on the body of her son who was slain by Indra -- *danuh saye sahavatsa na dhenuh*.

The Vedic mother was very proud of her children. Indrani in her hymn boasts about her sons and daughter: *mama putrah satruhanah atho me duhita virat* -- "all my sons are brave and my only daughter is simply great!"

The Vedic woman seems to be at her best and happiest during this phase of her life -- as a wife and a mother. But sometimes ill-luck struck and she became a widow -- a state which, in the Hindu world means, by definition, torture, suffering and deprivation.

But the position of a Vedic widow is far from this misery. The funeral hymn (*Rgveda* X.118) gives details in this regard. The widow was made to lie on the funeral pyre, next to her dead husband. Then, her brother-in-law or an elderly person would go to her, hold her hand and ask her to get up and face life anew -- *udirsva nari abhijiva lokam...*! She then went along with the other women and entered the house. She would be henceforth considered as a wife of the man of the house. Obviously, the fact that she did lie on the funeral pyre is reminiscent of an older practice of *sati*. *Atharvaveda* refers to the *sati* in no uncertain terms as the age-old custom -- *puranam dharmam*, which must have been the law of the day before this.

But, the Vedic society did not approve of this gross injustice to the woman. It was sensitive to her personal loss and social insecurity. It therefore devised a way by which the widow would get back her status as a wife and enjoy the pleasures of life. The Vedic society must have thought -- why should the women suffer? Why should she be denied happiness? Why not give her another chance? With these great thoughts, the society tried to be just and fair to the woman.

This was a bold social reform. And for this, the Vedic society deserves praise. No other society after the Vedic one – not even the present one – has been so sensitive to a woman's grief, so angry at injustice to her and so supportive of her rights. If we compare the status of a Vedic widow to that of her Hindu sister, the difference is shocking. The Vedic society realised the identity of a woman and so, it respected and protected her.

This woman, who was assured of protection and insured against injustice, developed two major qualities – self-confidence and self-respect. The affectionate treatment she received since childhood gave her the self-respect, whereas good upbringing and education made her confident. The Vedic girls, like their male colleagues were initiated into formal education. The girl child too received the *upanayana* ceremony and had proper and formal education. *Atharvaveda* (XII.3.) tells us that a maiden will get a beautiful husband because of her education – *brahmacaryena kanya yuvanam vindate patim*. *Asvatayana Grhya Sutra* says that when *upanayana* is performed for a girl, no mantras should be chanted. This goes on to prove that even a thousand years after the *Rgveda*, girls still underwent the *upanayana samskara*. A later text named *Haritasmriti* talks of two types of maidens: *brahmavadinis* are those who keep studying all through their lives whereas there are *sadyo vadhus* who pursue studies only till they get married.

In the *Rgveda*, there are a score of hymns composed by women seers like Apala, Lopamudra, Sraddha, Indrani etc. This shows that not only were the women intellectually compatible with men, but also that the male ego of the Vedic seers was not 'hurt' to include hymns composed by the females! Another text named *Jaiminiya Brahmana* mentions a kingdom where even the women composed *Vedamantras*! The Upanisadic references to Gargi and Maitreyi are too well known to be repeated. But there is also a dark side to the story. When Gargi Vachaknavi kept on asking deeper questions about the ultimate reality, Yajnavalkya, the great philosopher, quietened her by saying: "Do not ask too much, Gargi, or else, your head might burst." I personally interpret this answer not only as an expression of male chauvinism but also as a hidden fear in his mind of being superseded by a female! The answer must have come as an insult and embarrassment to Gargi, both as a philosopher and as a woman. Even in the Yajnavalkya-Maitreyi dialogue in the *Chandogya Upanisad*, Katyayani, the second wife of Yajnavalkya is spoken of as *stripradnya*. The word is used with much sarcasm and humiliation to that lady. However, we cannot forget that the list of seers to whom *tarpana* is offered at the time of *sraddhas* includes the names of three women Sulabha, Gargi and Maitreyi.

Apart from academics the women knew many other arts and used them. They were true companions of their husbands even outside the domain of the house. Vispala who (in all probability) was the queen of king Khela, accompanied him on the battlefield where she lost one leg. Another lady named Mudgalani drove the chariot of her husband on the battlefield and "as she drove her upper garment fluttered on the wind like a flag".

But of all the Vedic women, the strongest of them appears to be Indrani, wife of Indra and daughter of Puloma. She was a very strong-willed person. She suffered because of the various other consorts of Indra. Though monogamy was the accepted social norm this did not deter the nobles and wielders of power and they always practised polygamy. But Indrani strongly disapproves of this and is active in finding out ways to conquer her co-wives. She is very sure that her physical appeal would win Indra over. She confidently says *aham keturaham murdha ahamugra vivacani* -- "I am the banner of the house, I am the head of the family, I indeed speak very strongly". She says so because she is aware – and she expresses it in no uncertain terms – that it is because of her that her husband is what he is. Even today, we say that behind every successful man there is a woman. She could either be his mother or a wife. Indrani asserts her individuality to a great extent. I dare not say that she represents the Vedic woman, but I must admit that her thoughts and feelings echo at least those of a fraction of the women.

Thus, the overall position and role of a Vedic woman is very satisfying. A loved daughter, a trusted maiden, a beloved wife, a respected mother and most of all an honoured individual are the facets of the Vedic woman.

But the greatest compliment that the Vedic society paid to this woman is something else.

All through the epic and classical literature, descriptions of heroines and women abound. But, every time a woman is described, the poet looks only at her physique. *Pinasronipayodhara* is a very common description. They talk of women only by way of describing her breasts, her hips, her waist, her navel, her lips, her hair. Even poets like Kalidasa could not escape from this. In *Mahabharata*, at one place, Draupadi is described as *trirgambhira sadunnata rakta pancasu pancasu*, i.e., she was deep at three places, raised at six ones and red at five. This description is made in very low taste and to say the least, amounts to vulgarism. To add insult to injury, the commentators keep discussing and guessing which three parts of her body could be 'deep' and which six ones could be 'raised'. The entire scene is repulsive and sickening. In spite of all the poetic embellishments, I have a strong complaint against the classical Sanskrit literature about its tendency to limit its vision only to the body of a woman and never look beyond!

Again, in this field too, the Vedic woman scores over all others. Nowhere in the *Rgveda* do we find any obscene reference to a woman. The seers never talk of her breasts and hips, but think of her feelings and emotions. This does not mean that there was dearth of a young connoisseur amongst the Vedic seers. Certainly not. As they describe the beautiful dawn, they do think of a bathing beauty. They also describe the sun who always follows Usas as a young man following a maiden. In fact, sun is called the lover of Usas. At times, while describing the 'dis-covered' beauty of Usas, a seer does go astray but immediately realizes what he is doing and uses proper and decent words.

This, according to me, is the greatest felicitation to the Vedic woman. This is the highest honour the society offered her. This was the most coveted respect that she got. This in itself is an eloquent statement of the prestigious position and role of the Vedic women.

One wonders why this respect for her individuality and this honour for her womanhood was never endowed upon the later women both from history and literature.

3

The *Satapatha Brahmana* on Women

Nirmala Kulkarni

Samhitas (i.e., collection of the Vedic *mantras* and sacrificial formulas) survived with a *Brahmana* text. A *Brahmana* text explains methods of sacrificial ritual, divergent opinions on ritualistic details and mystic explanations of them. Besides explaining the ritual, these texts furnish etymologies of various words, religious taboos prevalent and mystic explanation of the social behaviour. These texts certainly serve as a great literary source to the cultural history of India. These were spread in the ancient Indian *aryavarta* at the advent of Vedic sacrificial religion. To some extent these are normative, as the later Indian tradition of the *Mimamsakas* has acknowledged them as an authentic guide of the 'right behaviour'. By utilizing the technique of ancient *Mimamsakas*, even the modern researchers can obtain the picture of the then prevalent society by transforming or eliminating the mythical account into rules of behaviour. Though partial, one may get a picture of the then living society, their norms and social customs. By analyzing the symbolism found in these texts, the underlying concepts could be understood. In similar lines an attempt is made in this paper to arrive at the image of woman in the minds of people living at the time of the *Satapatha Brahmana*.

The *Satapatha Brahmana* occupies prime position in the *Brahmana* texts not just because of its extent, but for various other reasons. It belongs to the white school of the *Yajurveda* founded by Yajnavalkya. It is more elaborate in comparison to the other *Brahmana* texts and is often called a "mine of important information". Though it is very difficult to decide the chronology of the text, the writing style and systematic treatment suggest a late origin of it, that is around third or fourth century B.C. This date could be confirmed on the basis of its reference to Ajatasatru (son of Bindusara) and the word *mleccha* which certainly refers to ancient Greeks. It gets importance for another significant reason as it "provides with legendary and terminological links between the Vedic culture on one hand and India of the Great Epic and of ancient Buddhism on the other" (Gonda 1975). Vedic India synthesized with Buddhist and Jaina ideologies forms the basis of medieval Indian culture. Therefore, it becomes relevant to compare the modern concept of woman with that of the medieval one reflected in the *Satapatha Brahmana*. An attempt is made in this paper to document in detail the account of the image of woman in the heart of the society which was on the threshold of Vedic and Buddhist India. Occasional comparison is made with the modern one wherever possible. The discussion in this paper may look incoherent, as the references to woman in the main body of the text are scattered. Yet, the prime aim is just to focus on some important concepts about women and not to arrive at any theory. The documentation (though not done in detail) would provide a background to scholars working in the field of feminist thinking to arrive at certain theoretical positions.

The Context

The main context of description of any *Brahmana* text is *yajna*. *Yajna* is a miniature model of creation. Since the primitive man was very curious about creation, all ancient worship patterns centre around it. *Yajna* is a pattern of worship wherein a human being tries to create a world like the given world. Furthermore, he observes that in the world of creation there are two elements, one male and another female. Therefore, by using two elements -- a male and a female -- he is trying to create the desired effect. Therefore, the objects utilized in the ritual are often classified as male and female, for example, if water and fire are used in the ritual, water is labelled as female and fire as male. To quote -- *yosa va apah, vrsa agnih*. Such classification is based generally on the linguistic gender.

Secondly, a particular procedure followed in the ritual is justified by citing local customs. As the procedure has something to do with creation, generally a woman is involved in the ritual and thus the then prevailing and supposed to be prestigious customs or thoughts could be gathered. The present article focuses mainly on such details.

As stated above, a woman was included in the ritual because *Yajna* was a worship pattern based on creation. Manifestation of creation is impossible without a female. Therefore, though secondary, she was given some place. But, it seems that whenever any ritual is motivated beyond creation, to be more specific, whenever it goes beyond the material plane, a woman is excluded. The *pravargya* ritual could be the best example of it. The *pravargya* ritual is a secondary ritual of the *Soma* sacrifices. The motive of it is to bestow a divine body to the sacrificer and moreover, to be identical with the sun. Thus, the idea comes a bit closer to the idea of salvation, which is entirely spiritual in nature. Women and *Sudras* are not allowed to watch this particular performance. Can we interpret it as an indication of seclusion of women in the spiritual field? Is it just because creation is impossible without women that they are included in the ritual, but when their presence is not necessary they are excluded from the ritual? A legend of the *Taittiriya Samhita* also shows that gods wanted to exclude their wives from obtaining heaven. Can we interpret these legends as indications of spiritual seclusion of women?

Participation of Women in the Ritual

1. Participation as a religious necessity: As pointed out in the previous paragraph, the *yajna* pattern of worship being ancient pattern is central to creation. As in the physical world a creation takes place by the union of two elements, male and female, even in the *yajna* both these elements must be present. Without a male or without the female counterpart the *yajna* will not come into existence. Therefore, *yajamana* (male sacrificer) and *yajamanapatni* (wife of the sacrificer) together have to perform the ritual. As they share the performance, they share the fruit of it. If *Yajna* is performed to obtain heaven, both of them are supposed to reach heaven. Therefore, a wife is often called *jaghanardha* -- a thigh. Since the context of participation is creation, even the metaphor refers to the organ participating actively in it. The same metaphor continues in the word *ardhangini*. However, the original context is forgotten. In the later usage the context is widened, it means a wife who shares all activities of life.

2. A man or a woman singly is not entitled to perform sacrifice. Therefore, a man without a wife is condemned as *ayajniya* -- not having a place at the sacrifice (*ayajniyo va esa yah apatnikah*). Though a woman, i.e., having status of wife was involved in the ritual, all wives of a person were not involved. Only *savarna* wife (wife of the same caste) had the right of participation. Thus, the participation was not equal.

3. The upper hand of men can also be seen in the adjectival words *ahitagni*, *diksita* etc. These words indicate performance of a particular rite done by a particular person. *Ahitagni* is a person who has kindled the sacrificial fire in his house. *Diksita* is a person who has undergone a particular rite. These and similar adjectives are not seen being used in case of a woman. One may understand that *ahitagni* is a person who along with his wife had kindled the

sacrificial fire. Yet, by the same word one never understands that it is a wife who along with her husband had performed the same rite. Thus, the role of a woman in ritual participation was secondary, and never independent. D.R. Bhandarkar had tried to prove from the Nagnika cave inscriptions that Naganika had performed sacrifice on her own. According to me the sacrifice was probably sponsored by the queen. She, being a widow had certainly no right to perform the sacrifice. Thus, it is beyond doubt that though performance of sacrifice was not taking place without the presence (later on symbolic presence) of the wife, her role was always secondary.

4. The secondary role of women could also be determined on the basis of another custom often referred to in the *Srautasutras*. If a man who has kindled the sacrificial fire in the house dies, all the sacrificial instruments are burnt on the pyre. In his presence the wife used to take part in it. If her role would have been independent or equal, the instruments would have been kept in the house. But, this practice is never seen. However, if the wife dies, the sacrificer had to remarry and never vice versa. The reason put forward for such a custom seems obviously partial to men. They say that the kindled fire should never be kept without any oblation, and a single sacrificer has no right to offer oblations, therefore he should remarry. If a woman would have had an equal role, she would have been given permission to remarry, but such a custom is not seen or referred to at all. This is an indication of her secondary, rather complementary role in the ritual.

Physical Description

1. The altar wherein the offerings are offered is shaped after the female bodily form, since it is considered as the seat of creation. Further, since a woman broad about the hips, somewhat narrower between the shoulders and contracted

in the middle was appreciated for her physical form, it was recommended that the altar should be broader on the west, contracted in the middle and broad again on the east. Contrary to this, we do not get a description of the male form that was supposed to be ideal. A man fair with blue eyes, or a man tawny with light eyes or a man black with red eyes is described, but these are associated with their learning capacity, and not with the ideal male form. Thus, probably beauty had become an identifying mark of a woman and learning that of man. Yet we cannot say it for sure, because the later *smrti* texts do refer to the ideal male body, as even a bridegroom is to be selected very carefully.

2. At another instance the deity Sinivali is praised as *sukaparda* (having well plaited hair), *sukurira* (having a good headdress) and *su-aupasa* (having good form). The text further says, "Sinivali is a woman, a woman is praised if she is such." This is a general expectation from a woman, to a certain extent from each human being. But, it is also true that a greater stress is put on women being neat and clean.

3. Feminine body is impure: As explained above in detail the *yajna* is meant for creation and that is why the sacrificer's wife has to take part in it. When she is ready to do her assigned role, a cord is fastened to her waist. The text says, "impure is the part which is below the navel". The impure part of her body is concealed with a girdle and only with the pure upper part is she participating in the sacrifice. Even here, we do not find anywhere censure of the male organ. It is also interesting that the other older *Brahmana* texts like the *Taittiriya Brahmana* do not think of such an interpretation. According to the *Taittiriya Brahmana* (3.3.3.2-3) the girdle is fastened to the waist as it is a mark of initiation ceremony. In the *upanayana* ceremony, a girdled is tied to the *brahmacarin*. Thus, it is a mark of initiation, that he is ready now for study. Since, the girdle is made of *munja* grass, the ceremony is alternatively called

maunjibandhana. Similarly, the wife of the sacrificer is initiated in the rite. Thus, the girdle is the symbol of initiation. Since the older texts do not associate this particular act to the impurity of sexual organs, it certainly is not the original motive of the rite. The *Satapatha Brahmana* is a post-Buddhist text. Asceticism had entered in the religion by this time. Therefore, the feminine body was regarded as impure, as it is considered one of the major impediments on the way to salvation.

4. A female does not have strength: It is an age-old and worldwide belief that a female is not strong. The text says *avirya vai stri*. In the *Taittiriya Samhita* she is called *nirindriya*, i.e., having no generative organ and hence powerless. For that reason, she is not entitled to inheritance (*tasmat nirindriyas striyah adayadi*). It is an indication of further inferior status of women. On the same ground, the later Jaina texts have rejected salvation for women, probably by equating physical strength for the mental one.

Inferiority of Women

There are many instances where the inferior status of women is indicated:

1. A day before the actual performance of the *Yajna*, the main priest of the sacrifice keeps all vessels etc. ready. Many types of spoons are used to pour *ghee* in the fire. The dipping spoon is called *sruva*. The word is linguistically masculine. The other smaller spoons are called *sruc* which is linguistically feminine. The main priest brushes the dipping spoon first and then the small spoons. The text also explains the reason, one must honour men first and then women. It further gives an example, if several women go together and even a small boy is accompanying them, he is the leader and the women are followers. Similarly, one must clean the dipping spoon first since it bears masculine linguistic

gender. The cleaning of other spoons should follow as they bear feminine linguistic gender. The passages from any *Brahmana* text look illogical. This particular passage is also not an exception. Yet the reality which it speaks of, i.e., inferiority of women to men is eye-catching and worth noticing as it is a part of our day to day experience. A similar concept is found in the Jaina religion. A nun – even if she is eighty years old – must bow down a younger monk, just because he is a male ascetic. Her experience, her age, nothing is counted. Just because she is female, she has to forego whatever she has achieved by age or experience. The religions, for which humanity was the foremost principle could not go away from the prevailing notion about women, because it was not simply a notion; in reality a woman did have an inferior status.

2. Her inferior status is further indicated in the creation myth. The text says: "The earth is the essence of all beings. Water is created on earth, water produces trees, trees flowers, and flowers fruits; a man is created by fruits (probably, by the seed) and a man has semen. Prajapati thought, let me create some substratum, basis, shelter for the semen. Therefore, he created a woman". Thus, the myth indicates that a woman is simply a bearer of the seed. She has no independent role in creation. When the role of the male in creation was not known to the society, the credit was given to women. Therefore, the matriarchal societies came in to existence. When the role of male partners was known, the status of women became low. They were simply regarded as the bearers of the seed. Just here, probably the metaphor of seed and field (*Beeja* and *Ksetra*) came into existence. The sole importance was given to the seed and never to the field. The field has just to grow it.

3. The text further says that since a woman is a substratum (*pratistha*), i.e., *adhara* in the sexual intercourse she has to be below. One who makes a woman lie down during sexual

intercourse enjoys the fruit of *vajapeya* sacrifice. He and his
wives gain merit.

4. The same passage further says: "The fertility period is the
   wealth of women. A man should call such a fortunate lady
   for sexual intercourse. If she denies, he should buy her (i.e.,
   lure her by promising clothing or ornaments). If she is still
   obstinate, he should overpower her by beating her either
   with his hands or a stick and also curse her to be
   unfortunate. The curse involves the words: "I take away
   your fortune by my fortunate organ." This passage clearly
   indicates the secondary role of women in sex. Her will is
   not taken into consideration rather it is terminated forcibly
   if goes against that of the male partner. It is true that in
   ancient times, creation played an important role. Much
   importance was given to the fertility period, yet the force
   or violence not verbalized in the ancient Vedic literature is
   openly stated in this text. This is an indication of
   deterioration in the status of women.

5. The whole paragraph cites various formulas to fulfil various
   wishes of men -- if he wants to beget a child, if he does not
   want to beget from sexual intercourse, if he desires to
   destroy his wife's paramour, if he wants to beget a learned
   daughter etc. Nowhere in the paragraph is there an
   indication of the fulfilment of the wishes of a woman. In
   the *Rgveda* women poets are bold enough to ask for sexual
   intercourse, they are free enough to choose their husband,
   rather such ladies are praised (*bhadra vadhur bhavati yat
   supesa samanam mitram vanute jane cit*). In the *Atharvaveda*
   certain rites are prescribed for women to fulfil their sexual
   desire with the desired partner. But the *Satapatha
   Brahmana*, a post-Buddhist text expected to bestow more
   liberty on women does the opposite.

Various Beliefs about Women

The *Satapatha Brahmana* discusses many other beliefs such as,
women are not true (*moghasamhita vai yosa*) or women could be

lured by singing etc. It also says that whenever a woman is called for sexual intercourse she first denies and could be lured afterwards. Very often she is compared with speech (*vak*). Many mythical accounts of *vak* are suffixed with generalizations of women.

Observations

The *Satapatha Brahmana* is a post-Buddhist Vedic text and is important for understanding the transitional period. The Vedic image of a woman is certainly changed in this period. Probably, she is deprived of freedom of speech. Gargi and Maitreyi are two exceptions to it, yet we cannot say that these are representatives of the then women in general. They are exceptional. We may go further and say that Indian society certainly reveres such women who go beyond normalcy. The queen of Jhansi was never looked at as a woman, she could perform at par with her male counterparts. Yet we cannot call her a representative of women. When she was admired in the society, other women were sitting on pyres of their dead husbands. Similar is the case of Gargi and Maitreyi who are often cited as examples of Vedic women in general. Other women certainly had a secondary role in every aspect of life. Furthermore, their general freedom was restricted. Because of the advent of asceticism she was conceived as an impediment in the way of salvation. This is a new dimension added during the period of *Satapatha Brahmana*.

References

Bhandarkar, D. R.: "Were Women entitled to Vedic Sacrifices?" in XII All India Oriented Conference Summary of Papers. Altekar A.S. (ed.) (1943) BHU Press, Benaras.

Gonda, Jan: "Vedic Literature (*Samhitas* and *Brahmanas*)", *A History of Indian Literature* (1975). Vol.I, fsc.I, Wiesbaden, pp.351-356.

Weber, A. (ed.): *The Satapatha Brahmana*, Chaukhamba Sanskrit Series (1964), no.96, Varanasi.

4

Images of Woman in the *Mahabharata*

Mangala Athalye

Behind any inquiry into the nature of woman's problems there is a question, "What it is to be a woman?" The answer to this question is not simple.[1] There are different ways of answering the question, a part of the answer is given in terms of images of woman.

Images of woman in Indian culture emerge mainly from the ancient epics such as the *Ramayana* and the *Mahabharata*. These epics exert a powerful impact on our modes of thoughts and feelings and fellowship. A woman is depicted in a variety of ways in *Mahabharata*. All these depictions have such an impelling force that in the later period they have been coloured and couched in literary elegance and have been used as images. From the modern point of view, whether *Mahabharata* is a history or not is a debatable question. The modern history makes a distinction between history and myth. Ancient Indians never really believed history to be a separate branch of knowledge. What is termed as *itihas* is so called because of its relative position in the time series. The *Mahabharata* had been therefore termed as *itihas*. It is a mixture of history, myth and morality. However, it cannot be said that the *Mahabharata* is the exact representation of that period, or that it represents all the women of that period. It does hint at the human goals and values that were lived in that particular phase of human life.

The need to study the images involves two considerations. The first is methodological and the second is interpretative.

Images have an important role to play in human sciences. One of the reasons for the primacy of images in social sciences is the uniqueness of the object of inquiry that is central to social sciences. The primary goal of natural sciences is to obtain knowledge of the world as it is given to us. The objects of natural sciences are physical objects. In order to know them man has to evolve certain categories that are more or less objective. It is through the framework of these categories that man tries to understand the world. But in the case of social sciences, mere knowledge of the objective categories is not sufficient. The objects of social sciences are acts of living beings, who have their own pre-interpreted understanding. An inquiry regarding man therefore invites subjective understanding of the life-world in which real individuals interact, e.g., in order to understand a certain custom or ritual, knowledge of the actual performance of the ritual is not enough, one has to also know the values that govern the ritual. More importantly, the so-called objective categories of science are evolved out of the everyday form of life. It is only in the social world that man's unclarified acquaintance with the world at large is transformed into the meaningful understanding of the world. The categories of understanding emerge through the subjective thinking on the part of the human being.

However, the process of giving meaning to and interpreting the meaning of the world is very complex. In this complex process, images play an important role. In this process, images help human beings to understand significantly their own life-world. They act as a tool of understanding their own private subjective worlds and also the social world that constitutes the diverse elements of history, culture, art and literature. Images crystallize the diverse and diffused aspects of human history and culture. They not only represent the exemplifications of how men actually act and live in the socio-cultural world but also project the ideal ways of conduct that could set a standard or criteria for the generations to come. This does not mean that descriptive and normative aspects of images could be separated from each other. The given image simultaneously acts as a live picture of human nature and also as an ideal that points to a possible transcendence of human weakness. Progress consists in making a transition from the actual state of affairs to the ideal state of affairs. Hence, it is the unity of what is natural and normative that provides the content of what we call an image.

At this level, it is necessary to make a distinction between what may be called a representation, an image, a fantasy and a concept. A representation is more or less a portrait. It pictures the facts as they are. It is rooted in the life-situation. A fantasy, on the other hand, does not correspond to anything real. It is an expression of the subjective play of imagination and to that extent is independent of facts or life-situation. An image is different from both of these. An image is not a photograph. It is also not merely oriented towards the values that are perceived and internalized by human beings in the real world. Thus, there are both the components -- the fact and the value, the natural and the normative. The narrations in history are records of events and happenings as they occurred. The fantasies are probings into the unseen events and happenings. Images on the other hand are crystallizations of the patterns of perception that are rooted in the lived situations. Concepts have definite, precise meaning which is more or less objectively accepted. Images do not have such definite boundaries of meaning. Their meaning changes in accordance with subjective understanding. Images are relevant from one more point of view. The specific illustrations of images also bring out the failure in concretizing these images into real life. For example, the image of a woman in terms of an ideal housewife brings out the enormous difficulties in concretizing the entire womanhood as such.

In the light of the dominant images, one can assess the present-day attitudes towards women. Whether a particular point of view really captures womanhood or not, can determine the value and significance of that point of view. On the other hand, the dominance of a certain point of view may also create new images. The modern woman lives and interprets her life through the images that have become a part of her life. She also looks upon the entire social life in and through the images that have been cherished.

The *Mahabharata* describes womanhood in all its complexity. I have not considered all the images of woman but selected only five. It is not by an arbitrary choice that I have selected them. One of the reasons is that none of them falls within the stereotyped images of woman. Secondly, all of them represent women who have played different roles, i.e., the womanhood is exhibited in different roles and in different situations. Thirdly, all these women in a sense have tried to reach perfection in their own way.

Of all the women in the *Mahabharata*, only Draupadi has been called as one of the exemplifications of womanhood. She is one among the five daughters who had set examples of what a woman could be. Draupadi reached the heights as a *dharmapatni*. A *dharmapatni* was not just a housewife but an intimate friend who shared all the commitments and dedications of her husband. No other woman could surpass her in the role of *dharmapatni*. However, if Draupadi could be said to be the ideal image of Indian womanhood one can think of other images in terms of deviations up or down a 'scale'. One such image is that of a beautiful woman whose life was governed by sensual pleasure, who was an object of pleasure and that was the only role which she had to perform. Pancacuda represents this image. On the other hand, there is another extreme – that of an image of woman who exemplified total detachment and disinterest towards sensuality. She was an intellectual who refused herself the joys and sorrows of the mundane world. She was a *sanyasini* called Sulabha.

Pancacuda and Sulabha represent the two extremes on the scale. Between these two, there is Amba, who wanted to compete with men and was willing to reject her femininity. She wanted to become a man. One more image which could be placed between Pancacuda and Sulabha is that of Suvarcala. She did not care for physical beauty. She represented the intellectual wife. She did not want to reject her femininity and compete with men as Amba did.

I have tried to present these images in all faithfulness, without doing any harm to what *Mahabharata* states about them. It is not necessary to cite all the situations and events in each woman's life because almost everyone knows them. The way every woman speaks and acts at various times in her life is more important. Her speech and actions indicate the texture and fitness of her character.

The images I have chosen for analysis and interpretation though different from each other, have a peculiarity common to all of them. They are the objects of a male-dominated perception. They are the ways man has perceived woman. But if we look at them from a woman's point of view, each image unravels a different and new facet of a woman's nature and opens a new way of understanding human nature. There cannot be one single definition of man or woman. There also cannot be one image of woman given the complexity of human social life. It is not possible to reduce all these images to one single image.

However, it seems that some images have been more emphasized, more stressed and propaganda has been made that woman has to be a good housewife, i.e., *dharmapatni* and a good mother, otherwise she is not a good woman. This did not happen out of an arbitrary choice but out of a systematically misleading decision. Which images of women are to be cherished and propagated also depends upon the interests and the so-called requirements of society. The society expected women to be good housewives and good mothers. At present, the expectations are the same. When a woman looks at these images, she also feels that these images are her images, in the sense that they are genuine authentic representations of herself. She also starts perceiving herself through these two dominant images. As a result, some images are handed down from generation to generation. Some images fade in the background and some become blurred with the passage of time. Those that are handed down over generations are stabilized and institutionalized to such an extent that even though the rest of the social environment changes, these images of woman remain untouched and still exercise their power on the minds of men and women. Thus, in the modern world, the image of woman as a mother and as a housewife has not vanished. On the other hand, it is being justified on the basis of the so-called new theories. The myths of the ideal housewife, ideal mother, ideal helper continue to haunt Indians. The television, the theatre, literature, films, rituals, education, everything that man has created helps propagation of these images. These images act like moral percepts.

Draupadi is seen in many different roles in the *Mahabharata*. In the *Adiparva* of the *Mahabharata* she figures as Drupada's daughter. After her marriage her character is sketched with only two colours, i.e., with two characteristics – one that she is a *pativrata* and the other, a mother. She was cited as one of the exemplifications of womanhood, as she was the ideal *dharmapatni* of the Pandavas. Draupadi's life is full of dramatic situations. It is not necessary to cite all of them because almost everyone knows them.

Though *Mahabharata* describes Draupadi's beauty in the most alluring manner, she was not a showpiece. She was a queen and she talks and acts with that stateliness that was characteristic of a queen. But this was not her distinguishing role. We do not remember her because she was a queen of Pandavas. We also do not remember her as a *pativrata* because there had been other women who could be compared with her in that capacity. Draupadi was an ideal *dharmapatni* and it is this role that gives her a place in the *Mahabharata*. A *dharmapatni* was not just a wife who shared the joys and sorrows of the mundane world but also participated in the achievement of higher goals of *dharma* and *moksa*.

Draupadi was so famous and well-known as a *dharmapatni* that Satyabhama, the wife of Krsna asked her the secret of the control she had over the mighty Pandavas. Draupadi explained to her the *pativratadharma*. In the *Vanaparva* there is a lengthy dialogue between Satyabhama and Draupadi.[2] Draupadi describes at length her own practices to make her family a happy family.[3] These passages show that Draupadi performed her role of *dharmapatni* in the best possible manner. She surpassed almost everyone in that capacity.

However, Draupadi was not just a *dharmapatni*. Her real nature came to the foreground when she had to face the situation of crisis. This was the time when Yudhisthira played the game of dice and lost everything in the game. He staked Draupadi and lost her. He had to give her away to the Kauravas. Duhsasana sent a servant to bring Draupadi. She sent back the servant with a few questions to Yudhisthira. She asked whether it was right to stake one's own wife like this in the game. She added that only mad people bet like this. Her second question was whether Yudhisthira had any right to stake her. She said, "Ask that gambler who lost and was enslaved first? Let me know this, then only I shall come."[4] Yudhisthira could not answer these questions. She sent the servant back to ask the senior people in the gathering who knew morality or *dharma*. But in answer she was forcibly brought into the *sabha*.

Bhisma after a long pause answered her question. He said that one who has become a *dasa* or slave has no right to stake and sell his wife like this but women are under the control of their husbands.[5]

Draupadi sided with her husbands. She wanted to free her husbands from the slavery. She pleaded that her husband did not know the game of dice properly and was tricked into staking her and the kingdom and that he was cheated by the Kauravas.

Draupadi was a dignified and sensitive woman. All the pride of her life lay in her being a *dharmapatni* and playing the different roles of a housewife, a friend and an adviser. When she realised that she had to succumb to the Kauravas as a *dasi* she told everyone in the *sabha* that she did not deserve what was happening to her because she was a daughter-in-law of Kurus, wife of the Pandavas and sister of Dhrstadyumna. She was praised by Bhisma that, despite being in great distress she followed the *dharma* of *pativratya*. When Dhrtarastra asked her to request for a boon, she requested her husbands to be freed with their chariots and weapons and they were freed.

All these questions asked by Draupadi were not just emotional expressions, they indicated a deep understanding of morality on her part. Draupadi had revolted against the passivity and indifference on the part of wise men. She revolted against the immoral conduct, deceitful action and malice exhibited by the Kauravas. Draupadi feels sorry for the downfall of morality and for the fact that no man performed his obligations in his respective role and guarded her against the insults inflicted upon her.

Draupadi had to follow her husbands in the forest in the twelve years of exile. She is seen burning with anger, sorrow and insult in the *Vanavasa*. Her sorrow was not that she had to toil but that she had to lose her honour. She could not bear the loss of her honour because she was confident that she had never failed in her conduct. She tried to convince and encourage Yudhisthira to recapture the kingdom. There is a long dialogue between Draupadi and Yudhisthira in the *Vanaparva*.[6] Draupadi tried to revive the spirit of her husband by telling him the philosophy of a warrior's duty. Draupadi advocated

Ksatradharma because she identified herself with the image of a *Ksatriya* woman. This dialogue between Draupadi and Yudhisthira shows very clearly that she was very conscious of her role as *dharmapatni*. She thought of herself as a superior lady as she was daughter, sister, friend and mother of brave warriors who owned a kingdom.

The different situations mentioned above depict the character of Draupadi. There are other places which also highlight her personality. For example, Vaisampayana mentions her as *tapasvini* while describing the incident of Duhsasana dragging her into the *sabha*, when Draupadi freed her husbands from slavery. Karna remarked that she had done a wonderful job. He compared her with a life-saving boat. Kunti mentions her as a person who always spoke the truth. Kunti admires Draupadi because she values *patilok* more than *putralok*.

Draupadi was considered the ideal of *dharmapatni*. But I find an inner contradiction in her role as *dharmapatni*. In spite of being a dutiful housewife, Draupadi had to fight for her rights as *dharmapatni*. She had to demand her rights and had to remind her husbands of their duties towards her. This fact makes it clear that Draupadi was not treated by her husbands or other men as their equal. She was expected to serve her husbands selflessly. The justification of this slavery is found in the ideal of *pativratyam*.

The idealization of woman as *pativrata* is a male-created idea about woman. The slavery of woman and the inhuman treatment she gets from man is rationalized by the thought that woman's ideal should be *pativratadharma*. *Pativratyam* is a moral duty of women. The creation of an ideal like *pativratadharma* is like giving the woman a throne after taking away all her weapons. Man deprived woman of her human rights and then pretended to give her everything by making her the queen of his heart. Man convinced woman that all her rights are ultimately rights of having a husband and children. He assured her that she would get everything desirable in life by surrendering herself to the husband. She has been taught by him that the fulfilment of womanhood lies in achieving *patilok*, by giving selfless love to the husband and children and sacrificing everything for the family. The crux of womanhood lies in the blind acceptance of the inequality imposed on the woman.

Draupadi, while describing her everyday routine to Satyabhama, tells her that a woman should behave according to the changing mood of her husband. An ideal wife is one who is wise enough to read the face of her husband. In other words, it is not necessary for a woman to study and understand the psychology of men but she is expected to know the mind of her master. Following the duties of *grhini* is the source of her pleasure and the fulfilment of her right as a wife. A *pativrata* is like a servant who does not care for her own wishes. She just follows her master. She has no identity of her own. As Draupadi narrates -- "I have kept aside anger and lust and pride. I serve my husband's (other) wives with great care. I always try to get the admiration of my husbands. My husbands are like gods so I serve them happily. I do not eat unless my husbands and their servants eat. I never adorn myself when my husbands are away from me. I am obedient to my mother-in-law. While serving my husbands, the day and night are same for me. A pleased husband is woman's heaven and success because she will get all good things by serving him."[7] This speaks for the hierarchical ordering of man and woman. A woman has to complement and help man. She cannot have an independent life of her own. The image of *pativrata* has been created to make woman a symbol of man's wealth, status and honour. That is why Draupadi was proud as a queen of Pandavas and a mother of five brave sons. The image of woman as a *pativrata* acts as a manifesto of the rights of man over woman. *Pativratyam* makes woman the property or possession of man.

Draupadi, in spite of being a queen was staked like any other material thing by her husband. She was an invaluable thing possessed by her husbands. She was a *nyasa* -- a protected valuable. That is why Yudhisthira staked her without asking her. He described her physical qualities as he would describe an object, while giving her away to the Kauravas.[8]

In a patriarchal society a woman was treated as an object of sexual gratification and reproduction. The power of man over woman is related to the idea of patriarchy. When man realized that there is a biological relationship between himself and his child, the child becomes his own by preventing his wife from having children from other men. For a man, his child is an expansion of his soul, there is the concept of the perpetuation of race. A man becomes immortal by creating a child.

In the process of perpetuation of race, a woman is given the role of only a protector. To ensure the identity of his own child, man controls his woman. A woman is controlled both mentally and physically. Physical control is expressed by many 'don'ts', such as not leaving the home, not talking with other men, avoiding their touch etc. This is what is meant when Draupadi said that she was unseen even by the sun and the moon when she was living in the palace. Mental control is achieved through the sexual taboos imposed on women. These various taboos also control other men in their relation with women. In the patriarchal society forms of control slowly become subtle -- they become internal. The image of a good woman is related to motherhood and image of a bad woman to lustfulness and cruelty.

A good woman will first be a good wife, then a good mother. An ideal wife means a woman who has totally surrendered herself to her husband, home and motherhood, a totally humble woman. The image of a woman who follows her husband in all respects is created by man for the continuation of male-power and male-superiority. The male power always fears that if woman is not controlled through these taboos there will be havoc. This is why a woman's life has meaning only if she follows a particular way of life.

This way of life is the *pativratadharma*, a noble ideal of woman's life. Without following *pativratadharma*, the life of a woman, whether queen or an ordinary woman, becomes meaningless. An appeal to and approval of the housewife's way of life works as a medicine on the ailment of bad morality. It is said that a woman is basically vicious and immoral. The observance of *pativratadharma* is a cure for this vicious nature. That is why the image of woman as a *pativrata*, as an ideal mother has worldwide sanction. In Indian tradition, the chanting of the names of the five *pativratas* is regarded as sacred. The duties of these roles and the thought behind them have ultimate importance in a woman's life.

The ways of enslaving a woman in the patriarchal society are very subtle. The total sacrifice of personality is framed out in such a way that if she doesn't follow the code of conduct prescribed for her, she will underestimate herself. The great tragedy is that the intention of man to enslave her is transformed into her own intention to become a *pativrata*. For example, if a woman selfishly loves her husband and sons she will feel ashamed of herself. She will underestimate herself because she is taught that giving motherly love and forgiving is the *streedharma*. So by dishonouring her own life she gains honour and prestige. The contradiction in woman's life lies in the fact that dignity of her ideal way of life demands total lack of dignity. She gains freedom by becoming a slave.

Pativratadharmapalana is idealized for continuation of woman's enslavement. This code of conduct has two aspects: The first aspect is regarding the physical work a woman is expected to do. For example, as Draupadi said, she cleaned the house, and the vessels, used to get up early in the morning and go to bed late at night. The second aspect concerns mental enslavement on her part. This lies in total subordination, and justification of this subordination. For example, as Draupadi said, it consisted of regarding husband as God.

The image of *pativrata* gives woman a moral sanction for her enslavement. This image is created by men to teach a woman to be "passive, timid and humble". A queen like Draupadi said that she was scared of her husband like she would be of a poisonous snake. The intention of creating the image of a *pativrata* is to teach and justify the acquisition of these special qualities of womanhood. It is a tragedy that Draupadi put forward *pativratyam* as the ideal of womanhood. This ideal has two aspects. It advocates *pativratadharma* and also invites exemplifications like that of Draupadi. She was a staunch advocate of the patriarchal values. She thought that she was an ideal wife and she guided others to become an ideal wife.

This is why the real friend and adviser of a woman was a great *pativrata* like Draupadi. Prescription of any role other than of ideal wife and mother to a woman becomes sin. Making man's life happy is woman's ultimate goal of life, it is her *moksa*. This is why by becoming a *pativrata* she pleased her husband, by becoming an ideal daughter she pleased her father and by sacrificing her own self she became an ideal mother. Following *pativratadharma* is the ultimate heightening of woman's life in the *Mahabharata* and generally in our tradition, *pativratadharma* is said to be a *moksa* for a woman.

It is interesting to note that along with the ideal of *pativratyam* there is no corresponding idea of *patnivratyam* which could be applicable to man. This makes clear that the prescribed moral principles and the code of conduct were not the same for man and woman. A woman was not only bound by the general moral principles and by the corresponding code of conduct but she was enslaved by the special moral principles and the code of conduct prescribed only to women. Even today ethics of duties is not same for man and woman.

The second image of Pancacuda is an extreme deviation from the first. Pancacuda was an *apsara* (nymph). In all ancient Indian literature *apsaras* are mentioned in different stories. The main duty of an *apsara* was to dance and sing in the *Indrasabha* to please the gods and heavenly souls by giving them sexual pleasures. Another important duty was to interrupt the penance of a person by the order of Indra. That is why *apsaras* were called heavenly prostitutes. (स्वर्वेश्याः). *Apsaras* also acted as servants of superior goddesses. Kamdeva was the god of *apsaras*.[9]

So Pancacuda represents woman in her capacity as a creature inviting and influencing men. She creates an image of woman as a carnal beast. Pancacuda describes women. The description of womanhood we come to know through her dialogue with Narada is an answer to the question, "What is it to be a woman?" She was a little ashamed of telling bad things about woman as an answer to the above question because she herself was a woman. It appears that Pancacuda was free to talk what she felt and thought about women because she was an *apsara* and *apsaras* were considered free women. *Apsaras* were neither wives nor mothers. But, the freedom they had was only apparent and not real.

Pancacuda acted and talked like a puppet because what she said were not her own thoughts. Draupadi had the freedom to talk, to express her opinion or to raise questions about the social practices. Pancacuda was made to accept man's classification of women and criticize them. She said what men thought about women. Pancacuda was used as a censorious woman, an agent of male dominance. The reproaching of women has the intention of creating a morbid image of woman. It is morbid because the characteristics which are described as women's vices are unreal and excessive. They are hardly seen in any person. Pancacuda was victimized. She was the victim of male-dominance. The thoughts she expressed about women were accepted by her as valid. Her mental enslavement was very obvious.

Pancacuda descried women in an obnoxious, straightforward manner. She said: "Women are the root cause of all the vices. No one is as sinful as women are. The gravest sin committed by women is that they accept and worship the most sinful men without feeling ashamed about it. Women do not have self control. No man is inapproachable for women. They do not have will and determination. Women, when their husbands are away and when they do not get any man, indulge in homosexuality. Women are fickle and quarrelsome by nature. They are difficult to understand. Women are obtuse, like a learned man's speech. The secret about all women is that whenever they come across a handsome man, by just looking at him they are excited. For women, the most important thing is the propitiation and favour done to them in exchange for sexual pleasures. Women are equal to the sum total of the cause of destructions like the god of death, wind, poison, an edge of knife, serpent, fire, hell and underwater fire. Since the beginning of the creation of the world these faults exist in woman. These are their natural faults."[10]

The image of a woman which takes shape out of the characterization of Pancacuda becomes very vivid now. This image of woman-reviling prostitute serves two purposes. One, as she is a superhuman being, what she says about human beings or about women automatically gets sanction. The second is that what she says about women is validated because she is a woman. Such an image of a woman-reviling *apsara* is used to intimidate all the women to follow the *pativratadharma*. Such an image becomes a necessary device for the patriarchal culture. Man has projected his weakness over woman and made her the abode of vices. By doing this, man tries to prove himself ethically stronger and superior. It shows the inner fear of man that woman will dominate man. The central presupposition behind this image is that the sexuality of woman is the cause of man's fall. The fear in man's mind about woman is the fear of losing self control because of woman. It is thought that relations with women would lead to loss of 'manhood'. It is believed that wealth, power and sexuality are valuable things to be preserved and a woman is always a sexually dissatisfied creature and hence a continuous threat to man.

In the *Mahabharata*, there are many dialogues and passages decrying women. The dialogue between Narada and Pancacuda is one of them. In all these passages there is an explicit message that by nature women are mean, low, deficient and good women should overcome these vices by surrendering themselves totally to man. Then only they become pure and faultless. This is a psychological treatment for women.

The image of Pancacuda represents a thought about women in general. For example, in the *Mahabharata* immediately after the Narada-Pancacuda dialogue, there is a story told by Bhisma. The story is told by Bhisma as ancient history. This story of *itihas* is as follows: In the beginning of the world all the people deserved to be gods. All the women were *pativratas*. Gods feared that human beings will become their equal because of their high morality. They all went to Brahmadeva. Brahmadeva created women for the downfall of men. He created women who are *Krtyarupa*. He bestowed lust to them, because they wished so. Brahmadeva also gave them food, drink, beds and ornaments. He gave them ignobleness, improper talk, *rati* (sexual love), lack of reason and lack of senses. This is why women are senseless; they do not have self-control, so they are not allowed to perform the Vedic rituals.[11]

This image of woman projects her as useless for the cultivation of culture and basically against noble ideals in life. The ideal of *brahmacarya* for man emerges out of this presupposition. However, woman's vicious nature, cruelty, her ever-dissatisfied sexual urge, her intellectual inferiority is not real but it is the creation of man's mind. Pancacuda is a mouthpiece for patriarchal dominance. Pancacuda's image is an attempt to offer a moral justification of woman's slavery to man.

The image of woman as sexually ever-dissatisfied creature perpetuates very faulty and unreal concepts about woman's sexuality. I think that characterizing woman as a lecherous creature gives justification to the thought that in sexual relations, it is not necessary to give her satisfaction. Man is supposed to 'take' it.

Any person, be it a man or woman, requires an ideal image for the development of personality. Such an image will help to increase self-respect, will heighten the humane qualities in that person and will reassure his sense of value and importance. Men have many such images as ideals. But in case of a woman, the image of womanhood as total carnality is very negative. It negates woman as a person, a human being having wish and will. It tells the woman that she is body, not soul, and sexuality is the end of all her existence. This image of woman as total carnality is very dangerous because this has been treated as a reality.

The third image is also in a sense a deviation from the first. Sulabha's character represents the image of an independent woman. The character of Sulabha is mentioned in the *Santiparva* of the *Mahabharata*. She is mentioned as *bhiksuki* meaning a woman who has abandoned everything and has become a *sanyasini*. A *bhiksu* or *bhiksuki* is a person who has control over his/her body and mind, who is full of spirituality and who is single and contented. A *bhiksuki* is a well-educated woman who does penance (*tapa*).

Sulabha had chosen to be a *brahmavadini*. It seems that Sulabha was influenced by the *Sramana* tradition. Sulabha was neither a carnal woman, nor a wife. She was an independent person seeking knowledge. She had remained unmarried because she could not get a proper match. She had refused to marry someone for her livelihood. Sulabha did not have the qualities which are ascribed to women by men. Sulabha represents the image of an intelligent, strong-willed, noble woman which is in contradiction with the image of woman in the traditional patriarchal society.

That is why the image of woman as a *sanyasini* was not wholeheartedly accepted in the society. The king Janaka blamed her for the misuse of the yogic powers she had and told her that the real strength of woman is her beauty, youthfulness and her status as a married woman.[12] Janaka wondered at her beauty and charm and said that her appearance was contradictory to her lifestyle (i.e., of a *yogini*). He said that "beauty, youthfulness do not go with yoga. How come that you are having both? I have doubts about you."[13]

The fact is that Sulabha never rejected her femininity and she regarded herself as equal to men like Janaka. She was well-aware and confident that she was superior to Janaka as a person. She proved her superiority by her knowledge, hard-work and thinking power. She was self-assured. Before answering his doubts and questions Sulabha first told Janaka what is meant by a 'proposition' because proper talk consists of true propositions. She tells him: "I shall utter a sentence which is meaningful. This sentence will not have ambiguous words. I shall use excellent words and propositions. I shall utter sentences which are true enough though they may be unpleasant. I shall not use a sentence which has no intention, which will require further explanation."[14]

Sulabha did not tell Janaka that he did not talk with her properly. Instead, she told him calmly that "I never talk out of anger, lust, fear or greed. I never talk indecently. I never talk out of contempt or pride." She further told him: "A person who neglects the listeners, looks down upon the listener is not a good orator. A good orator is one whose speech percolates into the heart of the listeners."

This speech of Sulabha reveals her self-confidence and her scholarship. She was not a book-worm. She was very firm and had good control over her mind and body. Her conduct was that of an integrated and devoted scholar. She was a completely developed personality. She had revolted against the patriarchal social system and along with it the value structure which provided the basis for patriarchy.

The image represented by Sulabha is not a sanctioned image in the traditional patriarchal society. That is why in the *Mahabharata* the image of an independent woman like Sulabha is not liked. A woman who desires to have a serious talk with a king need not be beautiful. In the philosophical debate it is enough that both the parties are equally learned. Yet because Sulabha was a woman it is shown in this story that she herself became a beautiful woman to visit the king Janaka. This clearly is an attempt to wipe out the image of woman. This is an attempt to deny that Sulabha was superior to Janaka.

Again it is said that Sulabha entered the *buddhi* of Janaka by yogic power, and then started to have a talk with him. Sulabha could sit in front of Janaka and talk with him. There was no need to enter his *buddhi*. But Sulabha, though learned and confident, was a woman. So, she needed the help of a man's intellect to discuss with men. This also indicates the intentional distortion of woman's independent character. That is why the image of an independent woman has not survived in our tradition. The traditional patriarchal society finds the intelligent woman as dangerous. The character of Sulabha is distorted so that this image is not perpetuated.

The fourth image is of Amba. It is an image of an abandoned woman, a *parityakta*. It is evident that Amba's total failure in life, the rejection of life itself by her, her penance resulted in giving her a man's body and mind in the next birth. The stigma of having been a woman in the previous birth persisted even in her rebirth as a man and leads to further insults. All these can be attributed to her being a woman who was no man's wife and her refusal to take shelter with her father, the king Kasiraja.

Amba was a possession of her father. Kasiraja arranged a *svayamvara* of his three daughters – Amba, Ambika and Ambalika. Bhisma, though he had vowed never to marry, went to the *svayamvara* and abducted the three sisters for his invalid brothers. Bhisma says "understanding that the price of these daughters is bravery, I placed them in my chariot after defeating all the kings." And "I bought them by paying their price."[15]

Amba refused to marry Bhisma's brother. She told Bhisma that she was in love with King Salva and wanted to marry him. She asked him to send her back to king Salva. Amba was a woman who had a mind of her own and was aware of her right to shape her own life according to her own thoughts and wishes. Here Amba appears as any other ordinary woman who wishes to be a wife of somebody. In the traditional patriarchal system, the ultimate aim of a woman in love was to marry the man she loves. Amba wanted to achieve the status of *pativrata* by marrying Salva. She refused to marry Bhisma's brother as she did not consider her mind and body as a commodity for sale in the market of marriage. She valued marrying the man she loved more than accepting the husband thrust upon her. Salva refused to accept her as a wife. Neither could she become a mother. She had no alternative of taking shelter with her father. She said that Bhisma deprived her of *patilok* and she was deprived from gaining a husband and serving him. She was neither a man nor a woman.

That is why she desired to be a man in the next birth. It was expected that Amba would follow the advice of the elders, obey them and follow the normal convention of the society and stay with her father. But she did not want to be conventional. Amba analyzed the cause of her misery. She stated very boldly "I blame my father because he fixed my price and made me stand in the market of marriage like a prostitute and Bhisma is solely responsible for the injustice done to me."[16]

Amba did not blame her fate as other women would. She realized that she could not fulfil the desires in her life because she was a woman. She said, "I feel dejected with my existence as a woman."[17] She desires man's body and mind. She could not get that, so she ends her life by entering into the fire. Amba refused to turn her femininity into any of these images acceptable to the patriarchal society. She has no place in such a society and hence she destroyed herself.

Why did Amba destroy herself? I think the answer is that she was not a person with a dead mind. She was fully aware of her mind and her right to fulfil the desires. She was burning with a feeling of being a full-fledged person. She destroyed herself because of the patriarchal attitude towards women. The greatest tragedy is that Amba wanted to have a man's body and mind to fulfil her desires. She thought it necessary to sacrifice her womanhood for the fulfilment of her ambitions.

In the patriarchal social system a woman who wished and tried to shape her personality as a human being was scorned at. An aggressive woman was always perceived as a threat to man's power and superiority. A woman who did not regard that the fulfilment of her personality lay in becoming a wife and a mother was thought as abnormal. The so called 'natural' description of woman and the natural roles a woman has to play were imposed on her by training and culture. That is why when a woman tries to overthrow the male-power, she finds herself in a dilemma. A woman who denies her femininity has to accept the disapproval of man and society. Either she has to be like other women, or else she has no place in the society. Such a woman has to deprive herself from every kind of love and care from man. The patriarchal social system has laid down the sanctioned ways of expressing womanhood. A woman should live as daughter, wife, mother or as a prostitute. A woman who refuses to live these roles is thought of as worthy of punishment. Amba is such a woman.

Amba was caught in the man-woman dilemma. This outward struggle becomes her internal struggle. The society tells such a split woman to end the struggle by herself. The male-dominated society expects that in such a struggle a woman should end the struggle by accepting the traditional role. If she does not accept the traditional role assigned to her, then the society tells her that she is not a real woman.

I call Amba a rebel because she refused to 'become' a woman when she was caught in the man-woman struggle. She felt dejected of her existence as a woman and burnt herself to death. It was the tragic defeat of her femininity that she thought that by abandoning a typical kind of femininity, she would be able to live like a human being. Accepting femininity as typically illustrated by the patriarchal society or becoming man by abandoning femininity or destroying oneself are not the real ways of assertion.

A woman living in a traditional patriarchal society of the *Mahabharata* period, calls the system of *svayamvara* a market of selling girls, blames the men who put up women at the *svayamvara* and men who win them by defeating others at the *svayamvara* like a commodity in the market place, and declares very boldly that she feels dejected with her existence as woman. It is very difficult to give a correct judgement of the values of the society in which we live but Amba did that. She represents a brave and self-respecting woman.

However, the image of such a rebellious woman has no place in the minds of scholars or laymen. The Indians have faithfully forgotten a woman like Amba. Women like Draupadi, Kunti, Gandhari are remembered. Their sufferings are glorified. In the eyes of the society there was atleast a possibility that their sufferings had some kind of meaning. Their suffering made some sense to themselves and others. Amba's suffering was thought of as meaningless, because it was a suffering of being a woman. It was not recognized as a suffering of being a woman. It was not recognized as a suffering at all. It was not a sanctioned or acceptable form of suffering.

The *Mahabharata* and the other texts like *Puranas* have idealized women as wife, as mother and they have rejected carnal women and witches. But a sensitive, uncompromising and rebellious woman like Amba is not known much in our tradition. This shows that certain images are not allowed to perpetuate.

I think today's woman also feels dejected with her existence as a woman. I think there is an Amba alive in each woman's mind -- an Amba who is well aware of the injustice done to her and an Amba who wishes to mould her life according to her own mind. Today's radical woman who refuses to enter into the institution of marriage and family is an image of Amba.

The fifth image is an image of a learned housewife. An image of a learned housewife emerges out of the image of a *dharmapatni*.

Suvarcala represents a woman who is different from both Pancacuda and Draupadi. Pancacuda represents total carnality. Draupadi represents an ideal wife with a worldly point of view. Suvarcala is also an ideal wife, with a spiritual point of view.

There is a story in the *Santiparva* of *Mahabharata* of Suvarcala and Svetaketu. In the story, Svetaketu is mentioned as a man who went beyond the dualities of life by tolerating them and who surpassed all the worldly restraints by following them. Suvarcala is mentioned as Svetaketu's wife. Svetaketu is described as an ideal *grhasta*.

Suvarcala was the daughter of sage Devala. Sage Devala did not arrange a *svayamvara* for his daughter. The peculiarity of Suvarcala's marriage is that instead of her father, it was she who declared the condition of her marriage. She told her father "Give me to a man who although blind, is with vision."[18] She told her father that her husband should be well-versed in the *Vedas* and that he should be able to feed and protect her well. Suvarcala told her father that she has given much thought to this condition of the marriage.

Suvarcala's father invited many *Brahmans* and told his daughter to choose one as her husband. Svetaketu came and declared "I am physically blind but the all pervading soul is my vision." Suvarcala was pleased with his answer and was ready to marry Svetaketu. Svetaketu said "I have decided to pay your price to your father. I will be able to feed and protect you. Accept me as your husband."[19]

Suvarcala in answer said "I have accepted you as my husband. Now you can ask for me to my father."[20]

Suvarcala's father handed her over to Svetaketu as *kalyanmayi sahadharmacarini* and Svetaketu accepted her as *sahadharmacarini*. This marriage reflects the personality of Suvarcala. It shows that Suvarcala respected intelligence rather than physical strength or physical beauty.

Now, in what sense were the expectations of Svetaketu from Suvarcala as his wife different? Svetaketu expected his wife to perform all the Vedic rights along with him. She should follow him and he will do what she likes and loves. He expected her to share with him the selfless and egoless acts (duties). This means that Svetaketu did not regard his wife Suvarcala only as an enjoyable object. He accepted her as his partner, *sahadharmacarini*. For him, she was his partner in the spiritual path of transcending the worldly affairs. Svetaketu was a man with high ideals and he wanted a partner to share his ideal. Svetaketu's expectation was not one-sided because Suvarcala expected the same kind of sharing from her husband. Her expectations in life were not limited to acquisition of material things and pleasures. She was a learned woman and that was why she decided to marry a man like Svetaketu.

It is said in *Mahabharata* that Svetaketu and Suvarcala were a good match for each other. It is mentioned that they lived together very happily and were successful in transcending this world, i.e., they attained the spiritual goal.

I find a peculiar kind of equality in the relationship of Svetaketu and Suvarcala. I say a 'kind of equality' because it is not a kind of equality given to a person as an independent human being. It is not an equality independent of sex-difference. The equality given to Suvarcala as wife *varnasramavisista grhasthasrama* is a stage in the married man's lifespan. The rights and duties of a married man and woman are fixed. In the *Anusasanaparva* of *Mahabharata* the duties of a married man are described.

A married man should follow non-violence. He should follow and speak the truth. He should be kind to animals. He should not have any extramarital affairs. He should protect other's property and women. He was expected to accept the things given to him. He should not eat meat or drink wine. In addition a married man, i.e., *grhastha* had three debts: *Dev-rna*, *pitr-rna* and *samaja-rna*. He was expected to pay back all these *rnas*.[21]

The help of a wife is necessary and inevitable to pay back the *rnas*. A wife is a means of attaining *trivargas*. So the ideal of *pativratyam* is prescribed for a married woman.

A man, if he paid back the three debts by following *grhasthasrama* and if he desired could attain *moksa*. A man was free to become a *sanyasi* or *grhasti* by observing the prescribed duties. This was not the case with a woman. Her *moksa* was her husband and the household work. A man had limited freedom in the framework of *varnasramadharma* but a woman had absolutely no freedom. The ethics of *varnasramadharma* insisted on the obligations of a person playing a particular role, but there was little stress on the rights of a person. In the *grhasthasrama* equality of husband and wife lay in fulfilling duties of the respective roles they had to play. Suvarcala was treated as Svetaketu's equal in the framework of *grhasthasrama*.

Suvarcala and Svetaketu were learned individuals. They discussed the basic philosophical questions with each other. In these discussions Suvarcala asked Svetaketu many questions. For example "What is the relation between word and its meaning?" or "What is the intention of contradictions?" He answered all her questions. It seems she was able to interpret and analyze what Svetaketu said. She asked for the explanation of different and apparently disconnected points in his answer. She was also able to correct him at certain points. For example, she said, "It is not proper to use the word *aham* in this context."

She had her own viewpoint about philosophical questions. She says, "I think that words alone can't prove anything. Vedic words can be meaningless."[22]

Suvarcala had accepted the framework of *grhasthasrama*. She was neither rebellious like Draupadi nor did she want to compete with man like Amba.

If we look at the relation between Suvarcala and Svetaketu carefully we notice that Suvarcala was a favourite student of Svetaketu. When the student and the teacher were men, the relation between the teacher and the student and the question of superiority in this relationship was on a different level. When the teacher and the student were both men, a superior student always adorned the teacher. There are many examples of students who had surpassed their teacher and the teacher felt proud about it. When the student was a woman and the teacher a man their relationship was on a different level. In such a relationship the teacher was always convinced that his lady-student would not surpass him in knowledge or in practice. A woman was never expected to surpass her teacher. In this teacher-student couple, the teacher was the husband. The tone of the whole story is that though Suvarcala was a learned woman she should consider herself as being in a secondary position. Svetaketu was superior, first as her husband and then as her teacher.

Suvarcala was a slave-cum-assistant of Svetaketu. She was different from other *pativratas* in one respect namely, she was a well-read student of her husband. A woman was not allowed to become an independent scholar in that social structure. The glorification of woman's status as a housewife was misleading because if a woman preferred to stay alone she was never praised as a good housekeeper. The image of woman as housewife and as favourite student therefore are more eloquent of the implicit patriarchal bias. Svetaketu was leading the spiritual life, that is why Suvarcala also became his partner in spiritual life.

Suvarcala represents an image of an ideal housewife who is intelligent, learned and yet inferior to her husband.

Today's intelligent, learned housewife is an image of Suvarcala. Even today, such a housewife is glorified for her devotion to family. The present-day society expects that educated women should use their education and intelligence for the betterment of family life.

If we look at all these images, we see that in each image there is an inner contradiction. Out of these images the image of a *dharmapatni*, the image of a learned housewife and the image of woman as carnal being (*apsara*) are perpetuated in the society. The image of woman as a *sanyasini* and as an abandoned woman are not perpetuated. Why it that each image contains an inner contradiction and why are some images perpetuated and some not? The answer to these questions is that the standard of womanhood is set by man, not by woman. This is the reason why there is no relaxation of standards. A woman can either be an ideal woman or no woman at all; she is totally rejected by the society if she is not an ideal woman. This is the reason why the male image of woman has a tendency to split into two – into black and white. She is either an ideal wife and mother, or a prostitute. This is why the image of woman as a *dharmapatni*, as a learned housewife and carnal being are accepted by the society. These are rigid images and that is why there is a split. It is difficult even for a most submissive woman to fit to it absolutely. The main reason for this remarkable split is the desire to maintain the male supremacy.

Many factors have served to perpetuate a patriarchal society. Of all these, the code of morality is the most important factor. The code of morality produces the moral standards for women. These moral standards are effective only when they are accepted by the whole society; by both women and men. The patriarchal society sustained itself for so long because women willingly accepted the roles prescribed for them. Women were never made aware of any other alternative.

The alternative can never be to be a woman like Sulabha or Amba, as the image of woman as a *sanyasini* and as a rebellious woman, are not perpetuated in the society. These two images of woman are used by the patriarchal society as a threat to the woman. These images give the message that if a woman refuses to accept the traditional roles, she will be destroyed like Amba or she will have to sacrifice the pleasure of marriage and family-life.

I think in today's Indian society, the greatest hindrance to the free development of a woman as a human being is the image of a woman as an ideal housewife, as an ideal mother or as a prostitute. The woman in our society does not consider herself as a human being. She has no duties except her duties as a daughter, a wife and a mother. She has no God except her husband. First she is a woman, a daughter, a mother, a wife or a prostitute. Her whole existence is for man. Her life-long duty is to love and therefore serve man. It is assumed that she is by nature unstable and irrational. These images of women do the job of justifying the present status of women in the society. Women with a refined self-awareness and a stable mind must have realised the causes of their status but these women were insulted by the society, a few had to destroy themselves.

It is often said by men that women themselves are responsible for their slavery and their secondary position. This argument is based on the statements that women are basically (by nature) full of passion and emotion, they lack the intelligence and stability of mind which men have; and that women have not proved themselves as equal to men, that women have not become anything except a mother, a wife or a prostitute. In my opinion the first proposition is absolutely false. The nature of 'women' as defined by men is imposed on women.

About the second proposition I would say that it is a one-sided truth. This means that women merely accept the traditional role given to them by the society. Why do they accept this role? Why do they not assert themselves? The answer to these questions is that they accept the given role because they have been trained for thousands of years to accept the tradition. A person's self-image is deeply affected and influenced by the society's image about that person. Any individual in the society forms ideas about self and his/her relations with other individuals through the roles assigned to that person by the tradition. This is the reason why women find the aim of life in becoming an ideal wife, an ideal mother or in giving sensual pleasure to man.

The necessity is of looking at ourselves very objectively. Women must make efforts to stand outside the stream of traditions and look at themselves. Women must ask themselves deep-rooted and perhaps hard and painful questions. I am aware that this is a difficult process. But if women want to make something worthwhile of their lives, and of their capacities as human beings, going through this difficult process will be essential. Our society is changing very fast. It is changing in many respects. Science, technology, the system of production, education, political systems – all these are changing rapidly. But the attitudes towards woman remain ancient – as ancient as the *Mahabharata*.

The basic traditional role of women has not changed. The traditional images of women are at the base of this stagnancy. We need to change them.

Notes

1. Feminist theory is mainly concerned with the question of defining femininity though it is not precisely formulated by the feminists.
2. Pandeya, Ram Narayandatta Sastri (Trans.). *Mahabharata: Vanaparva*, Gorakhpur, Geeta Press, 1956, pp. 1618-1623.

90   *Mangala Athalye*

3. Ibid., p.1621.
4. Pandeya, Ram Narayandatta Sastri (Trans.). *Mahabharata: Sabhaparva*, Gorakhpur, Geeta Press, 1956, pp. 895.
5. Ibid., p. 898.
6. Pandeya, Ram Narayandatta Sastri (Trans.). *Mahabharata: Vanaparva*, Gorakhpur, Geeta Press, 1956, pp. 1028-1038.
7. Ibid., p. 1621.
8. Pandeya, Ram Narayandatta Sastri (Trans.). *Mahabharata: Sabhaparva*, Gorakhpur, Geeta Press, 1956, pp. 891-892.
9. Joshi, Mahadevsastri (Ed.) *Bharatiya Sanskriti Kosh: Volume I.* (Pune, Bharatiya Sanskriti Kosha Mandal, 1962).
10. Pandeya, Ram Narayandatta Sastri (Trans.). *Mahabharata: Anusasanaparva*, Gorakhpur, Geeta Press, 1956, pp. 5598-99.
11. Ibid., p. 5601.
12. Pandeya, Ram Narayandatta Sastri (Trans.). *Mahabharata: Santiparva*, Gorakhpur, Geeta Press, 1956, p. 5281.
13. Ibid., p. 5280.
14. Ibid., p. 5282.
15. Pandeya, Ram Narayandatta Sastri (Trans.). *Mahabharata: Udyogparva*, Gorakhpur, Geeta Press, 1956, p. 2494.
16. Ibid., p. 2497.
17. Ibid., p. 2525.
18. Pandeya, Ram Narayandatta Sastri (Trans.). *Mahabharata: Santiparva*, Gorakhpur, Geeta Press, 1956, p. 4989.
19. Ibid., p. 4990.
20. Ibid., p. 4990.
21. Pandeya, Ram Narayandatta Sastri (Trans.). *Mahabharata: Anusasanaparva*, Gorakhpur, Geeta Press, 1956, p. 5918.
22. Pandeya, Ram Narayandatta Sastri (Trans.). *Mahabharata: Santiparva*, Gorakhpur, Geeta Press, 1956, p. 4994.

5

Beeja-Ksetra-Nyaya: Some Considerations

Meena Kelkar

The aim of this article is to examine the *Beeja-Ksetra-Nyaya* and find out its significance in the feminist theory. This is done in three parts. The first part deals with the theory, the second with the factual aspects and the third with the philosophical problems.

Theory

One of the central issues involved in the feminist debate is the question of the presumed dichotomy of male and female character types. The dichotomy is articulated in terms of biological contrasts, personality traits, social roles and such other roles.

The Indian tradition has articulated this dichotomy in terms of a model called *Beeja-Ksetra-Nyaya*. *Nyaya* means an analogy or a metaphor. Usually a metaphor is used in order to explain complex objects so that day to day functioning of life becomes smooth and easy. *Dehali-Deep-Nyaya, Suchi-Katah Nyaya* and *Sthalipulak Nyaya* and many such metaphors have become a part of Indian literature.

The metaphor of *Beeja-Ksetra* is used in order to explain the relationship between man and woman. This metaphor was not only used as a literary model but even as a scientific truth and it became a tool of justification of the supremacy of man over woman. An essentially unequal relationship between man and woman is reflected and emphasized through the use of *Beeja-Ksetra-Nyaya* and it is utilized by culture to underrate the significance of woman's contribution to biological reproduction.

The *Beeja-Ksetra-Nyaya* is presented in *Manusmriti*, in chapter 10, Shlokas 68 to 70 and in Chapter 9, Shlokas 32 to 52. *Beeja* means seed or semen and *Ksetra* means field or land. A woman is called a field that acts as a nourishing agent for the growth of a seed. Man is called a seed that has the power to reproduce its own kind.[1] Manu states three possibilities of *Beeja-Ksetra-Nyaya*. He says that some experts give greater importance to *Beeja*. Some others regard *Ksetra* as prominent and some give equal importance to both *Beeja* and *Ksetra*.[2] The solution of the problem is as follows: Normally a seed sown in a defective field (or non-field) gets destroyed without giving any result. A field without the seed being sown into it is simply barren land. However, that the seed is given greater importance can be seen in the cases in which, due to the influence of good seed, sages who were praised and worshipped were born even from animal wombs.[3] Thus, even though in principle *Beeja-Ksetra-Nyaya* contains three possibilities, Manu rejects the other two and puts forth his view that *Beeja* is superior to *Ksetra*. The identification and equation of *Beeja-Ksetra-Nyaya* with this view itself is suggestive of the existence of male-dominance.

The whole of *Manusmriti* speaks for the supreme importance of *Beeja*. The rationale is given in terms of the similarity between the seed and its offsprings. The natural biological law that like begets like supports it. Manu also justifies it by giving an illustration that a person born in *Tiryakyoni*, i.e., animal species also could become a *muni* simply because it was an offspring of a worthy seed.[4] A perverse form of this view occurs in the *Mahabharata* which mentions that a human being is born without the semen carried or nourished by a woman so that the existence of a woman or a female animal is not needed at all. Dronacarya's birth illustrates such a case. This implies the view that irrespective of the quality of the field the quality of the seed shows itself and perpetuates itself.

This particular articulation of *Beeja-Ksetra-Nyaya* invites important issues like the genesis of the metaphor, the way it influenced the actual individual and social life and the normative problems that arise out of it.

Genesis and Practice

To be very precise, this metaphor represents a relation between man and woman. The fact that the metaphor compares man and woman with seed and field could be said to suggest that it comes from that period when human beings took to agriculture. Certain laws of nature govern the whole of the biosphere. That like begets like must have been easily observed and a known fact. The law that governed the plants and animals must have been extended to human life. However, the so-called superiority of *Beeja* and inferiority of the field must be a human construction. When human beings started cultivation of land, land became a property or a possession. Man owned the land and he also owned the woman. As soon as man's role in the reproduction system was realized, the mystery about motherhood evaporated and woman was looked upon as a bag of leather that carried the baby. Just as earth became land, woman became a bag of leather.[5] An agricultural model was superimposed on human life and there was an identification of the process of production with the process of human reproduction. Man owned the land; he sowed the seeds and reaped the harvest. But who owned the crops? Naturally, the owner of the land and not necessarily the one who sowed the seeds. The logic that governed the process of production was virtually extended to the process of reproduction. A woman's body was identified with the field, semen with the seed and the rights over the children were identified with the rights over the crops. Just as produce belonged to the owner, children belonged to the father. In most of the cases, the one who owns the land sows the seed; in that case the owner and the sower might be the same. But if this is not the situation, crops belong to the owner because the land belongs to him. In the same manner, the man owned a woman and children, but if she has children from some other man, the children rightfully belong to the husband. It is only in these non-normal odd circumstances that seed and field are treated on the same level, both of them being subservient to the owner of the field. This peculiar strategy relates the *Beeja-Ksetra-Nyaya* to the idea of ownership, which operated within the socio-cultural world.

The social structure that was based on the hierarchy was gradually built and guarded by a variety of implicit defence mechanisms that worked in the most subtle and complex manner. The social stratification, the duty-centered code of conduct that prescribed duties on the basis of *varna* and *asrama*, special insistence on the integrity of the society and execution of the moral rules with the help of *dandaneeti* and *anvishiki* all imply a well-knit framework that operated both at the surface level and at the deeper level.

Thus, *Beeja-Ksetra-Nyaya* in the form of supremacy of *Beeja* was not only confined to the theoretical level but it pervaded the whole form of life. Its glorified cosmological expression occurs in *Geeta* where Krisna calls himself the father of the world because he is the giver of the seed[6]. But on the practical level, morality, art, culture, daily rituals, religious practices, marriage systems; in short every aspect of life came to be structured around this *Nyaya*. The *Nyaya* not only endorsed but justified man's rights over woman and children. It determined the hierarchical structuring of the family wherein man was thought of as the head of the family and woman and children became his property. Woman came to be regarded as a commodity, an object to be given or accepted as a gift. She was to be protected just as wealth is to be protected. Owning a beautiful woman became a point of prestige, a status symbol. Subduing women, capturing them in war, exchanging them for something else became a symbol of a man's gallantry. "Woman is a jewel",[7] "Woman has to be protected in childhood by her parents, in youth by her husband and in her old age by her children" and such other verses speak for this view. In the *Mahabharata* there is a story as follows: Yayati, a king presents his daughter Madhavi to a hermit Galav who in turn sells her four times to four kings and gets two hundred and fifty horses from each one of them and then fulfils the wish of his teacher. The four kings one by one get sons from her and return her to the hermit. The story symptomatically highlights the woman's place in the society.[8]

This attitude towards woman is further expressed in the rules regarding the marriages, particularly in terms of *anulom* and *pratiloma vivaha*. A *Brahman* could marry a *Sudra* woman and their child could become a *Brahman*. But if a *Brahman* woman married a *Sudra* or any other class the child could not become a *Brahman*. His status was decided by the status of his father. An interesting point is that later on such children were not given this legitimate status also. They were called children born out of *varna-sankara*. The concept of *varna-sankara* too seems to be an extension and expression of the idea of primacy of *Beeja*.

Similarly, the practice of *Niyoga* was established and man could use woman as a means of reproduction. The very idea of *Niyoga* was a further extension of *Beeja-Ksetra-Nyaya*. It reiterated the comparison of land and woman. In the case of the land, whosoever owned the land owned whatever was there in the land. Similarly, it was thought that whosoever was the husband owned all the children of woman. The children born out of *Niyoga* did not belong to the person concerned but to the rightful owner or the husband. If a woman had children before marriage they also could become the property of the husband.

At one place, Krisna persuades Karna to join the Pandavas saying that Pandavas would accept him as one of their brothers because he was a son of Kunti.[9]

More importantly, the psychology of men and women came to be dominated by the belief that man is superior and hence he must rule over woman. On the one hand, as a mother, woman was respected like a goddess but as a wife she was treated like a slave. Such an ambivalent attitude expressed itself in different rituals and customs which otherwise appear to be very different. Even now in certain so-called advanced societies giving away one's own daughter (*Kanyadan*) is thought of as a holy act that achieves great *punya* for her father but in certain tribal societies, the father actually sells his daughter and the bridegroom has to pay the price for the girl. In the first case there is a glorification, in the second case there is a clear-cut barter system at work. But both are based on the same presupposition that woman has an instrumental value and she can be exchanged. The ambivalence has led to a split in the personalities of men and women. Man respects his mother but he may ill-treat his wife. He cannot respect her. Similarly a woman favours her sons but she cannot have the same attitude to her daughters. This ambivalence thus signifies a decadent and unhealthy state of society.

The standard practice even today is that the son remains with his parents but after marriage the girl leaves the house. This practice too rests on the belief that a male-child is looked upon as the giver of seed, *Beeja-data* and a creator of culture. On the other hand a girl is looked at as the field and a carrier of culture. This has trivialized her status, her life is spent in giving birth to children, taking care of them until they grow up, training them for their roles and doing the household work. Like barren land, a woman who cannot bear children is thought of as useless and it is thought of as natural for the husband to go for another woman. This has resulted in the sharp boundary line and division of labour between the domestic life and the public life, domestic life being the woman's world.

Master-slave relations got considerable weightage and importance so much so that it was thought of as natural for man to rule his wife and children, natural for a king to rule or dominate his subjects and natural for a man of power to dominate those that were weak. It justified the slave mentality to such an extent that to enslave others and to become slaves became a way of life. This is best expressed in the following verse: "It is not the horse, not the elephant, not the tiger that should be sacrificed but the he-goat because even fate does not favour those that are weak."[10]

Some Philosophical Problems

However, apart from these consequences, the *Beeja-Ksetra-Nyaya* leads to certain philosophical problems at the theoretical level. As a metaphor for explaining gender distinction it confuses between two types of concepts. The very comparison between an inanimate object and a living entity is wrong. It tries to establish links where no links exist. Connected with this is another difficulty. The comparison confuses between the process of production and the process of reproduction. The agricultural law "reap as you sow" does not work at the human level because reproduction at the human level is not producing of a prototype but a making of a new unique individual organism. The *Beeja-Ksetra-Nyaya* not only underrates the woman's contribution in the reproductive process but also misrepresents it.

Modern science has falsified the *Beeja-Ksetra-Nyaya* on scientific grounds. It has proved that there are in all 46 chromosomes, 23 from a male and 23 from a female that unite to produce one single cell that grows into a human baby. This indicates that woman is not only a nourishing agent but also an active participant in transmitting 50 percent of the child's characteristics and hence her contribution is more compared to the contribution of the male. The new genetic theory is revolutionary in this regard. That is why in the wake of the 21st century it is not a matter of debate whether *Beeja-Ksetra-Nyaya* is scientifically accepted or not. Why do we still reck up the old issue again? The reason is that at the level of thought, feeling and action we have not rejected the *Nyaya*. Even now we are not free from the prejudice that man is superior to woman. In the name of law we have accepted that everyone is equal irrespective of sex, religion and race but in actual practice we do not follow what we have accepted as our commitment. One of the reasons for this is that we are afraid of losing the patriarchal system. Men are not ready to lose their rights and women are not ready to lose their so-called secure life and face the world. Secondly, many of us are still under the impression that matriarchy would provide an answer to all our problems. Many are under the swell of this myth and hence refuse to face the situation. Thirdly, we have not been successful in evolving a system that would transcend and avoid the dangers of either patriarchy or matriarchy. We have offered a mirror not a vision.

As a result, substitution of one biological model by another one has not brought any change into our life. Another question connected with this is the question of the very use of biological models in social sciences. Long back biologists had told us that men are stronger than women but they have not told us why male strength and male activities in general are valued by people in all cultures. Biological sciences put constraints but they do not determine the behaviour of the sexes. The differences between male and female reflect an interaction between physical constitutions and patterns of our social life. Recent studies of human hormones indicate that changes in one's hormonal levels themselves are highly sensitive to changes in one's social environment.

If this is so, then the very practice of using scientific models for explaining social phenomena needs to be reconsidered. If the practice of science does not admit of any normative theory there is always a danger of its being used for bad purposes. We had allowed fanatic theories of purity of race and culture under the name of Social Darwinism. We had allowed the so-called scientific theory of *Beeja-Ksetra* to structure the Indian form of life for centuries. Today we expect that along with the falsification of *Beeja-Ksetra-Nyaya* emergence of the new theory of genetics would change our life and there would be a revolution in all aspects of life. But this is a debatable issue. What is more important is the issue of making a choice between our fidelity to science and our commitment to life. No discovery and no theory in science has finality about it. There is always a logical possibility that the given theory may be falsified tomorrow. Hence our form of life need not be rigidly committed to scientific theories or models. Whether a contribution of man or woman is more important is not the real issue at hand. The issue is what values are we going to follow in our individual and social life. It is not commitment to this or that science that makes our life a truly human life but it is our commitment to normative values that makes us true human beings.

I do not know whether there could be a feminist theory, which would throw light on the gender distinction in the most desirable manner. Maybe in the long run we may not formulate any such theory at all. But if at all we are thinking in that direction we must have an integrated theory of life -- a theory that is neither scientific nor utopian. A scientific theory lacks or ignores the normative element. A utopian theory retains the gap between the 'is' and 'ought' elements. A normative theory not only deals with 'what ought to be the case' but it deals with it in the light of 'what is the case' and 'what can be the case'. Such a normative theory may not give us any decisive answer to all the problems of individual and social life but it should at least give us a meaningful way of organizing our experience, thoughts and practices.

Notes

1. *Manusmriti, Shloka* 32, *Adhyaya* 9.
2. *Manusmriti, Shloka* 33 and 69, *Adhyaya* 9.
3. *Manusmriti, Shloka* 69, 70, 71, *Adhyaya* 10.
4. *Manusmriti, Shloka* 71, *Adhyaya* 10.
5. *Mahabharata, Adiparva, Shlokas* 74, 110.
6. *Bhagvatgeeta, Shlokas* 3, 4, *Adhyaya* 14.
7. *Manusmriti, Shloka* 39, *Adhyaya* 2.
8. *Mahabharata, Bhagvatyanaparva,* 115 to 120, *Adhyaya* 15.
9. *Mahabharata, Shloka* 8, 9, *Bhagvatyanaparva.*

6

Man-Woman Relationship in Indian Philosophy

Meena Kelkar

One of the important issues in the present-day Indian context is to discover the space for a possible theorization in feminism. The articulation of man-woman relationship provides a nexus of such and other related inquiries. This relationship is expressed by three different models in ancient Indian philosophy. The models are not separately given but they occur in the context of metaphysical theory of the classification of reality. Most of the classifications of reals speak of two types – the living and non-living. The classification of reality into male-female type is something, which is unique in itself. Whether reality can be classified in this way or whether such an attempt presupposes a different kind of perspective are problems that need serious consideration. This paper attempts to evolve the possible perspective for making this type of classification and in the light of this perspective tries to elaborate the three models of man-woman relationship and suggest their implications for feminist theory.

According to the Indian tradition, the knowledge of any object is not only through reason but also through experience. Most of the classical Indian philosophies (*darsanas*) accept direct

First published in *Indian Philosophical Quarterly* Vol. XXVI, No.1, January, 1999.

sense-perception as a means of knowledge along with others. The so-called exclusive commitment either to reason or to perception does not arise in this context. Everything is an object of both perception and reason. There is no experience that is exclusively rational or exclusively perceptual but every bit of experience is a gestalt of the interplay of both the rational and the perceptual.

The description of reality that comes from the classical Indian philosophy not only refers to the conceptual classification of reality but it also refers to the perception of reality. The direct experience of reality many a time has been expressed in the naive and childlike language of perception. This language is the language of sound, touch, physical form and smell.

Logically, a distinction can be made between conceptualization and perception.[1] Thus, Schopenhauer makes a distinction between concept and what he calls an idea, so as to distinguish between philosophy and aesthetics. According to him, the domain of philosophy is the domain of reason, reflection and conceptualization. The domain of art, on the other hand, necessarily involves perception, feeling and imagination. Concepts which play an important role in philosophy have a determinate and fixed meaning. The meanings of the concepts do not change so often. But they are barren and unproductive in art. Concepts are to be understood and not to be perceived. Ideas are used in the field of art. They resemble living organisms as they have a generative force, which brings forth that which was not previously put into them. Ideas are not to be understood but they are to be perceived. Yet both philosophy and art are interrelated in that both seek to answer the question "What is life?" by different means, art by percepts and philosophy by concepts.

However, as has been said earlier, the logical distinction between conceptualization and perception does not in any way disfigure the description of reality made by ancient Indian philosophers. The conceptual classification of reality is simultaneously pregnant with imaginative awareness of reality. This imaginative awareness of reality is suggestive and is expressed through various models and images. Such descriptions of reality are the best exemplifications of aesthetic sensibility.[2]

All Indian philosophical theories are called *darsan*. The term *darsan* not only implies knowledge but direct experience of reality. The models and images that speak for the reality are such that they are related to the form of life. They are made from actual lived situations by a process of abstraction. They act as heuristic devices for pointing to some form of life. At the same time models also act as exemplars for present day living of men and women who consciously follow and practise them in their own ways. Thus these models hint at the man-woman relationship that existed and was lived sometimes. They also act as guides for the man-woman relationships in the future. Indian philosophy consists of three models of man-woman relationship: (1) The *Brahma-Maya* model, (2) the *Purusa-Prakriti* model, and (3) the *Siva-Sakti* model. These models have important implications for feminism. At this point, it is necessary to see as to how models are different from symbols. In a sense, models are also symbols. Symbols are used for representing objects. Models not only represent the objects but also have a formal structure by virtue of which they can be used as heuristic devices for analysis and justification of new thoughts or theories. Yet they can be said to have two aspects which the symbols have. Paul Ricoeur narrates two aspects of symbols – the regressive and the progressive.[3]

The regressive aspect refers to all those suppressed desires and ambitions of which a human being is not conscious. The progressive aspect throws light on new ideals and moral points of view and, in this sense, symbols have a prophetic flavour. The above mentioned models can be considered from these two aspects. From the psychoanalytic point of view, a search can be made for all those personal and racial memory impressions that have imprinted their marks on the unconscious mind. From another point of view, a search can be made for exploring new horizons of ideals and new normative forms of life that emerge from these models. The construction of utopia would become a challenge in this context. But there is one more reason for treating models as means of research. Models, being symbolic, are means of discovery. As psychiatrist Rolo May had pointed out, they progressively reveal a structure in our relation to nature and our own existence. They reveal a new ethical form and by drawing out inner reality they enable a person to experience greater reality in the outside world as well.[4] The *Brahma-Maya*, the *Purusa-Prakriti*, and the *Siva-Sakti* models can be considered from this point of view.

Most of the classical western philosophers have classified reality into mind and matter but there is no attempt to make use of the pair of male and female (the Pythagorean classification includes references to masculinity and femininity but they are treated as qualities and not as substances). The intention behind this exercise is to classify reality. Naming the elements is followed by personifying them. Personification of reals is the unique feature of classical Indian metaphysics. It is because of this imaginative exercise that the elements of the world not only become concepts but also become models. In this way, the domain of philosophy and art merge into one another and do not remain apart as has been suggested by Schopenhauer. Such an exercise provides a wide space for two altogether different theories of modern aesthetics. One of them, namely structuralism, emphasizes the basic structure of the theory and consequently gives more importance to concepts. The other one, deconstructionism, emphasizes the changing shades of meaning and hence gives more importance to everchanging interpretations. It is interesting to see how both these extreme theories almost converge upon one another. The models used are not models from science. They are not devices to represent some abstract entities but are models from aesthetics. They are not only representations but superimpositions or projections on reality. They presuppose a particular perspective of understanding and interpreting the form of life. The personified elements thus become the vehicles of meaning. They capture a segment of reality and open up a new way of living. If unmasked, they exhibit layers of meaning. The meanings are never determinate and stable. Different agents at different times and places interpret them in different ways. According to Derrida, this technique is called "active interpretation" and it is contrasted with the technique of passive classification which takes the form of conceptual analysis.[5] However, conceptual analysis can go hand-in-hand with interpretations, including new ones. The contrast made by Derrida becomes more complex because the models of *Brahma-Maya*, *Purusa-Prakriti* and *Siva-Sakti* are not mechanical models but are organic. The Derridan distinction cannot be applied to these organic models. The two techniques -- the active classification and the passive classification cease to remain unrelated and separate. On the other hand, their everchanging, continuous interplay and configuration add one more dimension to the total complex of meaningfulness. The models are founded on a framework that is rooted in real life situations. The 'inner design' itself becomes flexible and everchanging. The models get a new context and a new meaning everytime. Both the processes of making models and of interpreting them are carried out continuously and this exercise becomes a part of our living.

The consideration of the three models from this point of view may highlight neglected areas of Indian philosophy. The models of reality now should not only be considered from the conceptual point of view but they have to be appreciated from the aesthetic point of view also. In order that such an appreciation becomes fruitful and philosophically relevant, the models and the foundational form of life have both to be taken note of. In the normal form of life, the man-woman relationship is very complex. Sometimes they are taken to be equal. Sometimes a woman is treated as subordinate and sometimes a woman is given greater importance.

The *Siva-Sakti* model of *Sakta* philosophy refers to a form of life where woman's position is stronger and more pronounced. The *Siva-Sakti* model of the *Saiva* philosophy suggests that both are equals. The *Purusa-Prakriti* model gives more importance to the differences between man and woman. As *Maya* is non-different from *Brahman*, the *Brahma-Maya* model does not give any separate status to woman.

The *Brahma-Maya* Model

The *Advaita Vedanta* describes reality in terms of *Brahman*. *Brahman* refers to the pure existence that has no qualities, no form. It is pure consciousness and it is free. It is the source of creation, growth and destruction of the world.[6] Whatever exists in the world is the expression of *Brahman*. Existence, dynamism and livingness are the properties of *Brahman*. When human beings attempt to understand *Brahman* from the human point of view, they impose human attributes on the reality that has no such attributes. *Brahman* which has no qualities, no form, now becomes a personified God. The God *(Isvara)* is also a manifestation of *Brahman*. It is because of ignorance that a human being forgets the real nature of oneself and identifies oneself with one's body. This identification further gives rise to distinctions like you and me, yours and mine and the whole web of human world is fabricated.[7] This phenomenal world is the world of names and forms. This is called *Prapanca*. The human world, along with the notions of truth and falsity, rightness and wrongness, and the everyday form of life that is based on distinction, are products of human creation. The origin of this anthropocentrism lies in the process of superimposition *(Adhyasa)*. However, just as the whole living and non-living world is the expression of *Brahman*, so also God is but one expression of *Brahman*. It is because of the superimposition of human qualities that *Brahman* appears to be God *(Isvara)* that has a human form. The power of God is called *Avidya* or *Maya*. It is because of *Maya* or ignorance that one forgets one's real nature and thinks that one is a physical body. Ignorance or *Maya* is not created by humans, although human beings are governed by it and are subject to its functioning. The creator of *Maya* is God, hence he is called *Mayin*. *Maya* functions for the playful enjoyment of God.

Maya does not have independent existence but it cannot said to be non-existent either since human beings are affected by her. *Maya* is said to be indescribable. *Maya* functions in two ways. It envelops an object so that it cannot be perceived properly,[8] consequently an object appears different from what it is. It obstructs the knowledge of an object. The phenomenal world of names and forms is illusory and not real in the true sense of the term. Sometimes a rope appears to be like a serpent. The cognition that it is a serpent is an illusion and when the illusion vanishes, only the rope remains. The phenomenal world is also illusory like a serpent.

The term *Brahman* transcends all notions of femininity or masculinity. It stands for existence par excellence and various forms of gods and goddesses are nothing but manifestations of *Brahman*. However, these gods and goddesses have phenomenal existence. *Maya* depends for her existence on God. God is the creator of the world that is real in the true sense of the term. On the other hand due to *Maya*, the illusion of the phenomenal world occurs. *Maya* is lifeless and does not have any purpose of its own existence. It is created for entertaining God.

The model of *Brahma-Maya* is important in many ways. *Maya* does not exist in the true sense of the term. She is not substance proper. The very mode of her existence is of a lower order. A woman also belongs to the lower level of existence. She does not have an independent existence in the sense that she does not have her own purpose for life. Her whole existence and living is for the sake of man. The *Manusmriti* and other ancient treatises state that it is woman's duty to give sexual satisfaction to the male and procreate. The *Manusmriti* also narrates laziness, fickleness and lying as the natural, inborn qualities of woman.[9] It is said that she is not at all worthy of trust. It is emphasized that she has always to be under the control of her parents, husband and sons. All this implies attributions of wholly dependent and slave-like existence.

Many implications about man-woman relationship follow from the above male point of view. The relation between a man and a woman is never taken to be a relation between two equals. A woman has no identity and she is also not supposed to have her identity. Whatever identity she is supposed to have is conferred on her by males. She is like a slave and a male is like a master. A slave does not have his own wish, similarly a woman cannot act according to her wish but has to follow the duties that are prescribed by man. The moral code of conduct, which is almost followed religiously, looks upon woman as property. Ancient Indian law speaks of women and children as the property of the male. The clubbing together of women, *Vaisyas* and *Sudras* in *Geeta* implicitly presupposes the prejudice that woman has no mind and hence no capacity to think. This prejudice is presented in the *Brahma-Maya* model.

The *Purusa-Prakriti* Model

The second model is the *Samkhya* model of *Purusa* and *Prakriti*. The *Samkhya* philosophy speaks of *Purusa* and *Prakriti* as two independent substances. Both are pure existents and cannot be perceived directly. *Purusa* is sentient and eternally existent. He is the seer and one who witnesses everything *(Saksi)*. Having no qualities, he is not subject to the experience of pleasure and pain. Sentience is the mark of *Purusa*. He is neither the doer nor the enjoyer. He is neutral and indifferent towards the experiences of the world. He is above bondage and liberation in the sense that he never falls into bondage or gets liberated. The experience of pleasure and pain are of the body-mind complex *(jiva)* and never of the *Purusa*. The *Purusa* identifies itself with body-mind amalgam and hence experiences sorrow. The moment he understands that he is wholly and radically different from the subtle body-mind organism, he is liberated. According to *Samkhya* philosophy *Purusas* are many and because of their contact with the *Prakriti* they get the forms of subtle body-mind organisms.

The second substance is *Prakriti*. *Prakriti* is inert and is wholly devoid of consciousness. Yet she has to go through the cycle of birth and death. The distinctive quality of *Prakriti* is that she is active, although she has neither consciousness nor knowledge.[10]

Prakriti is made up of three qualities: *Satva, Rajas* and *Tamas*. *Sattva* produces knowledge of doing many things. *Rajas* initiates the tendency to act and *Tamas* stops the tendency to act and promotes lethargy. The three qualities act and interact with one another, sometimes helping one another, and other times dominating one another. They behave and co-exist like man and woman. The state of their equilibrium is called primordial *Prakriti (Mula-Prakriti)*. The coming together of these three qualities is not for one's own self because *Prakriti* is lifeless (unconscious). It is activated for the sake of enjoyment and liberation of the *Purusa*. Her activity is as natural as the occurrence of milk in the cow for her calf.[11] The mere existence of sentient, neutral *Purusa* activates *Prakriti*. The coming together of *Purusa* and *Prakriti* is like coming together of a lame person and a blind person.[12] The whole world of phenomena is produced out of this coming together of *Purusa* and *Prakriti*.

Purusa comes into contact with *Prakriti* and identifies himself with *Prakriti's* experiences of pleasure and pain. He becomes unhappy and quests for liberation. Ultimately, he understands that he is radically different from *Prakriti*. The knowledge of his true identity (being) liberates him. If there is no one to see and enjoy, the very functioning of *Prakriti* has no meaning. The minute body that comes into contact with different gross bodies acts like an actor. In this way *Purusa* has to undergo sufferings of birth, old age and death until the minute body is destroyed. The dancer goes to the back side of the stage as soon as her dance is over. Similarly, once the world has been created, *Prakriti* becomes indifferent towards the world. *Purusa* is always pure, free and conscious. Only *Prakriti* has bondage or liberation.[13]

The model of *Purusa-Prakriti* refers to two independent substances. If unmasked, it exhibits one more form of man-woman relationship. Man and woman have each their own identity. They have their own independent existence and their own distinctive qualities. Their existence, however, is qualitatively different. *Purusa* has consciousness but *Prakriti* is devoid of it. She does not have an iota of consciousness. The distinctive quality of *Purusa* is knowledge, and the distinctive quality of *Prakriti* is capacity to act.[14] Yet their coming together is purposive. They come together in order to compensate for their own imperfections. *Purusa* does not undertake any activity. He is basically pure and free. But because of his contact with *Prakriti*, he is dragged into the cycle of phenomenal world. He does not act but, being conscious, his mode of existence is of a superior kind. Similarly, a man, by nature, is supposed to be superior. A woman, being on par with unconscious inanimate objects, has no intelligence. Her mode of existence itself is of a lower level. Yet she has the artistic qualities of an actress like that of charming the people. The concept of *Prakriti* expresses the view that a woman lures and hypnotizes. Yet, the status of *Prakriti* is higher than the status of *Maya* in *Brahma-Maya* model, for *Prakriti* has an independent existence. She is the cause of the world and the God does not participate in the creation of the world. This model presupposes that the roles of man and woman are basically different. Yet their coming together is governed by pragmatic considerations. The view that both of them co-operate in order to fulfil their missions suggests prudence in practical life. Here the utility consideration becomes more important than the understanding between man and woman. No understanding and cooperation between them is hinted. Apparently, the relation between them looks like the relation between two equal beings – but the qualities attributed to woman are such that she is almost like preordained executive who carries out the plan of the board of directors. She has no identity of her own nor has she the power of making decisions. She is also not supposed to know that one must have such an identity. She is a slave-cum-machine.

Such a view implicity presupposes the modern biological and psychological determinism in terms of which the differences between man and woman are projected to be basically natural and hence unavoidable.

The third model is the *Siva-Sakti* model.[15] This model comes from *Kasmir Saivism, Sakta* philosophy and from the philosophy of Jnaneshwara.

Kasmir Saivism

In this philosophy, *Siva* is believed to be all pervading, eternal and pure consciousness. He is beyond perception and conception. The word *Siva* is beyond the comprehension of language and thought. The realization of *Siva* is never through words or thoughts. There is no idea or symbol that fully represents *Siva*. No human intellect can understand it. He is not an object of knowledge and yet can be directly experienced.

Kasmir Saivism believes *Siva* to be personal God *Isvara*. *Isvara* is full of love.[16] *Sakti* is an inseparable part of the loving God. *Vedanta* does not give an independent status to *Maya*. *Samkhya* takes *Prakriti* to be lifeless. In keen contrast *Saivism* states that *Sakti* is not inert but living. She is *Siva's* energy. She is the knowledge, activity and desire of *Siva*.[17] Sometimes she becomes the power of will. Volition is the grace of God and it creates desire for emancipation. The power to know is a means to know God. Sometimes she becomes the power of activity. It is in and through the power of activity that the whole world continues to survive and grow.[18]

Sakti is the cause of both bondage and liberation. It is through the medium of *Sakti* that *Siva* becomes one with the whole creation or world. It is through the exercise of *Sakti* that *Siva* becomes the creator, caretaker and destroyer of the selves. The whole universe is created through *Sakti*. *Siva* is not created by *Sakti* and *Sakti* is not created by *Siva*. In fact, *Siva* and *Sakti* are just two names. Both the names refer to the same existence (reality). *Siva* is the quiet, silent and neutral state of *Sakti* and *Sakti* is the dynamic, active state of *Siva*.[19] The relation between *Siva* and *Sakti* is like the relation between the Sun and the rays of the Sun.[20] They are one.

The attempt to trace the roots of this model leads us to a form of life where man and woman are equals. Yet on the metaphysical level, they do not refer to two separately existing realities. It is only on the level of attributes that they are different. Both of them are expressions of one and the same existence. There are similarities and differences in them. They are similar in respect of being living and conscious. They are different in the sense that man is neutral and passive but woman is active and dynamic, she takes interest in everything. Their coming together is something that is neutral.

This model places man and woman in a wider context of 'being human' but this context does not produce any new thought. The suggestion that both are human beings does not lead to forming a specific relationship between the two. From the grammatical point of view, man becomes the subject and woman as his power becomes either a quality or an activity. Thus there is a one-sided dependence of woman on man. This dependence is expressed by treating her like an object. Hence *Kasmir Saivism* does not provide any foundation for equality between man and woman.

Sakta Philosophy

The *Siva-Sakti* model is also used by *Sakta* philosophy. Yet the *Sakta* model and consequently the model used by *Tantrism* is very much different from *Kasmir Saivism* model and also from other varieties of *Saivism*. According to *Sakta* philosophy, the reality on which the existence of the world depends is both the formal and efficient cause of the world. The belief that there is a feminine element at the root of every creation is central to the *Sakta* philosophy.[21] This basic reality or energy behind the creation is everpresent. There is neither creation nor destruction of energy, but only transformation. This reality has no beginning and no end. It is eternal, self-luminous and dynamic. The *Sakta* philosophy calls this state as *Siva-Sakti Samarasya*. In this original state of unity or oneness, *Siva* element is inactive, neutral and just perceives everything. But the *Sakti* element is free and active. On the empirical level, even the element that is called is *Siva* is also a form of *Sakti*. One cannot talk of *Siva* without *Sakti*.[22] The world is grounded in the oneness of *Sakti* and *Siva*. Both are independent and yet they are together. There is an implicit harmony between them. There is a feeling of oneness and a sense of belongingness between them. This is the original primordial state of existence. At the next level, the feeling of oneness is replaced by the feeling of one's own distinctness. This creates the feeling of one's own identity against the awareness of the other. Both the elements then start acting and reacting against one another. These two forms of energy are called fire *(Agni)* and the moon *(Soma)*. Fire produces suffering and death. *Soma* (the moon) produces happiness and life. The function of fire is to destroy and that of the moon is to create. The whole world is the play of *Siva* and *Sakti*. It is the throbbing of energy or *Sakti*. *Sakti* is non-different from *Siva*. When she desires to see the functioning of *Siva* and *Atma*, the creation of the world takes place.[23]

The whole universe is implicitly present in the womb of this great power *(Mahasakti)*. The origination, growth and decay of the world is but the play of this power. *Siva* is sentient and luminous, *Sakti* is dynamic. The *Sakta* philosophy states that *Siva-Sakti* is both sentience and dynamism *(Sat, cit)* harmonized together. *Sakti* is free, she produces livingness which gives rise to the awareness of one's own self. This awareness of oneself is a form of *Siva*, but *Siva* is also an inseparable part of *Sakti*. *Jiva* or individual self is identical with *Siva*. When the self forgets its identity and becomes aware of its physical body, it develops ego and becomes proud. It is only by the grace of the teacher that it becomes aware of its real nature. In its unity with *Siva*, the power of worship *(bhakti)* on the part of the self becomes one with the sentience of *Siva* and a feeling of oneness is created. The self becomes *Siva*-like but not *Siva* himself. The worship of *Siva* *(bhakti)* is not converted into *Sakti* but it becomes like *Sakti*. In this state, there is no question of either bondage or liberation. What remains is the self-luminous, harmonious and everflowing existence par excellence. This is the perfect state of the existence of the universe.[24]

This model of *Siva-Sakti* would have given a new turn to feminist thoughts. All other philosophies presuppose a male's point of view. Central to *Sakta* philosophy is the thesis that the world is produced by the female element. *Siva* is also considered as the form of *Sakti*. Here woman is considered to be the mother of everything. She is neither inert nor like an animal but living and intelligent. She is not the object of enjoyment but like a man she is an enjoyer, an agent. She does not act as an obstruction to liberation but she helps in liberating the self. There are many beautiful names of the goddess in the *Sakta* philosophy. *Moksada* (the giver of liberation) is one among them. The *Sakta* philosophers believe that realization of self is also the result of the awakening of a power *(Sakti)* which is called *Kundalini*.

A woman not only gives birth but she also brings up the young ones. In the *Markandeya Purana,* the goddess says that she would nourish the whole world with the life-sustaining vegetables, which would grow out of her own body and that after the heavy rains, she would again come on earth, as *Sakambhari.* The *Sakta* philosophy glorifies the woman. Motherhood has always been a matter of respect for the Indians. The various forms of *Sakti* occur in the different forms of goddesses and their worship. The model of *Sakti* at least gives us a clue to infer that sometimes there must have been matriarchal societies in which woman reigned supreme.

At the practical level, the model implies that man and woman are on par with one another. They have their own distinctive qualities and yet none of them is either superior or inferior. The model is suggestive of a peaceful, harmonious coexistence of man and woman. It explicitly expresses equality that is demanded by the feminists. But, more importantly, the model supplies hints to develop a possible ontology and epistemology of feminism. Freedom, dynamism, power of creation, luminosity, the throbbing of life are some of the qualities that would be necessary for such a theory. This theory would look upon nature not as a resource but as a source of life. If a mother's point of view is generalized nothing remains except love and benevolence for the world. However, if feminism would take this stance, there is the danger of creating the female counterpart of male chauvinism, where, instead of man, woman would dominate, and do everything that is done by man in a male-dominated society. On the other hand, the *Siva-Sakti* model opens a new possibility wherein transcendence of male chauvinism as well as feminism itself becomes a necessary step. Here transcendence does not mean destruction of masculinity or femininity but awareness of a limit -- a point of perfection beyond which the differences cannot be stretched. Such a transcendence would provide for the creation of a new kind of world, a world in which man and woman are in perfect harmony, joy, and peace with each other. The *Siva-Sakti* model is thus the symbol of the ideal man-woman relationship.

Siva-Sakti Model of Jnaneshwara

In *Anubhavamrta*, Jnaneshwara talks about the creation of the world as the result of the coming together of *Siva* and *Sakti*. According to him *Siva* and *Sakti* are independent and equal yet because of love they cannot remain away from one another. Pradeep Gokhale presents Jnaneshwara's description of *Siva-Sakti* at four different levels.[25] On the first level, both the elements are independent. The essential properties of *Siva* element are existence, capacity to perceive, enjoy and act. The essential properties of *Sakti* element are the capacity to be perceived and to become an object of perception. Both come together and a child in the form of the world comes into existence. *Siva* and *Sakti* can stay away from one another but because of their attraction and love towards one another they live together and not separately. At the next level, it is impossible for them to live separately because *Sakti* becomes the quality of *Siva*. Both are expression of existence par excellence, both are luminous. They live so happily that their so-called separate existence is also illusory. They are one and the same. At this level *Sakti* cannot be separated from *Siva*, just as sweetness cannot be separated from jaggery. This view is similar to the *Kasmir Saivism* model. At the third level, *Siva-Sakti* are not separated but they are one. Both are just two names of *Siva* or, just as well of *Sakti*. Jnaneshwara states that the difference between man and woman is also the expression of one single *Siva* element.

At the fourth level, the whole world is split into two parts, *Siva* and *Sakti*. Both of them refer to separate substances yet they are not mutually exclusive. They are so experienced together that one cannot understand whether it is the experience of *Siva* or of *Sakti*. Jnaneshwara also believes like

Kasmir-Saivism that the whole world is produced out of *Sakti* in the form of knowledge, desire and action. He says that the world is the expression of *Siva*. Just as the moon and its light, the ocean and its waves cannot be separated, similarly *Siva* and the world cannot be separated. The world becomes a sportive play of *Siva* and *Sakti*.

The consideration of these four types of relationship with reference to feminism evokes four different types of man-woman relationships. At the first level, man and woman are independent and equal. Both have consciousness and intelligence. Man is capable of action, he is the doer, enjoyer and observer; woman, on the other hand, is the object of action, an object of enjoyment. Both of them have their own distinctive natures but their love for one another does not allow them to remain separate. However, there is a logical possibility that they can live separately. In this context, the love and understanding becomes more important but the relation of the enjoyer and that which is an object of enjoyment does not vanish.

At the second level, woman becomes the power of man. The relation between man and woman becomes a relation between substance and quality. Thus, both are not on par with each other. There is no reciprocal relation between the two.

At the third level, man and woman are just two names of *Siva*, the difference between them is a matter of nominal, linguistic type. In reality they do not have an independent existence. Both are imperfect and unless they come together they cannot overcome their imperfections.

At the fourth level, man and woman turn out to be two different modes of existence. Their personalities and qualities are different yet they are interdependent. This view suggests that, although being equal and independent, they cooperate with one another. *Siva-Sakti* model in this sense can give rise to equality between man and woman because even after coming together their distinctive qualities are not destroyed. Their identity is preserved. On the psychological level, some qualities are common to both man and woman but some qualities are different and unique. This particular view springs from *Siva-Sakti* model of this type. The psychological questions about the uniqueness of qualities with reference to man and woman will have a different dimension from this model. Yet this model acts like a metaphor. It does not provide the determinants of heterogeneity or homogeneity, either explicity or implicity.

The discussion of these above mentioned models at least suggests that the articulation of man-woman relationship has anthropological, philosophical, psychological, social, political and aesthetic aspects. Any question of feminism in the context of Indian tradition demands serious attention to these various aspects.

The consideration of these three models also suggests one thing, that is, even within the male dominated discourse there is a possibility of progressive transcendence in terms of better attitude towards woman. The same discourse contains *Brahma-Maya* model that denies any status to woman, the *Purusa-Prakriti* model that grants independent existence to woman and the *Siva-Sakti* model opens up a new form of life wherein woman is respected. Both the glorified and the denigrated versions of the models highlight new areas of research in feminism.

Notes

1. Schopenhauer. *The World as Will and Representation*, Payne E.F. (trans), Dover Publications, 1969, Vol.II, p. 235 and p. 406.
2. These models are not expressions of primitive modes of thinking where language is not very important but they are expressions of a refined sensibility. At times, maturity in thinking leads to the

awareness of the limits of language. The classical Indian thinkers however did not think (like Wittgenstein) that one should remain silent where language falls short of expression. On the other hand, for them the limits of language open up new and novel ways of 'sensing' the things. The reality exhibits itself and the experience of reality is a matter of 'perceiving' and not just thinking.

3. Paul Ricoeur: "These authentic symbols are truly regressive progressive, remembrance give rise to anticipation, archaism gives rise to prophecy...Such symbols both disguise and reveal." (*Freud and Philosophy* trans. Denis Savage, Yale University Press, 1970, p. 497).

4. Rolo May (edited, Introduction), *Symbolism in Religion and Literature*, George Braziller, New York, 1961. p. 45

5. J. Derrida, *Writing and Difference*, Bass. A. (trans.), as quoted by Stuart Sim in his essay, "Structuralism and Post-Structuralism" in *Philosophical Aesthetics: An Introduction*, Oswald Hanfling (ed.) Blackwell, Oxford. 1972, pp. 426-427.

6. *Janmadyasya Yatah*, second verse, *Brahmasurtrabhasy Vaidika Sankar Advaitamatamuvada* (Marathi), edited and published by D.V. Jog., 1954, p. 589.

7. *Adhyasa-Bhasya, Brahmasutrabhasya*, p. 170

8. In the *Atharvaveda* and *Aitareya Brahmana* the term *Maya* is used in the sense of magical power.

9. The *Manusmriti, Adhyaya*, 9, Verses 17, 14, 13 and 16. From *Shri Sartha Manusmriti*, edited and translated in Marathi by Pandit Ramchandra Sastri Ambadas Joshi, Sri Gurudev Prakasan, Pune.

10. *Samkhya Karika*, Verse 19, edited by Dr. Ramashankar Tripathi (Hindi), Varanasi 1970.

11. Ibid., Verse 57.

12. *Sankaracharya* argues that *Purusa* is indifferent, passive and cannot activate *Prakriti*. Even a lame person has to act in order to help a blind person. *Purusa* is simply incapable of any action. So the analogy of the blind and the lame person breaks down. See *Brahmasutrabhashya* Adhyaya 2, Pada 2, Sutra 7. *Sankarbrahmasutra* Vol. 2. Vasudevsastri Abhyankar and Prof. Chandorkar (Marathi translation) Bhandarkar Oriental Research Institute, Pune, October 1957.

13. *Samkhya Karika*, Verse 59 and 62, edited by Ramasankar Tripathi (Hindi), Varanasi, 1970.

14. It is because of the dynamic, active nature of *Prakriti* Prof. D.P. Chattopadhyaya seems to hold the view that the *Prakriti-Purusa* model must have emerged in the matriarchal society.

15. *Siva-Sakti* were worshipped in the pre-Aryan Sindhu culture as the phallic symbols *Linga* and *Yoni*.

16. Wherever there is God, there is love and where there is love, there is God. *Tirumantiram*, Verse 151.

17. Sivajnana Siddhiyar, 1.66 *Saiva-Siddhanta Darsan* (along with the Hindi translation) by Dr. Kailasapati Misra, Ardhanarishvar Prakasan, Varanasi, p. 57, *fn 2*.

18. According to *Kasmir Saivism* power of activity which *Siva* has is the natural play, a throbbing of the Lord Siva. The *Saiva-Siddhanta* on the other hand holds that this activity is motivated by the noble desire to uplift the human beings.

19. Spinoza talks of two expressions of substance, 'Natura Naturata' and 'Natura Naturans'. 'Natura Naturata' refers to whatever has been created. It refers to the passive state of nature. 'Natura Naturans' refers to nature in its active form creating the whole world. To Spinoza, nature created (Naturata) is created by nature naturating, creating (Naturans -- the active state). Both are expressions of one single substance or God. *Saivism* goes a step further and defines the passive *(Siva)* and the active *(Sakti)* in terms of one another. So there is a reciprocity between them.

20. Siva-Jnnana Siddhiyar, Supakkam., 5, 9. *fn* 1, from *Saiva-Siddhanta darsan*, by Kailaspati Misra, Varanasi, 1982.

21. Deviprasad Chattopadhyaya in his *Lokayat* quotes the following verse from the *Markandeya Purana*. The verse expresses the statement by the Goddess herself "I shall support (nourish) the whole world with the life-sustaining vegetables, which shall grow out of my own body (*Atmadeshasambhavaihi*) during a period of heavy rain. I shall again fame on the earth, then as *Sakambhari*".

22. Gopinath Kaviraj. *Tantrik Vangamaya me Shaktadrishti*, Bihar Rashtrabhasha Parishad, Patna 1963. p. 133.

23. Cakreshvara Bhattacarya. *Saktadarshanam* (Sanskrit) 1968, p. 92.

24. Ibid. p.100.

25. Pradeep Gokhale. *Jnnanadevance Anubhavamrutatil Tattvajnnan* published by Alka Gosavi, 1985, pp. 15 to 18.

7

Empowerment of Women: The Buddhist Perspective

Lata Chhatre

Empowerment of woman is one of the important issues in women's studies. Many attempts have been made to solve and to dissolve this issue. But as it seems this problem has yet to be solved. Hence, in this paper I have made an attempt to understand and to solve the issue by excavating philosophical, metaphysical and epistemological considerations behind it.

Generally, empowerment of woman means the self-realization[1] of woman and her active participation in decision making, in her social and personal life.[2] At the level of theory, it is possible to think that woman can realize herself and can play a significant role in making personal and social life meaningful, but at the level of practice it is not possible because at this level, empowerment is not only related to her abilities and capacities but also to the customs, traditions and religious practices that either provide or restrict the space for her to bloom. They are the decisive factors, which decide whether a woman can participate in social activities. These factors not only do not allow her to participate in decision-making but to play an important role in her social life. This shows that although empowerment is theoretically possible, it is not possible practically. Here some problems arise; why is there a gap between theory and practice? How to bridge the gap between empowerment of the woman at theoretical level and empowerment of woman at practical level? Buddhist philosophy helps us to solve these issues. In Buddhism, it is accepted that there are two *avaranas* or perspectives, namely, *klesavarana* and *jneyavarana*. *Klesavarana* is that sort of perspective which is related to the individual's knowledge about herself and *jneyavarana* is that sort of perspective which is related to the individual's knowledge about the external world on one hand and to the external world's knowledge about the individual on the other hand. With the help of these concepts, I shall argue that due to the *klesavarana* and *jneyavarana*, there is a gap between theoretical and practical aspects of empowerment.

In this context, I shall argue further that if the *klesavarana* and *jneyavarana* will be removed then the gap between the two aspects of empowerment may be removed and a woman can enjoy her empowerment in the true sense of the term. Hence, in this paper, I am going to discuss following points:

1. Nature of empowerment.
2. Nature of *klesavarana* and its relation with the individual's knowledge about herself.
3. Nature of *jneyavarana* and its relation with the knowledge of the external world.
4. How do *klesavarana* and *jneyavarana* create the gap between the theoretical and practical aspects of empowerment?
5. How does the removal of *klesavarana* and *jneyavarana* bridge the gap between theoretical and practical aspects of empowerment?

I shall discuss these points in sequence.

Nature of Empowerment

Empowerment of woman is widely and specially used with reference to woman's holistic development. Holistic development means her social, cultural, economic, political, mental and spiritual development. Empowerment means woman's realization of her own capacities and power so that she can face challenges and overcome social and cultural barriers. It builds a positive image about herself. It creates enough confidence in her so that she takes an active part in decision making related to herself, and her family. However empowerment does not mean something that is external to her but it is built in her and hence it has to be excavated by her.

This shows that empowerment of woman has two aspects, namely, theoretical aspect and practical aspect. Its theoretical aspect deals with the issues like, how is it possible to empower the woman and after getting empowerment how can she use her capacities and powers? How can she participate in decision making etc.? The practical aspect deals with the actualization of her empowerment, her actual participation in decision making in her personal as well as social life.

In other words, the theoretical aspect of empowerment is related with different possibilities of empowerment and its practical aspect is related with their application in society where woman as well as society have important roles to play. For the actualization of woman's self-realization two conditions need to be satisfied, namely, change in mental attitude of woman and change in mental attitude of the society. Change in mental attitude of woman enables her to break social and cultural barriers and change in mental attitude of society enables the society to provide the opportunities to woman and also to encourage her so that she can explore her capacities. Both these changes are important and necessary because if a woman is not ready to utilize her capacities then there is no use of providing opportunities to her. Similarly, if the society is not ready to provide the opportunities to her then there is no use of her having empowered. Hence, if we are interested in bringing about woman's empowerment in practice it is necessary that

there should be mental transformation on part of woman and
the society.

   Theoretical and practical aspects of women's empowerment
are important and necessary because even if society is interested
in providing her with the opportunities to explore her
capacities in her personal and social life, but it does not have a
proper theoretical background, it is not possible to make use of
them. Similarly, even if though there is an ideal theory of
empowerment, but society is not ready to actualize it then such
a theory will become useless. So we can say that without
theory, practice is blind and without practice, theory is empty.

Understanding the Problem of Empowerment in the Context of Indian Culture

In our country, we see that women have rights in various fields,
and they are playing important roles in politics and
administration. However, it seems that they are not very
confident. It is because they are still under the pressure of
traditional and cultural values and mental make-up. It may be
the case that though by achieving highest success in various
fields of knowledge, she has challenged the male-centered
society and culture, yet she has failed to remove the cultural and
social barriers to which she has been confined for so many
years. Perhaps, while opening the opportunities for her,
male-centered society has taken enough care to not let her
forget her duties and mental make-up. Hence, it is necessary
that woman should have empowerment. Here a question arises:
why has woman not realized herself? There are basically three
reasons for Indian woman's not having self-realization, namely:

1. Woman's attitude towards herself.
2. Woman's attitude towards the society.
3. Society's attitude towards woman.

   1. *Woman's attitude towards herself:* Through the processes
of socialization and enculturation woman has formed some
images about herself in her mind; also some cultural values have

been taught to her. She is not ready to do those things due to which these images about her will be broken. It is because of these that while achieving the highest status in society, she has to follow her duties, which are prescribed by the society. She is trying to make herself fit in that image. For example, Sita is an ideal woman for her. Hence, we can say that woman cannot have empowerment because she is still ignorant about her capacities and powers. This makes her stick to the traditional and cultural roles. Thus the mental set-up of woman does not allow her to break the cultural and social barriers.

2. *Woman's attitude towards society*: Through the processes of socialization and enculturation, woman is taught that society in general and male in particular are her protectors. So it is her duty to serve the society and males in the society. Due to this reason also she is not ready to break the barriers.

3. *Society's attitude towards woman*: Sometimes we see that the society or social mind also has cherished some images about woman. As a carrier of traditional values and *samskaras*, social mind also examines and evaluates her achievements within the framework of these values. Hence, whenever the intelligent woman shows her calibre and revolts against the traditional values she becomes the victim of social ridicule.

This shows that the wrong attitude of woman towards herself and society and also the attitude of society towards woman have created obstacles in the actualization of her empowerment.

In brief, woman does not have empowerment because on the one hand she has a wrong understanding about herself and about the society and on the other hand society also has a wrong understanding about her. Hence, if we want woman to be empowered then her ignorance about herself and society as well as the ignorance of society about woman will have to be removed. When this sort of wrong understanding will be removed from the mind of woman and that of the society, they will realize that all the ideas of woman about her rights, duties, obligations, customs are man-made. They will realize that these rights, duties, customs etc. are anthropocentric in nature and hence they are human constructions. Yet whatever is constructed by humans can be changed. Hence, the anthropocentric world of values cannot really assess the ability of woman.

This shows that the significant empowerment of woman in Indian context requires three sorts of changes, namely, change in woman's attitude about herself, change in woman's attitude about society and change in society's attitude about woman.

However, the empirical evidence has shown that it is not possible because either Indian society or Indian woman or both are reluctant to accept that woman has the power to introduce her own independent existence. What are the reasons for this reluctance? There could be many reasons but with the help of two concepts from Buddhism, namely, *klesavarana* and *jneyavarana* I shall try to reveal the metaphysical and epistemological reasons behind that.

Any individual, in present context a woman has *klesavarana* because of which she is not mentally prepared to play the decisive role in her family, society and nation. Similarly, the society has *jneyavarana* because of which society is not mentally prepared to accept the true value of woman's role in the development and welfare of the society. Let us see the nature of *klesavarana* and *jneyavarana* in detail.

Klesavarana and Woman's Attitude Towards Herself

Gautama Buddha while talking about the problem of human suffering has pointed out that there is no permanent, eternal and unchanging principle like *atma* but individual's perspective about herself gives rise to self-love and also to her belief in *atma*. This kind of perspective is known as *satkaya drsti*.[2] According to Gautama Buddha, this is a kind of *trsna* or uncontrolled and unlimited desire of man, which is the basic cause of human suffering. This kind of *trsna* is called *klis'ta trsna*.

Vasubandhu, while explaining this thought of the Buddha, has elaborated the concept of *klesavarana*. According to him, *klesavarana* is *atmadrsti* or *atmiyadrsti*[3] or man's perspective about himself. Actually, every human being, independent of the gender consideration, is composed of five elements or *panchaskandha*, namely, *rupa skandha, samjna skandha, vedana skandha, samskara skandha* and *vijnana skandha*.[4] This is also known as *nama rupa*. But due to the ignorance and perspective about herself an individual assumes that there is a permanent, external and unchanging principle like *atma* that resides in human body. An individual further tends to desire those worldly things and affairs, which give her nothing but pleasure and avoids those worldly things and affairs, which give her nothing but pain. In this way, according to Vasubandhu, an individual's perspective about herself is *klesavarana*.

This *klesavarana* consists of four kinds of *klesas* or defilements, namely, *atmadrsti, atmamoha, atmamana* and *atmasneha*. *Atmadrsti* consists in accepting that there is *atma* that resides in *panchaskandha*. *Atmamoha* is ignorance about the nature of *atma*. *Atmamana* is the pride about *atma*. *Atmasneha* is self-love. According to *Vaasubandhu*, it is due to *atmamoha, atmadrsti* and *atmamana* that there is *atmasneha* or *asakti*. This *asakti* gives rise to suffering.

This concept of *klesavarana* can be used to understand the nature of the wrong understanding of woman about herself. Like any other human being, a woman is also composed of five elements. She has good and bad qualities. Besides that she does not have qualities like being a mother, a sister, a wife etc. built into herself. That is, she is not born with these qualities. But while living in the society, some roles are ascribed to her. On the basis of these roles she is named as a mother, a sister, a wife etc. All these names are nothing but kinship terminologies. However, due to the wrong understanding about herself, she thinks that all these are her characteristics and they are built into her. Accordingly, she tries to behave within the framework of that role and this sort of behavior gives her pleasure. Because she loves these roles, she is proud of them.

Indian social structure and epics are also responsible for this sort of wrong understanding of woman. No doubt that *asramavyavastha, purusartha* and *varnavyavastha* have important contributions in the formation of Indian society and also in shaping the individual's private and social life. *Varnavyavastha* has divided the society into four *varnas*; namely, *Brahmana, Ksatriya, Vaisya* and *Sudra*. These four groups have certain status in the society. *Brahmana, Ksatriya* and *Vaisya* are enjoying the higher or superior status and *Sudra* is enjoying the lower or inferior status in society. Thus *varnavyavastha* has provided a pyramid structure of the society where *Brahmanas* are on a higher strata and *Sudra*s on a lower strata. There are four *purusarthas*, namely, *dharma, artha, kama* and *moksa*. *Asramavyavastha* includes four *asramas*, namely, *brahmhacaryasrama, grahasthasrama, vanaprasthasrama* and *sanyasasrama*. With the help of *asramavyvastha* the span of human life has been divided into four parts.

However, there is inequality and injustice in society, especially with regard to the people belonging to *Sudra* caste and women. For the present, we restrict ourselves only to the consideration of women. When we thus restrict ourselves we find that woman does not have high status in the society. Woman does not have specific *varna* because her *varna* is determined either by her father or her husband. Similarly, she cannot peruse *moksa* as she cannot enjoy *sanyasasrama*. Besides that she does not have any share in the wealth of her father and husband.

Similarly, *Manusmriti* and the epics like *Ramayana* and *Mahabharata* have described the nature of woman in such a way that a woman thought that her nature is and should be according to this description. For instance, the description of woman's nature occurs in the *Mahabharata* in three different forms:

1. Both *Manusmriti* and *Mahabharata* have laid down certain norms of behaviour for an ideal woman with ample illustrations drawn from various sources. For example, Parvati, Savitri, Draupadi symbolize total devotion to the husband, a virtue necessary for an ideal woman.

2. It also goes on to explain how a woman becomes an object of ridicule if she violates the rules or refuses to observe the code of conduct prescribed for her. It is believed that the woman is a weak creature and needs to be protected. This is nothing but showing disrespect for the woman.

3. Lastly, it refers to how a woman achieves honour by strict observance of all the imperatives. There is no dearth of eulogies to woman in the *Mahabharata*.[6]

Due to this kind of hammering and brain-washing either by social structure or through epics, the woman started thinking that whatever is imposed by the society is her true nature and it is her duty to behave and to become a woman as described by social norms and values. She started thinking that the qualities imposed by society are her inborn qualities, that they are built-in-her. It is because of this that she forgets her nature, capacities and powers. Consequently, she is unaware and ignorant about herself. This ignorance has not only created the wrong apprehension about herself but has given rise to self-love and also a belief about herself that basically she is a mother, a wife etc. In Buddhist terminology, this perspective can be called as *satkayadrsti*. This *drsti* or woman's wrong apprehension about herself creates *trsna* or uncontrolled desire in her mind. Due to this *trsna* she tends to play only those roles which give her nothing but pleasure. Such roles may include the role of mother, wife, daughter etc. This *satkayadrsti* alongwith *trsna* forms the *klesavarana* of woman. Due to this *klesavarana* woman starts thinking that motherhood, wifehood etc. are her built-in-features and she acts accordingly.

In this way, *klesavarana* has an important role to play in the mental formation of woman.

Jneyavarana and Woman's Attitude Towards Society and Society's Attitude Towards Woman

Our epistemological inquiry is based on three pillars, namely, knowledge, known and knower. Generally, it is believed that the knower and the known exist independently from each other. It is further believed that the qualities and characteristics of the object that the knower knows are built-in-features of the object. However, according to Buddha, this is a kind of ignorance. While talking about the problem of human suffering, Gautama Buddha has pointed out that an ignorance of the self is not only the cause of *trsna* and thereby the cause of human suffering but man's ignorance about the nature of an object is also the cause of *trsna* and human suffering. In order to satisfy his desires, an individual imposes certain qualities on an object and assumes that an object has these characteristics. That is to say though that object does not have these qualities, due to the wrong apprehension and ignorance about the nature of an object, an individual thinks that an object has built-in-qualities and that it exists independently of the knower.

In this way, due to the ignorance about the nature of an object, an individual accepts the duality of knower and the known. This kind of ignorance is known as *aklista avidya*. This perspective about the nature of an object of knowledge is called as *dharmatmya drsti*. It gives rise to ignorance known as *aklista avidya*. In this way, due to the ignorance about the nature of an object, an individual accepts the duality of knower and the known.

While explaining this thought of the Buddha Vasubandhu has introduced the concept of *jneyavarana*. According to him, *jneyavarana* is *dharmatmya drsti*. He argued that the qualities or *dharmas* that an individual apprehends do not exist in the external world but they are *kalpanas* or conceptual constructions of the individual. But due to ignorance and wrong perspective about the nature of an object, an individual assumes that there is an object of knowledge having certain qualities, existing in the external world independently of its being known. This ignorance gives rise to the duality of knower and the known. This kind of ignorance is called *jneyavarana* which is due to wrong understanding of the nature of an object and its relation with the knower.[7]

In other words, *jneyavarana* is the ignorance on the part of knower, which gives rise to the duality of knower and the known. It is a perspective which is known as *graha-grahaka drsti*.[8] Generally it is accepted that whatever exists in the external world is the object of knowledge and whatever an individual experiences, exists in the external world. Similarly, whatever an individual talks about exists in the external world and whatever exists in the external world can be talked about. In other words, whatever is knowable is real and whatever is real is knowable. Similarly whatever is nameable is real and whatever is real is nameable. In this way to accept one to one correspondence between the knowable and the real is *graha-grahaka drsti* or *abhideya-svalaksana grahaka drsti*. It is also called *dharmatmya grahaka drsti*, because an individual is ignorant about the fact that whatever that he experiences or talks about does not exist in the external world. This perspective is also called *graha-grahaka drsti* because an individual or a knower believes that whatever he experiences is independent from him.

Thus, according to Vasubandhu, to accept the duality of knower and the known is a kind of ignorance, which is known as *jneyavarana*.

Now, let us see how this concept of *jneyavarana* helps us understand the attitude of woman towards the society and society's attitude towards the woman. In this context, we have to consider two sorts of epistemic relations between woman and society; first the epistemic relation where a woman is a known and the society is a knower and second, the epistemic relation where the society is a known and the woman is a knower.

We have to consider both these epistemic relations because many times it happens that woman has power but the society is not ready to accept it. On the other hand, it also happens that society is ready to provide the opportunities to woman to utilize her qualities but she is not ready to use them. Consequently, in either case, empowerment of woman does not become possible. Hence, by considering both the sorts of epistemic relations between woman and society, we can realize why empowerment is not actualized. I shall consider these two relations in detail:

1. *Epistemic relation where a woman is known and the society is a knower*: Due to social and cultural reasons, the society looks at the woman from the perspective of the traditional value framework which has been transmitted and supposed to be an ideal from generation to generation. From such a perspective woman is accepted as a mother, as a wife etc. and consequently a woman is introduced as a wife of or as a mother of somebody. Nobody introduces her without any reference to these roles. It is forgotten that being a mother, or a wife is not her inborn nature, but all these relations come into existence when she comes in contact with other members of the society. These descriptions of woman are human constructions. They are based on kinship relations. Many times it is forgotten that all these relational qualities are not inborn qualities of woman but are superimposed qualities and then it is believed that these qualities are essential qualities of woman. Similarly, it is assumed that a woman having these qualities exists independently of her being known. This ignorance gives to rise to the duality of man and woman. This is *jneyavarana* of the social mind in general and man in particular which is governed by man's or society's wrong understanding about the nature of woman. This is *dharmatmya drsti*. Due to this point of view, it is assumed that woman has those qualities which social mind apprehends and the qualities which social mind apprehends are supposed to be the essential qualities of woman. It is further

believed that whatever is attributed to woman is the built-in-property and vice versa.

2. *The epistemic relation where woman is a knower and the society is known:* In this relation we find that a woman is under the pressure of the social and ethical norms and values of society. Right from her childhood through the processes of socialization and enculturation, moral and social values have been taught to her in such a way that every time, she is dependent on others, especially on male members of the society either for her work or for her existence. Consequently she thinks that she has been protected all the time by men. Hence she thinks that it is her duty to serve them by all means.

Hence, we can say that due to the perspective that tradition has imposed on her to look at the society in general and man in particular, she is unable to see the appropriate nature of man. This perspective of woman is called as *dharmatmya drsti*. This *drsti* makes her think that whatever she apprehends as the qualities of society or man through the processes of enculturation and socialization are built-in in the society and man and that these built-in qualities of society or man can be apprehended by her. For example, she believes that husband is God. This type of relation between a woman and society as the knower and the known gives rise to the dualism of woman and man.

Because of this perspective, she is reluctant to break the traditional framework and hence she is not ready to accept the opportunities given by the society. Due to this *dharmatmya drsti* woman as well as society are not ready to go beyond the duality of man and woman. Both these sorts of perspectives can be called *dharmatmya drsti* because the minds of man and woman are both ignorant about the fact that whatever that he or she apprehends or talks about are not the inborn qualities of woman or man respectively. Consequently it is assumed that woman as well as man exist independently with their qualities. To accept duality between man and woman is ignorance. This ignorance can be called *jneyavarana*.

The Effect of *Klesavarana* and *Jneyavarana* on Aspects of Empowerment

Hence, we can say that due to the first sort of epistemic relation, though woman has capacities to be an individual, due to the conservative members of the society she cannot accept it. Similarly due to the second sort of epistemic relation, though society offers the opportunities to woman for her progress, but due to the impact of enculturation and socialization her mind becomes so dull and conservative that she is not ready to take advantage of these opportunities.

In this way, we have seen that *klesavarana* is related with the woman's attitude towards herself and *jneyavarana* is related with the woman's attitude towards society and society's attitude towards woman. Due to *klesavarana* and *jneyavarana*, we can talk about empowerment of woman on theoretical level but on the practical level it is not possible. Here a problem arises: how do we bridge the gap between these two aspects? To this issue I shall now turn.

Removal of *Klesavarana* and *Jneyavarana*

A bridge between theory and practice: Vasubandhu has not only talked about *klesavarana* and *jneyavarana* but he has also talked about removal of ignorance. He has pointed out that *jneyavarana* is *pratiyogi* or counter-adjunct of *dharma nairatmya* or unique particulars. That is, where there is *dharma nairatmya*, there is an absence of *jneyavarana*. In the context of empowerment of woman *dharma nairatmya* means to accept that just like any other human being, a woman is composed of five elements. She is just like a bare particular and hence whatever the qualities that are apprehended are not built-in-her but are human constructions.

In order to have knowledge of *dharma nairatmya* it is necessary that there should be an absence of *jneyavarana*. There will be an absence of *jneyavarana* only when an individual realises that whatever he experiences and names is nothing but the result of conceptual and linguistic constructions and further when he accepts that although he has an experience about the external world and woman and even though he talks about it and woman, they are devoid of *dharma*.

Jneyavarana of society and woman will be removed only when society realizes that whatever is imposed on a woman is nothing but a conceptual construction and a woman too is nothing but an aggregation of five elements. Similarly *jneyavarana* of woman will be removed when she realises that whatever she imposes on male in particular and society in general is nothing but a conceptual construction; male too is nothing but an aggregation of five elements. When *jneyavarana* is removed both society and woman have an appropriate knowledge of each other. In this situation, woman will be ready to take the opportunities provided by society. Similarly society will not hesitate to accept woman as an individual, an independent being.

While talking about the removal of *klesavarana* Vasubandhu has said that *klesavarana* is the counterpart or *pratipaksi* of *pudgal nairatmya* or no soul, i.e., where there is *klesavarana* there is an absence of *pudgal nairatmya* and where there is *pudgal nairatmya* there is absence of *klesavarana*.

In the context of empowerment of woman, accepting *pudgal nairatmya* will mean accepting that just like other human beings, woman is also composed of *panchaskandha*, she is just like a bare particular, she has her own qualities. Although she is performing certain roles in the society, the qualities which are necessary for the performance of those roles are not built-in-her. When she realises this fact, then her *klesavarana* will automatically be removed. In this way by knowing *pudgal nairatmya*, woman removes *klesavarana*. This could be called self-realization on part of the woman.

In other words, *klesavarana* of woman will be removed only when she realizes how to draw a line of demarcation between her own qualities and the qualities imposed by society on her. When she realizes her own nature, she is capable of using her abilities for the welfare of family, society and nation.

She is powerful enough to participate in decision making and play a decisive role in the world of politics.

In this way the removal of *jneyavarana* and *klesavarana* will bridge the gap between the theoretical and practical aspects of empowerment. This will pave a way for solving woman's problem. This is the important contribution of Buddhism in feminist philosophy.

Buddhist Contributions to Feminist Philosophy

While solving the woman's problem, Buddhism seems to be the first system of thought, which has given importance to the spiritual and intellectual development of society and woman. Generally it is believed that in male-centered society, a woman is subordinate and a man is dominant. It is further believed that in this society all social and ethical norms, rules and sanctions have been formed out of male interest and hence if we bring certain changes in social structure then woman will not have problems. For example, in this context, it may be argued that if we go from patriarchal society where a man is the central figure to matriarchal society where a woman is the central figure then woman will not have problems.

However, this is not acceptable in the Buddhist system. Buddhists believe that social structure is not necessarily responsible for woman's problems but the *jneyavarana* and *klesavarana* of the society and that of woman are responsible for her problems. Hence we can say that in the Buddhist system of thought, if the woman and society have *jneyavarana* and *klesavarana* then woman will have problems even if we go from patriarchal to matriarchal society. Hence from the Buddhist perspective if we want to solve the woman's problem, it is not enough to make a change in the social structure, it is also necessary to remove the *jneyavarana* and *klesavarana* of the woman and the society.

This is the important contribution of Buddhism to feminist philosophy that it does not give much importance to making certain changes in the society but it gives importance to making

mental and spiritual changes in woman and society. Whereas
the former are superficial and hence temporary, the latter are
fundamental and lasting.

Further, it is also believed that the woman can be
empowered if education is given to her and if she will be
economically independent. However, the empirical evidence
has shown that it is not the case. This is because she is still a
slave of customs and traditions. Hence mere education and
economic independence of woman are not sufficient. But it is
necessary, as pointed out in Buddhism, to make changes in her
mind so that she can have enough confidence to break
traditional and social barriers. It is also suggested in Buddhism
that if woman has to empower herself it is necessary that she
should take enough efforts to remove cultural and social
bondage by realizing her true nature. This thought is not only
advocated in Buddhism, but it is also actualized in it. *Therigatha*
is its striking example. *Therigatha* is a collection of the poems
written by Buddhist nuns. These nuns have described the social
and family background from which they have come. They have
explained how they have realized the ultimate truth and have
made themselves free from suffering.

This shows that Buddhism has not only advocated that
woman should be empowered but it has also provided the
opportunities for her self-realization. Buddhism seems to be the
first religion where woman's right for self-realization has not
only been accepted in principle but has also been actualized in
practice.

Buddhism, by accepting that every human being is
composed of five elements, has advocated the equality between
man and woman and thus transcended their gender difference.
It treats man and woman on par with each other. This shows
that Buddhist thought does not believe in the dualistic model of
man and woman for solving the problems of woman.

The dualistic model accepts that there is a gender difference
between man and woman, which is imposed by male-
dominating culture. It means gender difference is a cultural

construction and whatever is constructed or imposed is not accepted as the real nature of the object in Buddhism. Buddhists accept that whatever is real is free from any sort of constructions. Construction is a sort of *jneyavarana*.

Hence, within the framework of Buddhist thought, we can say that instead of solving the woman's problem through attempts based on a dualistic model it is better to transcend this difference and accept that each individual is an aggregation of *panchaskandha*, he is an unique individual. Each individual, either man or woman has good as well as bad qualities. Accordingly he or she is morally good or bad. Buddhism has not only advocated this thought but through the dialogues between Mara, one of the symbolic men and the Buddhist nuns Buddha has shown that it is possible.

Notes

The author is grateful for helpful comments and suggestions of Dr. Meena Kelkar, Dr. Vaijayanti Belsare and Dr. Deepti Gangavane.

1. In this context the word self-realization has not been used in the sense of *moksa* but in the sense of a woman's realization of her capacities and power.
2. Association of Indian Universities: *Education and Woman's Empowerment*, pp. X – XII.
3. Sthiramati, *Vijnaptimatrasiddhibhasya*, p. 87.
4. Vasubandhu, *Abhidharmakosa*, p. 34.
5. Sthiramati, *Vijnaptimatrasiddhibhasya*, p. 172.
6. M.A. Kelkar, *Subordination of Women: A New Perspective*, p. 47.
7. Sthiramati, *Vijnaptimatratasiddhibhasya*, p. 87.
8. Ibid., p. 341.

8

Salvation and Women in Jainism
(with special reference to Prabhacandra Suri)

Nirmala Kulkarni

All Indian philosophical traditions discuss the theme of salvation in their own philosophical tenets by designing the means and measures for its achievements. Some of them also enlist the eligible or the *adhikari* of this highly coveted path. In this context a question arises -- Is a woman eligible to attain salvation? If yes, what is her identity in that particular philosophical system? If no, what is the reason behind denying salvation to her? The present article centers on searching traditional answers to these questions and further analyzing them.

However, to our surprise, the only philosophical system to give crystal clear answers to these problems is the Jaina system. Both the offshoots of these systems -- the *Digambaras* and the *Svetambaras* -- have given cerebral answers to this particular problem by reserving separate chapters of their texts under the title *strimuktivada*. The Jaina authors focus on this problem because it is one of the differences which segregate these two schools of the Jaina philosophy. The *Svetambaras* advocate salvation of women, whereas the *Digambaras* deny it. Prabhacandra Suri, a prolific Jaina writer belonging to the *Digambara* sect has discussed this particular issue in two of his texts, viz., *Prameyakamalamartanda*[1] and *Nyayakumudacandra*.[2]

Both these texts differ little in the content and expression. Moreover, he reviews all the arguments advocated by the *Svetambaras* and refutes them. Therefore, to get an essence of the Jaina view in general and *Digambara* view in particular I have concentrated on the *strimuktivada* of the *Nyayakumudacandra*.

Many attempts have been made in this direction by researchers, especially by foreign scholars, since this particular problem is of serious concern to 21st century studies.

1. Nalini Balbir (1997) in her rapid review of the position of women in Jainism writes a few words regarding women and salvation.[3] Her article is certainly useful in ascertaining the position of women in general in the Jaina religion.

2. N. Shanta (1997) in her extensive dissertation entitled, 'The Unknown Pilgrims' describes almost all aspects of female asceticism of the Jaina religion.[4] She takes a resume of the texts discussing the issue of salvation and women. She presents in brief the arguments of both the sects. Her most important contribution lies in the documentation of opinions of contemporary female ascetics on various issues. Certainly she has toiled a lot to give a thorough picture of the Jaina *sadhvis*.

3. The last and important author is Padmanabh Jaini. He has published two works on the subject:[5] (a) A paper entitled 'Gender and Salvation' (1997) takes into consideration the views of the *Svetambaras*. (b) He has possibly enlarged the same paper in book form under the same title. However, since I could not procure both these references I am unable to review them.

Thus, it seems that no attempt has been made to analyze the views of the *Digambaras*. The present article plans to review their position in the following line:

1. History of *strimuktivada* in Jaina philosophy
2. Analysis of Prabhacandra's arguments
3. Resume

History of *Strimuktivada* in the Jaina Philosophy

The Jaina *Agamas* are supposed to be the basic texts of the Jaina religion. But these cannot be said to be very old. Among the *Agamas*, the oldest texts do not discuss the problem of salvation of women. Only the late *Agama* texts raise this problem and try to argue from the *Svetambara* point of view. These texts are not considered authentic by the *Digambara* sect.

Kundakunda is the first *Digambara acarya* to deny salvation for women. *Pravacanasara*[6] and *Astapahuda*[7] are the two Prakrt texts written by him. *Pravacanasara* does not make any statement regarding salvation of women. Only at one instance it simply indicates it:

Kim kimcana iti tarkah apunarbhavakamino'tha dehepi |
Sanga iti jinavarendra nihpratikarmatvam uddistavantah ||

Here, Kundakunda just says that even though all persons desire salvation, still *Jina* has introduced some attachment to their bodies by intending partial destruction of their *karmas*. Here, he suggests that women are advised to be with garment; therefore they are not completely free from *karma*. Yet, it is not clear from the above verse whether he intends women to be with attachment or the householders. Yet, it seems that the verse is certainly conducive for the discussion of *strimuktivada*. Because, the commentator Jayasena quotes nine additional verses discussing the said topic. Probably these are suffixed later on to the above quoted verse. These are in the form of a dialogue between the *purvapaksa* of the *Svetambaras* and *uttarapaksa* of the *Digambaras*. These are as follows:

The *purvapaksa* argues:

Preksate na iha lokam param ca sramanendradesito dharmah |
Dharme tasmin kasmat vikalpitam lingam strinam ||

The moral order laid down by Jinendra does not expect anything beyond salvation. In such order, why is the feminine gender shown with option? (i.e., the Jaina order for women folk is different from that of the male ascetics.)

niscayato strinam siddhih na hi tena janmana drsta |
tasmat tatpratirupam vikalpitam lingam strinam ||

Certainly, women are not seen or said to have obtained salvation in the same birth. Therefore, the order given for them differs.

prakrtya pramadamayi etasam vrttih bhasita pramada |
tasmat tata eva pramada pramadabahuleti nirdista ||

By nature itself, women are full of erroneous behaviour. Therefore, they are called *pramada*, i.e., full of erroneous behaviour.

santi dhruvam pramadanam mohapradvesau bhayam duguncha ca |
citte citta maya tasmat tasam na nirvanam||

Certainly, lust, hatred, fear, and *duguncha* reside in them. Thus, untruthfulness is always with them. Because of that they do not obtain salvation.

na vina vartate nari ekam va tesu jivaloke'smin |
nahi samvrtam ca gatram tasmat tasam ca samvaranam ||

In this mortal world, no woman is without the above quoted faults. She possesses at least one of them. Moreover, the body in its natural condition is without garment. But, to cover her inherent faults she is ordered to wear garments.

Cittasravah tasam saithilyam artavam ca praskhalanam |
Vidyate sahasa tasu ca utpado suksma manusyanam ||

There is rise of lust in them, therefore, they do not have a strong mind. For the same reason they have menstrual flow and thus, they give birth to thousands of micro-organisms.

Linge ca strinam stanantare nabhi kaksa pradese ca |
Bhanitah suksmottpado tasu katham samyamo bhavati ||

Microorganisms take birth in the female organ, in between their breasts, in the navel, and below the arms. Then, how is it possible to keep restrain?

yadi darsanene suddha sutraddhyayanenapi samyaktah |
ghoram carati va caritram striyah na nirjara bhanita ||

Though she is pure by keeping right faith, though associated with right study, though practicing fierce behaviour, still she will never be free of complete destruction of karma.

tasmat tam pratirupam lingam tasam jinah nirdistam |
kularupavayoyuktah sramanyah tatsamacarah ||

The omniscients have introduced a suitable sign, i.e., covering garment for them. Female ascetics born in respective families, possessing beauty and youth follow the rules of behaviour accordingly.

These additional nine verses quoted by Jayasena speak the foremost logic applied by the *Digambara* Jaina monks to segregate women from salvation. According to them women are impure by nature, they cannot control *himsa*. Therefore, they cannot attain the state of *nirjara*, i.e., the state where complete destruction of *karma* takes place. For the same reason they cannot attain salvation.

Astapahuda is not yet critically edited. It shows similarity of expression with that of the *Pravacanasara*. The following verses of this text deny salvation for women. It says:

lingam strinam bhavati bhunkte pindam svekakale |
aryapi ekavastra vastravaranena bhunkte ||

A woman has garment as her sign. She takes meals once a day. Any female ascetic must take her meals by wearing a single garment.

Thus, by prescribing garment for women as their invariable sign, Kundakunda further says:

*Napi siddhyati vastradharo jinasasane yaddyapi bhavati
tirthankarah |
Nagno vimoksamargah sesa sesah unmargakah sarve ||*

In the religion of the Jainas a person, even if he is a *tirthankara*, cannot attain salvation with garment. The path to salvation is without garment, rest all are not the right paths.

Kundakunda further argues that a woman cannot even have *pravrajya*, i.e., initiation in the *sannyasa*.

*Linge ca srinam stanantare nabhikaksadidesesu |
Bhanitah suksmah kayah tasam katham bhavati pravrajya ||*

Since women produce microorganisms in their body, they cannot attain *sannyasa*.

*Yadi darsanena suddha ukta margena sapi samyukta |
Ghoram caritva caritram strisu na pravajya bhanita ||*

Though she possesses right knowledge, right faith, and follows strenuous behaviour, she cannot attain *sannyasa*.

*Cittasodhir na tasam sithilo bhavah tatha svabhavena |
Vidyate masas tasam strisu nasankaya dhyanam ||*

They do not have a clear mind. They are feeble-minded. They have menstrual flow, they are not free from fear. Therefore, they cannot meditate with full concentration.

Thus, Kundakunda applies the same logic as seen in the above quoted interpolated verses of the *Pravacanasara*. It is certainly astonishing that he denies even *sannyasa* for women because, it is said that the Jaina religion is the oldest religion to offer *sannyasa* for women. It is also true that Buddhism and Jainism are the two sects to allow women become ascetics. The statement of Kundakunda should be reviewed in historical perspective. Moreover, the Jaina female ascetics had contributed a lot to the Jaina religion. They were educated. They used to copy many manuscripts. But even though they had a very good position in the society, no woman ascetic had written a single book or commentary. Is it because she was not treated at par with the male ascetics or she was not allowed to write independently? The above remarks of Kundakunda need a different type of interpretation based on careful scrutiny of the Jaina religion.

These two works along with the commentary *Dhavala*[8] on *Satkhandagama* have paved the path for the *Digambara* view of *strimuktivada*. Prabhacandra has developed the theme in a more logical way.

Among the *Svetambara* writers Sakatayana[9] is the pioneer of refuting the *Digambara* view. The tradition is developed by Ratnaprabhasuri and many others. Ratnaprabhasuri mainly focuses on the *avisesitva*, i.e., nondifferentness (women are not different from men.)[10] This seems to be an important and relevant criterion felt by the *Svetambaras*. However, it was limited to the spiritual field, which never gained ground in the Indian soil. Otherwise, India could have given an altogether different and relevant outlook to the world even today.

Analysis of Prabhacandra's Arguments

As said in the introductory remarks, Prabhacandra argues against salvation of women in his two texts, *Nyayakumudacandra* and *Prameyakamalamartanda*. The *strimuktivada* from *Nyayakumudacandra* is translated along with notes by me.

Here, an attempt is made to analyze Prabhacandra's arguments to lay hold on his concept of women. By 'his concept of women' I do not mean his individual opinion, but that of majority of the then existing Indian society, which he represents. Again while using the word 'majority', I am aware that whatever he has painted is not the only picture of women, because the other side of the coin is evident in the views of the *Svetambaras* who consider men and women equal, at least in the spiritual field. Moreover, all other systems of philosophy do not take into consideration, rather go beyond the physical differences on the spiritual plain. But when Prabhacandra argues against spiritual salvation of women, he tries to prove the inferiority of women mainly on the material plain which represents a general opinion about women existing at his time. Such opinion is not abruptly designed, but gradually evolved due to various social, cultural, and political situations. Here, as far as possible I would try to show how this particular image is evolved in due course. Of course, my opinions are based only on the literary sources. Thus, the present section mainly tries to analyze Prabhacandra's beliefs about women.

Spirituality and Women

"Women do not deserve spiritual freedom, because they are inferior to men" (*purusebhyo hinatvat*) is the key argument of Prabhacandra. Inferiority of women in the spiritual field is directly discussed only in the Jaina texts. A brief historical picture of the position of spiritual freedom of women would be as follows:

The Early Vedic Period

In the Rgvedic period the highest intellectual activity, i.e., creating a new poem was not at all forbidden for women. The aim of the society was creation and not spiritual attainment. *Yajna* was the creative activity which was the miniature model of the universe. Even the wife of the sacrificer had to play a crucial role including the singing of *samans* in the *Yajnas* of the *Brahmanic* period. We have archaeological evidence to prove that women could perform sacrifices independently. (These must be reviewed critically. Furthermore, some light must be thrown on the thread ceremony for women because unless a person undergoes this particular ceremony he or she is not entitled to perform any kind of sacrifice. Thus, her independent entry in the field of ritual could be determined only with the help of her right to *upanayana* ceremony.) In the *Vajapeya* sacrifice, she actually used to climb the staircase along with her husband. Here, the staircase was the symbol of heaven. Thus, though she was treated as secondary here, her treatment was not very different from men.

The Late Vedic Period
The first instance of the concept of spiritual salvation could be traced back to the rite called *pravargya*.[11] It was a secret rite carried out in the forests. The wife and low castes were not allowed to watch the rite. A vessel was heated red hot along with a golden plate representing the sun. Then milk was poured in the vessel and boiled. The motive of the rite was to bestow the lustre of the sun on the sacrificer. It was supposed to be a mystic rite. Here, the wife of the sacrificer was secluded though the reasons forwarded by tradition differ. The early texts acknowledge the important place of women in the procreating activity and say that such a mystic and fierce rite kills the procreating capacity of women and therefore they should not see it. But, the *Satapatha Brahmana* says, because women are not true, they should not watch the rite. The *Satapatha Brahmana* is the early representative text advocating seclusion on such grounds. If *pravargya* is interpreted as the early iconic rite to manifest some idea nearing salvation, the *Satapatha Brahmana* is the text to show some germs of seclusion of women and *Sudras* in the spiritual field (vide another article by me 'The *Satapatha Brahmana* on Women' in the same book).

No text on *Dharmasastra* or *Purana* or that of philosophy in the *Brahmanical* tradition takes into consideration the issue of salvation of women separately except the Jaina tradition. Here, they group women in the group of human beings; thus, framing a common process of salvation for both of them and apparently considering them equal to men. Though the *Dharmasastra* texts prohibit women from taking *sannyasa*, they never say that women are not entitled to salvation. One has to infer seclusion of women in the spiritual field on the basis of citations like *striyo vaisyas tatha sudrah te'pi yanti paramgatim.* However, in the *Brahmanical* system, concepts like salvation were introduced concurrently when *bhakti* took a great stride. Thus, the temporary seclusion was ceased. Therefore, the question of salvation of women did not arise in the philosophies of the *Brahmanical* system. In the *Yogavasistha,* we come across Cudala, the wife as well as the teacher of Sikhidhvaja, who herself was a *jivanmukta.* No doubt, women were prohibited from taking *sannyasa. Jivanmuktiviveka* says that *sannyasa* is not at all prescribed for women, but without *sannyasa* they can attain salvation. But *sannyasa* was not at all must in the *Brahmanical* system. Moreover, no system was fastidious like the *Digambaras. Digambaras* with their unpractical views regarding *himsa* were more strict about inclusion of women in the spiritual field. Therefore, by taking resort to the material identity of women which was partially rooted in primitive beliefs and partially in social customs, Prabhacandra had to prove their inferiority in the spiritual field.

To project her inferiority, Prabhacandra compares her with an androgen. According to him, an androgen is inferior to men and similarly women too are. This is not a personal belief of Prabhacandra, but that of many patriarchal societies. He has just given logical form to it. In any ancient society, procreation is desired and given importance, thus naturally, the unproductive members of the society were looked down upon. In procreation, both male and female are important, but are viewed differently in various types of societies. When women are treated as the main participants in procreation, it takes a form of matriarchal society. When men are considered the important member in procreation, it turns into a patriarchal society. Here, they consider women just as the bearer of the embryo. Here, the metaphor of seed and field is used in many classical texts. Procreation and farming were often compared as the ancient community was well acquainted with farming, and because new arrival is common in both the activities. The Proto-Austroloids compared the male organ with the plough, which tills the land (i.e., woman) and sows seed. In patriarchal societies importance is given to the seed than to the land. Thus, woman is always considered as the secondary cause in procreation. Thus, naturally, as the man is given much importance, the reproductive organ of man was also given importance. Therefore, those who do not possess it are inferior. Women and androgens do not possess it, therefore, they are inferior. According to the *Aitareya Aranyaka* men possess something extra than women.[13] (*atiriktam vai pumsah nyunam striyai, Aitareya Aranyaka* 1.4.2.) On the same ground they are deprived of their right over property in the *Taittiriya Samhita, tasmat nirindriyah striyah adayadi* (*Taittiriya Samhita* 6.5.8)[14] Thus, the belief of Prabhacandra that women are equal to androgen is deeply rooted in the primitive society, it is not his own fabrication.

Another strategy used to weigh women, as inferior to men is to consider them as different from men. In the western countries she was considered as different from men because she did not possess the rationality possessed by men and therefore was deprived of the right to vote. Mary Wollstonecraft was the first woman to challenge this popular belief and advocate the equality of women with men. Sabara, an ancient commentator of 2nd century A.D. says that women are not comparable with men as a man studies the *Vedas* and a woman does not or cannot. Though Sabara and Prabhacandra are in favour of counting them as different from men, *Svetambaras* argue in favour of women on the ground that women are not different from men. Ratnaprabhasuri contradicts Prabhacandra and says, "a woman is not different from a man". Of course, the whole context is that of spirituality, the practical difficulties faced by women were not taken into consideration. But, it is noteworthy that a woman is conceived as equal to men even if in only the spiritual field in 2nd or 3rd century A.D. Just because the context was spiritual, such thinking could not launch a movement of feminism in India. Moreover, the overall patriarchal and male-dominating society could not cherish this thought, to such an extent that even in the 21st century the *Svetambara* women consider themselves inferior to men and not worthy of salvation. But, it is certainly remarkable that long back some members of the Indian society could think of women as equal to men at least in the spiritual field.

The inferiority of women is also judged on the basis of a typically Jaina belief that a woman is not capable of starting any good or a bad deed. This particular belief is based on the peculiar and complicated concept of *karma* adhered to by the Jains. For them any *karma* is matter and is accumulated on the soul which is basically a lightweight object moving upwards. Because of bad deeds it is soiled. The *pudgalas* (particles) of *karma* accumulate on the soul. Thus, the natural upward direction of the soul is obstructed and the soul becomes heavy. To get it back to its natural state the accumulated *karma* must be washed off. If the *karma* is not washed off, the soul will not be liberated. Moreover, the accumulated *karma* will be washed off only when it has reached its fruition (*bhogadeva ksayah*). No other factor contributes to free a soul from it. Certainly, it is through the cycles of death and birth. A more sinful person will get a more painful state of birth. Even fighting against *karma* is not possible in certain types of births as a being is not capable of even thinking of getting rid of *karma*. They just have to experience the fruits of the earlier accumulated *karma*. The Jainas have designed certain stages in accordance with their concept of *karma*. According to them, any being has to undergo certain stages to get rid of his earlier accumulated *karma*. They have produced a chart of ascending or descending order as per their *karma* design. According to the severity of the sin or *karma* either accumulated earlier or newly produced, a being may proceed up or descend down. Beings of hell will never be able to go to heaven because they are not capable of starting that particular *karma* which will lead them towards heaven. Similarly when a woman aspires for salvation, she cannot, because being a woman she must have accumulated considerable amount of *karma*. Unless much of that *karma* is washed off, she will not be capable of starting any kind of ultimate type of *karma*, best or worst (i.e., leading to salvation or to the seventh hell). By severe penance she has to suffer for the earlier deeds. Then she may be reborn in man's body. Then, she may be born as a god and enjoy heavenly pleasures. Thereafter, she is entitled to be born as a man whereby she gains the capability of getting rid of her *karmas* and attains salvation.

This particular Jaina belief associates two concepts, viz., *karma* and woman. Here, the word *karma* is nowhere meant in the sense of good deeds. It essentially means heinous deeds which are full of sin. Thus, sin and women are associated. Sin is associated with women because women have to undergo certain painful and 'dirty' situations such as menstruation and childbirth. In any primitive belief system such physiological situations gain importance mainly if are associated with procreating activity. Some extra-physiological value is attached to it. Of course, such a value differs from society to society. In the patriarchal societies these, though productive, are viewed as dirty and always associated with sin. It is because of a body of such basic beliefs spread all over the world since ages that a woman is viewed as a helpless object. Such helplessness is viewed as a result of some sinful deed. Therefore, woman is never considered as totally free from bad deeds. The other systems found some way out by introducing concepts like *pativratya* (being faithful to the husband) and *bhakti* towards

God to get free from the earlier *karma* and getting salvation. However, the basic viewpoint to consider a woman as a sinful being is the same. Because of such a conception, woman is never considered at par with men.

As she is associated with sin, and therefore possesses *karma*, she is painted as having lack of control over herself. Because she cannot restrain herself, she cannot possess extra-human capacities such as defeating a scholar in debate, transforming herself into another form, and flying in the air. These yogic capacities are supposed to be a result of ultimate control over oneself. This belief is also a peculiar Jaina belief because, in other philosophical streams, women are not said to be deprived of such capacities. According to a legend Sarasvati, Mandanamisra's wife had defeated Sankaracarya in a debate. In the *Yogavasistha*, women characters are described as possessing such Yogic capacities. Only the Jaina tradition is obstinate on such views as it places a lot of importance on extreme restraint, which cannot be followed by women because of some social reasons. It is surprising that these capacities are thought to be possessed exclusively by men. The Jaina tradition thinks them as yogic capacities and therefore associates them with restraint. Even when the position of women was degraded and they were deprived of education, often because of child marriages, women in general were said to be deprived of such talents. Here, the Jaina tradition fails to understand that the reasons are socio-cultural and not biological. The ability to win in debate depends upon the freedom of speech given to a person in the society. If a woman is advised from childhood not to speak much or loudly, not to argue, and moreover, if she is denied an opportunity to learn, how can society expect her to argue with men on the philosophical issues? The rest of the capacities are purely of yogic nature. This particular picture of women drawn by Prabhacandra seems to be very late. Because, the Vedic women had enjoyed a somewhat glorious position and not a humiliating one as depicted in Prabhacandra's description. They had the right to learn and discuss the philosophical issues in royal courts. Gargi was a member of Janaka's court and asks Yajnavalkya many philosophical questions. Maitreyi, Yajnavalkya's wife discusses *amrtatva* with him and wishes to go with him in search of the *amrtatva*. The female seers of the *Rgveda* were seen expressing some issues which are seen as formidable in later days. Thus, what Prabhacandra has painted is a late picture of women, when they are deprived of their freedom of speech. Why and when this happened is the question.

The next reason Prabhacandra puts forth for the inferiority of women is that they possess belongings (*parigrahavattvat*). Belongings or *parigraha* means they cannot remain non-attached in the world. For the *Digambara* Jainas, *parigraha* means wearing clothes. To call even rough clothing *parigraha* is certainly an extreme case though it fits in the logic and rules of behaviour of the Jainas. To be free from attachment is the prime condition of salvation. The popular means of attaining it is to renounce the world by obtaining *sannyasa*. The Buddhists and the Jainas have introduced this means to women. The Vedic tradition was not in much favour of asceticism in its early period because the ultimate goal was said to be achieved by *yajnas*. Both husband and wife performed any *yajna*. Later on, in the *vanaprasthasrama*, both the husband and wife used to devote time to philosophical discussions. Though, the formal structure of the *sannyasa* as *asrama* is not seen in the early *Vedas*, or in the *Upanisads*, speculative discussions on something beyond material wealth are definitely seen in the *Upanisads*. Sulabha Maitreyi rejects material wealth for the sake of *amrtatva*. Is it not *sannyasa*, though not formal? But the later texts deny *sannyasa* for women and for any incomplete being, i.e., lame, blind, impotent etc. However, though a woman is not introduced to *sannyasa* formally, her mental detachment was not discouraged or forbidden in the later Vedic tradition. Thus, the inferior picture of women on the basis of belongings as painted by Prabhacandra is strictly a *Digambara* Jaina notion.

Another important point of inferiority of women according to Prabhacandra is their association with *himsa*. The Jainas aspire for complete *ahimsa* in case of an ascetic. However, a woman wears garment, which does not bridle *himsa*, rather is conducive to it. A woman in her menstrual period is dirty and cannot refrain herself from *himsa*. Thus, even though she desires to refrain herself from killing, she is helpless. Such is not the case with men. They can refrain themselves from *himsa* and can follow the regulations in complete degree.

Here, Prabhacandra is associating a woman, especially her menstrual blood with sin which is conducive for *himsa*. Ancient patriarchal traditions from all over the world in some way or the other associate the menstrual blood with killing. Basically the fear of blood which lies in the primitive minds is the cause for such an association. According to another theory men tried to control women by tabooing menstrual blood. In Indian religions however, it was always tabooed and associated with sin.

Prabhacandra says as a woman is not paid respect by men, she is inferior to men. Even a young monk is bowed to by an old female ascetic. Even the *Satapatha Brahmana* speaks out a similar belief. In reality, such hierarchy is introduced by the society. In patriarchal societies men are the rule makers. Therefore, such rules are certainly intentional. It has nothing to do with her individual capabilities. Prabhacandra is speaking out a fact in patriarchal society. Here, she is inferior just because she is a woman. Her contribution or her experience is not taken into account. Even today Jaina and Buddhist monasteries follow the same custom. In common folk though we do not experience such hierarchy at the same level, it is experienced a at similar level. Men are given preference at many levels. At the time of birth the male child is given preference. Later on they are fed well. At the level of education and marriage everywhere they are treated as superiors.

Prabhacandra further accuses women on the ground of untruthfulness. This is a common charge against women that has prevailed since Vedic times. In the *Veda*, they are called as having the 'mind of a wolf' (*salavrkanam hrdayani etah.*) The *Satapatha Brahmana* says "as she is untrue, one need not allow her to see the *pravargya* rite". *Anrtatva*, i.e., untruthfulness is described as an inherent nature of her. Such qualities are contextual human qualities. These are not to be said only of women. These are common to both the sexes. But tradition attributes these only to women.

As she does not possess high qualities, she is inferior to men. According to Prabhacandra there may be some women who possess high qualities, but the degree of their high quality is certainly less than that of the men. This is also a general traditional belief. The culturally induced inferiority seen and observed in the world may be the reason behind such remarks. But psychologically this belief will not stand. This is an age-old belief expressed by Prabhacandra.

She is inferior to men because men can easily defeat her. She is named as *abala* (having no strength). Strikingly enough a woman was not known as *abala* in the Vedic times. We get some references of her involvement in wars as we come across some such examples in the classical period. Yet in the classical period she was invariably known as *abala* and the Vedic literature does not recognize her as so. It was certainly in the mind of people, but was not expressed as clearly as in classical literature. A son was called *vira*, but we do not get any similar term for the daughter. Modern feminists interpret that even the physical inequality of women is introduced by culture. Women were expected to be delicate in the patriarchal society. From ancient times they are trained to look at themselves as weak and dependent on men.

Prabhacandra advocates that women are inferior because they do not adorn special posts. In the monastery the special posts are given to men and never to women. Even in the society prime posts are given to men and not to women. This is taken as evidence of the fact that women are not capable of administering such important posts. This belief speaks of the drastically changed position of women at the time of Prabhacandra. At his time women were deprived of education. Since the conditions were insecure, women were confined to household activities. In the monasteries however, they had facilities of education. Yet, as the general picture of women was inferior to men, even here they were treated as inferiors. Though tradition does not speak of women adorning the highest posts, at the same time it does not even argue that a woman should not be given an important post. Being a patriarchal society it might have been an unwritten law that major decisions should be taken by men. Still, this is a custom and cannot be treated as the parameter of inherent inferiority. But as the status of women in the society was inferior, this was taken as the parameter of inferiority and not as a result of inequality. The changed status is seen in the examples which Prabhacandra produces. He says that in each house man has the power of decision-making and not the woman. Thus the right of decision-making which was conferred upon the newly bride in the marriage hymn was ceased by the time of Prabhacandra. Her position as *samrajni* was reduced to that of a servant. Mark the difference in the status of a newly-wed bride described in the marriage hymn and the same described by Kalidasa in *Sakuntala*. In the marriage hymn she is called the *samrajni* of all the family members, whereas in the *Sakuntala*, Kanva advises her to serve elders, tolerate co-wives and obey her husband. We do not feel the severity of his advice because it has become a custom to behave so. Yet both these passages mark the drastic differences in the status of women in the house. The Vedic woman was probably the sole authority in decision-making, whereas the classical woman had lost this important right and thereby her position in the family, probably because she was deprived of the necessary education and was too young to take decisions.

Prabhacandra further says a woman cannot claim the inheritance. In the Vedic times there was difference of opinion over whether a woman has right over inheritance or not. The *Taittiriya Samhita* (reference discussed above) flatly denies her as a claimant over property, but Yaska refers to a debate over this issue. In the *Smriti* literature there is controversy regarding her right over property. It is certain that at the time of Prabhacandra women were denied right over property. He further says, "even though they are elder and beautiful they do not have any say in the decision-making and in property". This certainly is a changed situation in the society. According to him even in daily life and in simple decisions women have to depend upon men. Men guide them in day-to-day behaviour. In my personal opinion, such a situation must have occurred only when women were deprived of education because of the slow rise in child marriage.

Thus, Prabhacandra projects a totally inferior picture of women. He bases his arguments on physical, cultural and philosophical parameters. All these parameters seem to be illogical today, but they give a complete picture of the deteriorated condition of life of women at his time. His opinions are based on the image of women prevalent in his period, which was almost drastically in contrast with the glorious image of Vedic times. I have tried here to weigh his views in a somewhat historical perspective. His major stress is on the physically impure nature of women, which is a result of some sin in earlier life. This is the mainstream view of all civilizations that associate women with sin and thereby to their present impure polluted status. It is curious on the part of

Prabhacandra that he rarely interprets women as luring men. But interprets the situation as a defeat of women by men. For example, he says that if women are seen by men, they are defeated by them because their body does not have the capacity to ward off men. Normally in such a situation women are blamed for arousing wild feelings in men. But Prabhacandra assumes the capacity of the male body to win over women. This interpretation though off the stream, tries to establish that complete power lay with men. Woman is painted not as tactfully luring men, but as a victim to his power, and thereby inferior.

Resume

The present paper concentrates on two key concepts, one that of ancient times, i.e., salvation and the other of the 21st century, i.e., women. It tries to associate these two concepts and see how far women were associated with it.

Salvation is an exclusive indigenous concept. It got its logical form in philosophical *sutra* literature and before that in the form of loud thinking in the *Upanisads*. Before, the Vedic religion was in a different form. The main aim of the *yajna* was to accelerate procreation, cosmic and material. *Yajna* was the miniature model of cosmic creation. Thus, in procreation, both the elements male and female have an equal role. In the most ancient primitive societies woman is actually seen as creating the new progeny. Therefore, they had an important position in the society. Slowly, the role of man in the procreating act was realized. In some societies, it was given importance. Thus, slowly the societies were formed along patriarchal lines. In such societies the role of woman became complimentary to man. Her role was just to bear the seed and rear it. Man was seen as the creator. The Vedic religion ascribes such roles to men and women. Here, the existence as a woman is never independent or as the sole creator, but it is complementary to men. Their position was always secondary to men. Because of the patriarchal pattern, ancestors were worshipped through sons and not through daughters. Therefore, male progeny was preferred to female progeny. Aryans got established in India with their patriarchal notions, yet they imparted equal importance to the creative counterpart. In mythologies these cosmic creative partners are addressed always in dual number with a stress on the male element.

As said above, *yajna* was the original ritual of Aryans formulated for accelerating cosmic and material creation; they were aware of the important role of women in creation. Therefore, she also had to play a crucial role in the sacrifice. She used to receive proper training for it, thus availing all facilities prescribed for men. As they were getting equal training, they used to contribute intellectually to the society. The female seers of the *Rgveda* have contributed in the most coveted field of intellect. Sulabha Maitreyi, Gargi Vacaknavi, and Atreyi are offered oblations as contributors of a particular Vedic branch. Slowly some mystic rites were added to the *yajna* system. *Pravargya* is the mystic rite introduced in the system of rituals by adding some new elements. It is the first rite to introduce the use of icons in the Vedic ritual. This iconic ritual was new to the system. Naturally it was kept away from the non-important persons. Moreover, it was a mystic rite aiming to give a radiant body to the sacrificer. Most probably, as it was something new to the *yajna* system, to assure safety of the progeny and that of the bearer of the progeny it was not revealed to the women. The ritual occurs in the transitional period from ritual to philosophy. Probably, in due course of time, this area was kept closed to women. The duo Maitreyi and Gargi who were properly trained in the system were the exceptions, and therefore Yajnavalkya satisfied Maitreyi's curiosity about eternality. We do not know what happened to other women. We do not get concrete references of women, other than Maitreyi and Gargi, involved in philosophical discussions in early literature. Later on, asceticism was introduced as a pre-stage of salvation.

The Jaina religion was never against asceticism for women. Buddhism unwillingly accepted the entrance of women in the *sangha*. This was altogether new to the *Brahmanical* ritualistic system which was basically oriented towards *pravrtti*. Yet it was assimilated in the religion, but as it was not convenient to women we do not find references to women ascetics in the Vedic religion. As Altekar has pointed out the wave of asceticism that occurred in ancient India introduced untimely *sannyasa* in men and women, and resulted in child marriages.[15] Child marriages resulted in complete removal of women from important fields, even her complimentary role was reduced to that of a servant. Later on, because of the constant invasions by foreign rulers the women were totally insecure. Many restrictions were imposed upon them resulting in their refraining from all intellectual activities. Thus, the personality of a woman from a happy lady governing the household, participating in all religious activities with almost equal importance, developing her own skills to develop her own personality was changed to a lady who has lost her hold on the family and become a submissive servant, killing all her interests and hiding in the house and working and serving just to please her husband. She had lost the straightforwardness of Lopamudra to express her sexual desire to her husband, she had lost the right to vent out her feeling of rage against her co-wives. She is projected as a lump of flesh and blood having no right over property, always being told as having no creative potency like a *napumsaka*. Her sole aim was to satisfy her husband and work as a reproductive machine. The classical literature gives us a picture of the elites, and not of a common person.

The importance of Prabhacandra's discussion lies here. He gives us the picture of a common woman. At his time, i.e., by 12th century A.D. India was ruled by Mughals. Men had also lost their freedom. The life of women was not at all secure. Prabhacandra, as a Jaina monk belongs to the area of Madhya

Pradesh and Rajasthan. History tells us about the pathetic condition of women in this period. The restrictions on women were tightened more. Once freedom is lost, everything is lost. Therefore, the woman painted by Prabhacandra has no right of decision-making and no right over property; further, she is considered as sin incarnate. Thus, she lost her freedom not only in society but also in the spiritual field.

Furthermore, another question puzzles us: why do we get contradictory ideas regarding salvation of women in the same strata of the society? The *Brahmanical* stream is totally silent about such issues. The *Svetambaras* though they associate women with sin are in favour of salvation for them on the ground that they are not different from men. It seems to me that as the *Digambara* Jainas are more fastidious about the physical side of everything, their views regarding *karma, himsa* etc. are more extreme. The other classical Indian philosophies including the *Svetambaras* are to some extent flexible. Moreover, India had both the sociological patterns, patriarchal and matriarchal. In the Vedic period itself the worship of mother goddess was introduced. Thus, the original ideas about women were two-fold: (1) Women are creators and sources of energy. (2) Women have a complementary role in the creation. Both these ideas were getting assimilated with each other. It had to reflect in the actual life. Thus, though in practical life the necessity of restrictions was felt, in the spiritual plain they were treated on par with men. Therefore, *Svetambaras* often advocated that a woman is not at all different from men. This particular thought arose in India around 2nd century A.D. Moreover, though the outward structure was changed, the inner stream was living in a different form. Thus, the creative and nourishing character of women viewed as important in the matriarchal societies and the complimentary, but almost equal character of women projected by the *Brahmanical* patriarchal societies advocated for the spiritual freedom of women. The

Brahmanical systems further found a way out for the spiritual freedom of women. *Bhakti* was the important doctrine which gave solace to the downtrodden, i.e., to women and *Sudras*. The adamant views of the *Digambaras* could not spread because the culture was formulated by both viewpoints. Moreover, both the views thought of women as an important part of the society.

We cannot claim that the position of women at present in India is desirable. Nor was it in ancient times. We cannot say that the achievements of Indian philosophical thought have percolated into practical life. The practical side perfectly squares the thesis of Prabhacandra. Women do not have access to salvation, though they are worshipped on the philosophical plane. We must thank Prabhacandra for painting a realistic picture of women, which is relevant even in the 21st century.

Notes

1. Mahendrakumar Shastri, (ed.) 1990 (1912). *Prameyakamalamartanda of Prabhacandrasuri*, vol.1&2, Satguru Publications, New Delhi.
2. Mahendrakumar Shastri, (ed.) 1990(1912). *Nyayakumudacandra of Prabhacandrasuri*, vol.1&2, Sri Garibdas Oriental Series, Satguru Publications, New Delhi.
3. Nalini Balbir, (1997). "Women in Jainism" in *Religion and Women* (ed) Sharma, Arvind, Indian Books Centre, New Delhi.
4. N. Shanta, (1997). *The Unknown Pilgrims*, Sri Garibdas Oriental Series 298, Sri Satguru Publications, New Delhi.
5. Padmanabh Jaini, (1997). "Gender and Salvation: Jaina Debates on the Spiritual Liberation of Women", *Journal of Indian Philosophy*, Vol. 25, no.5, Oct.1997.

6. A.N. Upadhye, (1935) (ed). *"Pravacanasara* of Kundakunda" with Sanskrit commentaries of Amrtacandra and Jayasena, Sri Rayachandra Jaina Shastramala, Bombay.

7. Pannalal, (tr) *Astapauda* with the commentary of *Srutasagara*, Shantivira *Digambara* Jaina Samsthan, Rajasthan.

8. *"Dhavala"* as quoted in *Jainendra-Siddhanta-Kosa*, compiled by Jinendravarni (1971), Bharatiya Jnanapeeth Prakashan, Delhi.

9. R. Birwe, (1969). '*Strimuktiprakarana* of *Sakatayana*', Bharaiya Jnanapeeth Prakashan, Varanasi.

10. Dalsukh Malvania, (1969). *Ratnakaravatarika of Ratnaprabhasuri*, L.D.Institute, Ahmedabad.

11. For a detailed description of the *pravargya* ritual see Buitenan, V.J.A.B.(1968) *The Pravargya Ritual*, Deccan College, Pune.

12. See any edition of the *Bhagavadgita*.

13. *Ta unatiriktau bhavatah, vrsa vai brhad yosa rathantaram, atiriktam va pumso nyunam striyai*. (Aitareya Aranyaka 1.4.2). On this Sayana comments, "The meter *Brhad* being like male has extra organ.(*Brhatasca pumrupatvena angadhikyam yuktam* |)"

14. The *Taittiriya Samhita* uses this particular sentence in a peculiar context. Gods wanted to achieve heaven leaving their wives here on earth. But they could not know heaven. When they saw the *Patnivatagraha*, they could know it. But, Soma could not accompany them as he was held by women, therefore, they made him powerless by pouring *ghee*. Therefore, women are powerless and hence cannot have right over the property.

15. A.S. Altekar, (1956) *The Position of Women in Hindu Civilization*, Motilal Banarasidas, Delhi.

9

The Doctrine of *Purusartha*:
A Gender Perspective

Vaijayanti Arun Belsare

The issues associated with feminism have aspects that are universal and culture-specific. Female subordination is universal. Women around the world share similar difficulties and experiences. It is essential that these similarities be demonstrated and specified and not be taken for granted. Although oppression of women and secondary status of women are a universal phenomena, the causes underlying them and the justification put forth may differ from culture to culture. It is therefore necessary to concentrate on the culture-specific aspects associated with feminism.

In this paper, I would like to view the doctrine of *purusartha* from a gender perspective. The paper is divided into four parts:

1. Discussion of the nature and significance of gender perspective.
2. Application of the gender perspective to the doctrine of *purusartha*.
3. Exploration of the presuppositions, principles and viewpoints underlying the doctrine of *purusartha*.
4. Pointing out the relevance of this attempt to the present day phenomena.

Nature and Significance of Gender Perspective

Gender analysis is more than the study of women. It is the analysis of gender relations and of gender as a structuring principle in all human societies. It is the study of gender, of the interrelationships between women and men and of the role of gender in structuring human societies, their histories, ideologies, economic systems and political structures. Gender analysis attempts to understand the different aspects and forms of relations that exist between men and women. It is an effort to find out the cultural norms that are prescribed for men and women by different traditions and societies in order to discover the ideologies that set these norms. Hence, with the help of gender analysis, it is possible to uncover the causes of the subordination of women.

The gender perspective is a major step and turning point in the development of the feminist movement. It helped to establish that the ground of inequality between man and woman is not biological. Men and women have obvious biological differences. But diversity is not the ground of inequality because equality does not mean uniformity. The closer study of the discrimination between men and women made it clear that one is not born but becomes a woman. 'Men' and 'women' are not natural categories; they are human constructs. The divide between man and woman is created by placing them into some fixed categories of roles and functions. The status of the woman in a family and society is determined by the functions and roles she performs. To understand the status of woman it is necessary to examine the structure of society. In a patriarchal and hierarchical society, normally a woman obtains secondary status because of the power relations that are part and parcel of the patriarchal society. Gender analysis helps to deconstruct the traditional value structure and brings to the fore the concealed aspects of tradition. It also helps us reach out to the hidden agendas or views accepted by the people.

A particular social system or a particular tradition and the value structures belonging to that tradition can be studied by way of applying the method of gender analysis. This application would help to find out the causes of oppression of women and subordination pertaining to that society. Once the causes are discovered it is possible to obtain the right remedies and solutions to the problem. Application of gender analysis thus paves the way for the development of women. I shall, therefore, like to view feminism both as a movement and as a methodology. Gender analysis is the methodology developed by the feminist movement which helps to deconstruct traditional value structure and social system from the standpoint of woman. It compels woman to assess what she offers to society and what in turn society offers her, the way she relates to her family and society and the way the family and the society relate to her etc. This assessment makes her realise whether the relation is reciprocal or one-sided. This awakening is the major objective of the feminist movement. For a free and uninhibited development of woman, awakening and empowerment are essential. A woman who is under the influence of traditional norms and values would not realise the kind of injustice tradition has done to her. It is the job of gender analysis to bring into proper focus the injustice inflicted on woman and to liberate her from the shackles of tradition.

Application of the Gender Analysis to the Doctrine of *Purusartha*

The doctrine of *purusartha* played a pivotal role in the socio-ethical development of the Indian society. It is accepted traditionally that *purusartha* is a well-knit doctrine that incorporates material as well as spiritual pursuits of man. It is a discussion of right ends and right means. It is believed that the doctrine is all embracing and takes care of the well-being of both individual and society. It is generally accepted that the doctrine is applicable to each and every member of society and is concerned with the good of all. As an ethical theory it presents a model of an ideal human society and ideal human ends. It declares what is desirable for an individual and what is not and also provides the causes for its declaration. The doctrine presupposes four facets of human existence: (1) man's existence as an individual; (2) as a member of society; (3) as a part of the natural world; (4) as a manifestation of the cosmic self. The four *purusartha*s, viz., *artha*, *kama*, *dharma* and *moksa* are supposed to take care of all these aspects of human existence.

The theoretical presentation of the traditional doctrine of *purusartha* no doubt makes one feel that the theory is morally adequate and satisfactory. This is so because the conditions of a good moral theory are that it should be applicable to each and every individual and should satisfy the basic human requirements. Traditionally at least it was believed that the doctrine of *purusartha* satisfied both the conditions. Application of the gender analysis, i.e., understanding or reviewing the doctrine from the standpoint of woman brings to the fore the inadequacies of the doctrine as a moral theory.

Let us try to view each and every *purusartha* from a woman's standpoint. Let us begin with the *moksa purusartha*. It appears that almost all religions that developed in India and especially *Brahmanic* tradition denied the right of *moksa* to women. What is more, like the *Sudras*, women were forbidden from studying the Vedic scripts. In the traditional Indian society, a knowledgeable person or one who pursued the path of liberation and had given up worldly pleasures was respected by every member of the society. *Moksa* was regarded as the highest kind of *purusartha*. But women were kept away from this *purusartha*. It was the highest goal of life which was not only not available to them but they were looked upon as an obstacle or a distraction in the path of man's liberation. Hence, this was the *purusartha* which completely excluded women.

Traditional Indian society was a caste-based society. Caste system was a socio-economic structure. In it the economic profession of a person was linked with his caste. A person belonging to a certain caste was supposed to follow the profession associated with that caste. Though it was believed that the caste system was initially based on the natural propensity of man, with the passage of time, the structure became birth-based. This being the case, the *artha purusartha* for every individual was primarily determined by his caste. All of us have assumed that whatever was true in case of man was also true in case of woman. But is that so? Let us ask this question: How was the caste of a woman determined? The answer is obvious. It was determined by the caste of either her father or her husband. She was not a member of caste on her own but through her father or husband. In the traditional Indian society a person could become a member of the society through his membership of the caste, i.e., an individual's citizenship was determined by his association with a particular caste. A woman in such a society ceased to be an independent primary citizen of the society. Hence, it seems that *artha purusartha* was also not available to her. It is the denial of the *artha purusartha* that made woman economically dependent on man, the family and in turn on the society. Her status automatically became secondary and subordinate.

Apparently it seems that the *kama purusartha* was available to each and every individual irrespective of gender. In practice, the society used woman's sexuality as a material resource for reproduction. The purity of caste was maintained by strict rules of marriage. Lower caste people were not allowed to marry upper caste women. The mechanism of control regulated the reproductive capacity of women. They were tied to household life and a special code of conduct was prescribed for them. Women who remained within the confines set by the society and accepted and followed the rules and regulations of the society were regarded as models and got the respect of the society, but those who attempted to flout the rules and regulations were condemned. A strict dividing line was maintained between a woman inside the house respecting the boundaries of the four walls and a woman who stepped outside the boundaries. The former got respect not as an individual but because of her power of reproduction and her submissiveness. The latter was either condemned or was treated as an object of enjoyment.

In traditional India, most of the times, woman was either viewed in the image of motherhood or in the image of a seducer. Different facets of womanhood went unnoticed in most of the cases. She was not viewed as a person capable of performing different roles and functions. Her personality was restricted to certain fixed roles, which were primarily confined to the household or were supplementary to that of men. The famous quote that a woman should be a friend, secretary, lover, wife etc. is normally interpreted as expressing a relation of complementarity between a man and a woman. But this is an example of pseudo-complementarity. The relation of complementarity is reciprocal. It also exists between individuals belonging to the same strata. It also assumes flexibility of roles and functions. But in the traditional society, flexibility of roles and functions was a rarity. The family structure was hierarchical in nature and hence man and woman did not belong to the same strata. Though the kind of functions that woman could perform for the man in different contexts were spelled out, the functions that man could perform for the woman were not offered. It appears that by spelling out the different roles that a woman was supposed to perform for a man, tradition had underlined woman's subordinate position in the family and society.

Kama purusartha understood as sexual enjoyment and as material well-being was not available to woman as an independent or a singular member of society. It was available to her within the boundaries laid down by society. She being economically dependent on the family, the approval of the family and society was absolutely necessary. There was thus no other alternative for a common woman than to act in accordance with the norms laid down by the society.

Understanding the nature, role and importance of the *dharma purusartha* is a complex process. It is complex because: (1) the term *dharma* has various connotations; (2) various activities are identified as *dharmas*; (3) in the framework of *purusartha*, *dharma* is associated on the one hand with the *artha* and *kama purusartha*s as the principle of organization and control and on the other with *moksa purusartha* as prescribing ways and means that would lead towards the path of liberation.

It is believed that the Vedic tradition initially accepted only the three *purusartha*s, viz., *dharma*, *artha* and *kama*; later owing to the impact of the Jaina and Buddhist systems, *moksa* as a separate *purusartha* was incorporated. From the very beginning *dharma* played a crucial role. *Dharma* functioned as a system of rules and governance by prescribing specific functions to each and every individual taking into account his caste, gender, status and place in the society. It worked as a religious, moral, social as well as a political agency. It therefore, prescribed different functions to the individuals as per the requirements of the social, moral, religious and political institutions. The functions prescribed by the institution of *dharma* were accepted as duties by an individual.

It was accepted that *artha* and *kama* only when controlled by the norms of *dharma* could be regarded as moral goals. *Dharma* hence was primarily viewed as the principle of morality. An act to be moral required the sanction of *dharma*. This institution of *dharma* tied women within the boundaries of four walls. It was done very skilfully. As stated earlier, there are different connotations of the term *dharma* in the Sanskrit language. One of the meanings of *dharma* is nature or character. The various functions and duties prescribed by *dharma* were justified by stating that it was in accordance with his or her natural propensity. This was how performing the household chores became the duty and natural propensity of a woman. It was believed that through the execution of different types of activities connected with the household she served and nurtured her family and her society. It was also supposed that this proper nurturing preserved the order, peace and happiness in the family and society.

By glorifying her role as a nurturer and preserver, her image was restricted to the roles of a caring mother and a dutiful wife. In actuality though, woman was confined to indoor activities to maintain the purity of caste. Encroachment on her freedom and independence was justified as a heuristic device to maintain the division of caste and the purity of higher castes. This was how women in India were victims of both a gender distinction and caste distinction. Womanhood was imposed on her as her essential nature.

It is appropriate in this context to distinguish between something which can be present as a 'potential' and something which can be present as a 'possible'. Potential is understood as the hidden or unmanifested power. Thus understood, it is associated with the essential nature or the core of a thing or the individual. A woman no doubt possesses the power of reproduction but that does not imply that she possesses the power of becoming a caring mother, dutiful wife, a household worker etc. Her having the potentiality of reproduction does not necessarily exclude the possibility of her being a caring mother, dutiful wife or a household expert but at the same time it does not necessarily imply the same. These roles were determined by tradition and were imposed on her and she performed them generation after generation. For this reason, again we have to say that in the true sense of the term *dharma*, *purusartha* also was not available to her. *Dharma* which was available to her was in the form of duty and not in the form of choice.

Interpreted from a woman's standpoint, the doctrine of *purusartha* ceases to be an adequate and satisfactory moral theory. Rather it becomes obvious that the doctrine of *purusartha* lent support and basis to maintain the secondary status of women in society.

Exploring the Presuppositions and Principles Underlying the Doctrine of *Purusartha*

The above analysis makes one notice that the meaning of the term *purusa* in the *purusartha* is not at all gender neutral. The term *purusa* in ancient days stood for man or male. Hence the application of the gender analysis reveals the ambiguity associated with the meaning of the term *purusa*. The analysis also makes us aware of the fact that a woman was not free to take decisions or choose among the alternative courses of actions or to select the goals of her life. Once we realise this it becomes easy to notice that the structure of the traditional society was not merely hierarchical; it was patriarchal as well. Gender analysis uncovers the truth that, that which is expected to represent the interests of each and every member of the society, in fact represents the interests of a chosen few. This revelation brings to the fore different possibilities: (1) Tradition represented primarily the interests of the higher caste men. (2) It was because of some socio-historical reasons that society has to impose restrictions on certain sections of the society. (3) It is possible that there were certain other traditions in which the interests of either the low caste people or women were represented but with the passage of time these traditions might have perished or got lost. (4) Or it is possible that these other traditions were destroyed by the *Brahmanic* tradition to keep its hold. The possibilities can be immense.

With the help of the gender perspective one could see the gaps and the ambiguities associated with what we identify as tradition. This understanding in turn helps us comprehend that there is nothing that we can call 'The Tradition'. Similarly, it may not be correct to consider something as the mainstream of society. The history of a particular society comprises of several traditions, i.e., several viewpoints or several interpretations of the individual and social life. This realization brings to the fore an altogether different relation between the past and the present or tradition and modernity. Tradition or the past can now be viewed as providing the sources of possibilities. It would be significant to view Indian tradition in this manner because it is made up of several Vedic and non-Vedic traditions. Every philosophical system or every caste and sub-caste represented a certain way of life. What is more, every philosophical system had its own interpretation of the doctrine of *purusartha*. Theoretical possibilities notwithstanding, on the practice level the *Brahmanic* tradition was dominant.

Despite several theoretical possibilities, one really wonders why *Brahmanism* held sway. Gender perspective can help one reveal the dynamics of interaction and interrelation that passed through these different philosophical systems. Gender perspective questions the divides created by tradition and uncovers the power relations that go along with it. In this context, I remember Barlingay's penetrating analysis of Indian tradition. He viewed different philosophical traditions (intellectual traditions) as a revolt against the action-oriented *Purva Mimansa* tradition. The rich Indian tradition was unfortunately dominated on the practice level by the *Purva Mimansa* system. Our analysis of the doctrine of *purusartha* is primarily built around the practice of *purusartha* which was mainly governed by the *Brahmanic* tradition associated with the *Purva Mimansa* system.

The analysis brings us to the next significant point associated with the Indian tradition. With the exception of certain philosophical systems, most of the systems in tradition accepted the distinction between the empirical world and the transcendental world, between the individual self and the cosmic self. It was supposed that the true essence of man lay in realizing the oneness of the individual and cosmic self. On the metaphysical level people accepted the oneness of all the individual selves irrespective of the distinction between caste, class, gender and colour. This freedom, this oneness has to be conceived on the transcendental, ahistorical level. Hence this metaphysical freedom and oneness becomes a mere theoretical myth. In the historical contexts, in practice, we come across attempts made to keep women away from such an intellectual enjoyment. Examples of women given their due rights are very rare, very exceptional indeed. In this context, one has to comprehend the dynamics of interaction and relation that must have passed through the two *purusartha*s – *dharma* and *moksa*.

As stated elsewhere, the *Brahmanic* tradition initially accepted only three *purusartha*s, viz., *dharma*, *artha* and *kama*. The *moksa purusartha* was incorporated because of the impact of the Jaina and Buddhist tradition. Though *moksa* was accepted as the *param purusartha*, it was also realised that not every individual could attain it. Hence, in the framework of *purusartha*, both *moksa* and *dharma* played a central role. Theoretically *moksa* was regarded as the highest goal but in practice *dharma* held a supreme position. *Dharma* functioned as the principle of the organization and order which helped society continue and preserve its values and principles, generations after generations. For the maintenance of society *dharma* functioned as the legitimate authority and as the legitimate authority *dharma* held power to control the individual wishes, aspirations and actions. Through the hierarchical caste structure on the social level and the hierarchical patriarchal structure on the family level, *dharma* bound each and every individual to specific functions and roles. In a way each and every individual suffered on account of this. The plight of women and low caste people was worse still. *Dharma* confined women to the household by claiming that they were positively hurdles and distractions in the path of liberation. From a woman's standpoint one could surely question the validity of considering *moksa* as *purusartha*. *Purusartha* by its very definition should be something which one could and should attain. If *moksa* is not made available to both women and *Sudras* then it ceases to be an ethical goal. It then functions as a device to exclude women and *shudras* from several social and public activities. It was through the *dharma purusartha* that *Brahmanic* tradition strengthened its hold on the individual and social life.

The *Brahmanic* tradition evolved a social structure in which individual life was divided into four parts. Apparently it looks as a model where individuals' individual and social, material and spiritual aspirations were acknowledged and taken care of. In the first stage of *brahmacharya* an individual was supposed to engage himself in cognitive activities; in the second stage, marriage and bringing up of the family; in the third stage guiding youngsters and detaching oneself from the material attachment and in the last stage staying away from the family in pursuit of knowledge. *Dharma* prescribed several activities and duties pertaining to every stage that an individual was supposed to perform. A close look at this structure reveals that the structure was built with man's life at the centre. The first as well as the last *asramas* were in the true sense of the term not available to women. There is no mention of what women were supposed to do at the stage of *sanyasasrama*.

The doctrine of *purusartha* along with the *varnasrama* system understood from the woman's standpoint reveals major inadequacies in the Indian socio-ethical system. This system attributed three primary functions to the individual self: knowing, doing and enjoying. Our analysis so far has made it clear that woman in Indian tradition was not allowed to perform these functions the way a man was. Ethical considerations demand that an individual be treated as a free and rational agent. Unfortunately, this was not the image of a woman which Indian tradition wanted to focus. For reasons of their own they confined her to the four walls of the household Gender perspective helps us see the injustice done to women by tradition. It also makes us see that there cannot be just one authentic interpretation of tradition. The views and ideas

imbibed through tradition no doubt have certain value but they
are not absolute and ultimate. One can review them, criticize
them and interpret them. Tradition is not a fixed, static entity
but something which is transmitted and preserved with the
passage of time. In the process of historical development certain
things remain, others perish. What is available to us as tradition
could be merely a fragment of it. If one acknowledges this then
one could relate with tradition in different ways.

Relevance of the Analysis to the Present-day Phenomena

In India, after the arrival of the British, due to the impact of the
renaissance values, some leaders started paying special attention
to the problems of women. Their attempts were surely
praiseworthy. But viewed from the point of view of woman,
what they offered were certain concessions and privileges
within the age-old traditional structure. Accepting those
changes and being satisfied with them is tantamount to
accepting the roles traditions had prescribed in different garbs.
The renaissance leaders acknowledged that injustice was done to
women but did not question or discard the traditional structure
which inflicted pain on women. Secondly, after independence
the constitution provided special considerations, to the lower
caste people because of the injustice done to them. However, no
such special consideration was shown to women. After
independence men automatically acquired the rights, freedom
and different opportunities, but women had to fight to get even
minimal rights. It is here that one realises the hold of traditional
ideas and norms on society in general and men in particular
because all of them believed that women are free to perform
roles and functions they are capable of performing. Gender
perspective makes one see that such a belief is groundless.

Reviewing the problems associated with the suppression
and subordination of women within the context of culture is
therefore necessary, especially so in India. In India, since the
arrival of the British, there was always the danger of a

confrontation between the two extreme positions, viz., revivalism and westernism. Neither position helps us have a proper understanding of the situation. In order to understand the specific nature of the problems of Indian women the study of traditional value structure and social system from the point of view of woman needs to be done. Women as well as men have to be freed from the hold of the traditional values and ideas. This freedom alone would bring a proper perception of the condition of woman and people would be ready to accept her as an individual and treat her as an individual. She would get her lost but rightful place in society if people recognize her worth as a rational and moral agent and treat her as a person.

As a methodology, gender perspective shows just what could be done to elevate the status of women and how. In doing so, it strengthens the feminist movement and substantiates its claims.

10

Feminism and Identity: Women Saints and the Question of Identity

Radhika Seshan

Identity is a vital aspect of one's position in both the natural and the social world. At the most elementary level, the identity we have is natural -- we are humans, belonging to the human species. But this elementary identity itself implies the complexities that follow, for, as part of the species, there is a sense of a group identity, or a social identity. As societies change over time and space, identity has to be constantly redefined. This redefinition often takes place within certain parameters, one of the most important of which is religion.

Religion has tended to be the most convenient method of defining identity. Given the fact that religion and society are necessarily intertwined[1] it is not surprising that religion, or rather, ritual, becomes the most important factor in locating oneself, both within one's own society, and with reference to other societies.

The structures of religion usually become more rigid over time and space. Rituals begin to be defined as knowledge; and monopoly over this form of knowledge becomes, in society, the domination of one group, class or caste over all others. This is true of all societies, western or eastern; the priestly class has, all over the world, claimed supremacy on the basis of its ability to dispense, through knowledge, legitimacy to certain groups. It is this legitimacy that provides the first level of identity. Identity is then sharpened with reference to, usually in contrast to, other groups – something that, in 20th century terms, is called a 'communitarian' or a 'communal' identity.

Medieval societies, much more than those of today, can be regarded as 'religious' societies, for religious structures defined the value system. By 'belonging' to a particular religion, humans accepted the ethics, morality, beliefs and norms of that religion, and could thus be differentiated from those not belonging to that group. This then becomes yet another aspect of identity – it is both inclusive and exclusive. To put it in different words, identity is necessarily based on the idea of difference: so, a different society, a different community, a different family, and a different individual (these being the levels of identity formation, i.e., individual, family, community and society). Thus, identity sharpens the 'different', and structures of society emphasize this. Different, however, does not mean deviant, for deviation is something outside society. Deviation, in the Indian context, meant non-observance of *dharma* (duty), which, in turn, referred to "the rules of social intercourse *(varna)*, stage of life *(asrama)*, and inborn qualities *(guna)*"[2]. Deviation thus came to mean the non-observance of a religious, and therefore a social system. When religion defined the value system of a society, non-observance of a religion meant, by extension, non-observance of those values, and so 'excluded' one from the group. As group identity would be affected by challenges, this exclusion was essential. Conversely, 'difference', lacking such implications of challenge, could be appropriated within a system.

Identity is therefore a fluid concept, which requires awareness both of traditional structures and of the possible challenges to them. It is in this context (of traditional structures and possible challenges) that three women saints of the medieval period have been selected for study -- Auvaiyyar (of the Tamil tradition), Akkamahadevi (of the *Virasaivite*

tradition), and Mirabai (of the North Indian tradition). They
tried to challenge the established patriarchal norms, but could
not avoid the idiom of the very norms that they challenged. In
fact, it could be argued that their challenge itself could be
accommodated within the *Brahmanical* tradition, where the
female aspect has generally found a place with reference to
Purusa-Prakriti or *Siva-Sakti*. In the former, the female aspect is
passive, requiring the active and the activating force of the
Purusa to release energy. The latter sees the two aspects as
complementary[3]. This was a philosophical plane, the "region
where the human spirit could soar to ineffable heights of
fancied perfection."[4] In the social realm, female identity was
usually lost, or rendered invisible, within the larger group
identities of family and community. Thus, women were, as has
been constantly pointed out, rendered faceless and voiceless. It
is perhaps because of this that the few women saints who were
'different' from ordinary women stand out -- if nothing else,
they had both faces and voices. As religion was, as pointed out
earlier, intertwined with society, these voices were raised
within society through religion. These women were, in a sense,
deviant, for they did depart from established norms. But at the
same time, they also reinforced certain aspects of religion, and
therefore, of society as well.

A discussion on women saints in medieval India could
perhaps be broadly classified on the lines of 'by' women and
'of' women. By this, is meant, discussions (1) by women saints
themselves, and (2) by others, not necessarily women, who, in
some manner, employ the female idiom or simile.

The first of the women saints, Auvaiyyar, belongs to the
South Indian tradition. She is remembered today as the greatest
devotee of Muruka (Kartikkeya). According to legend, she was
a beautiful girl, who was of marriageable age. Her parents
(father?) had found a suitable match for her, but she wished to
devote herself to worshipping her Lord. Before her marriage
could take place, she prayed, asking Muruka to prevent it

permanently. She was instantly transformed into an old woman, and thus, avoided the married state.

There are two striking features about the legend. The first is that divine intervention was necessary to avert marriage. To put it differently, paternal (or patriarchal) control over a daughter was so complete, that no girl could argue against marriage; that was her duty, no matter what her personal inclinations or desires. The second is the removal of the sexual element, implicit in the transformation of a beautiful young girl into a withered old woman. The old woman is, in a sense, asexual, and is then permitted to devote herself to prayer and song in praise of God. It could even be argued that she was, in fact performing the duty applicable to that stage of life – that of *vanaprasthasrama*. Auvaiyyar's songs, in both literary and chronological terms, actually belong to the Sangam rather than the medieval period, for she maintained the Sangam tradition of *akam* and *puram* (inner and outer)[5]. Generally, she wrote of war, politics and love, using similes evoking the first two to demonstrate the last. So, for instance, she wrote of a "king" (God), who took "many enemy forts with guarded walls"[6]. Another poem talks of the "man of many spears" who had "the strength to protect and care/though the times are troubled"[7].

Auvaiyyar's life, as depicted by legend, throws up many questions, to which I have no answers. For example, is it significant that she is remembered as a devotee of Muruka, the god of the hills? Muruka can be seen as the god of the forest/tribal people, who is worshipped by hunters and forest dwellers. The expansion of the political system of the plain areas, particularly under the Colas, resulted in the incorporation of these, perhaps older deities, into the framework of temple religion and *bhakti*, not just as worship, but as representative of a community of worship[8]. Unfortunately, the legends do not give us any details of Auvaiyyar's life prior to her transformation. So, while we could put forward, as a tentative hypothesis, the idea that Auvaiyyar in a sense 'peripheralized' herself by worshipping Muruka, we do not know whether this was the result of choice or of family background – i.e., we do not know whether she belonged to the hills or the plains. The only certainty is that, in contrast to the emerging pattern of the *bhakta* community, she preferred to be alone, away from other human contact. Does this then mean that, despite age, societal norms were strong enough to force a woman saint to isolate herself from that society?

The second woman saint who will be discussed is Akkamahadevi, of the *Virasaivite* (Kannada) tradition. *Virasaivism*, in its early stages, rejected both caste and gender differences. The debating assembly of the *Virasaivites*, the *Anubhava Mantapa*, was one in which all participants met on equal terms. Both men and women were entitled to initiation, through a ceremony called *Linga dharana* (usually seen as the equivalent of the *namakarma* ritual). The parents of a child were also initiated into the *ashtavaranas* (the eight spiritual aspects or coverings), that were to be passed on to all children. The sect laid emphasis on the *Siva-Sakti* tradition, which, as mentioned earlier, regards the male and female elements as complementary. This meant, on the one hand, that no bar was placed on marriage and on the other, that no emphasis was laid on pollution[9]. The latter automatically freed women from the three kinds of pollution that, in the Vedic system, are gender specific -- during menstruation, the period of 12 to 40 days after childbirth, and the permanent pollution of widowhood.

Akkamahadevi is only one of the many women saints within *Virasaivism*, but is possibly the most famous[10]. She was a contemporary of Basaveshwara, being initiated into the sect by him. Her poetry is often explicitly sexual, for the spiritual union tends to be described in terms of a sexual union[11]. She too, was reported to have rejected marriage (with a prince) in order to devote herself to worship. In other ways too, she was a rebel -- notably, she was the subject of a major discussion in the *Anubhava Mantapa* because she went about naked. She argued, in her defence, that truth itself was bare and needed no adornment, and was upheld by Basaveshwara[12].

Akkamahadevi's poetry emphasizes the complementarity of *Siva* and *Sakti*. When the two are seen as parts of a whole, then their independent identification becomes meaningless. *Siva* is *moksa*, to be achieved through the exercise of *Sakti*, which causes both bondage and liberation. In societal terms, this can be seen as a negation of gender -- that is, the gender of the *bhakta* is unimportant, for it is transcended in the process of worship. Akkamahadevi expresses this idea when she says, in one of her poems, "all the world is a wife".

The radical dimensions of this kind of thought are very clear. There is, here, a negation of the basic idea of identity as biological difference, and, instead, an emphasis on the androgynous nature of worship. *Bhakti*, in other words, transcends gender, for it involves giving up the sense of self, to seek sublimation in the object of worship. Unfortunately, this radical element did not survive in the later *Virasaivism*. While the 12th century *Virasaivism* had stressed the unimportance of caste and gender differences, from the 13th century, both were reinstated. The four-caste *Brahmanical* framework continued to be rejected, but in its place, three clear divisions emerged[13]. This was, perhaps, a necessary outcome of the institutionalization of the sect, but the dichotomy present within the movement can be seen earlier also. Mention has been made above, of the fact that no bar was placed on marriage. On the contrary, *Virasaivism* emphasized family life and the work ethic. The ideology of the movement stressed the need to live in the material world, and by meeting its challenges, achieve spirituality. But what is noticeable is that most of the women saints were not married. For all the radical content of the movement, it appears that the women saints found it easier when their attempts to achieve union with God were not impeded by husbands! We do not get much indication of the attitude of other women in the sect to these saints, but Akkamahadevi was apparently too much of a rebel to suit them, for much of the most pungent criticism was levelled against her by women.

The third woman saint is Mirabai, the only one in the North Indian tradition, and possibly the most famous. Legends about her are numerous enough to make it very difficult to distinguish between the historical and the legendary figure. Certain facts appear to be reasonably well-established – she was of a Rajput royal family, and was married into another royal family, but she rejected marriage, for she wished to devote herself to worship. As in the earlier saints, here too, one sees the rejection of marriage, but there is, so to say, a progression that is visible. Auvaiyyar appealed to Muruka, who saved her from marriage (the groom is unknown); Akkamahadevi rejected a prince (an identifiable groom); and Mirabai, unable to reject marriage, rejected the husband. Her rejection was on two levels: (1) she talked about the illusory nature of *jag suhaag* (worldly marriage), and therefore, (2) she rejected the material world that accompanied that married life. It is the latter that makes Mirabai, in many ways, a symbol of radicalism and rebellion, and so, as Parita Mukta[14] has pointed out, a symbol of "the public humiliation that Mira had inflicted on collective Rajput honour". Mira did challenge male authority to go her own way. She continued her challenge even after widowhood, when, in contrast to the accepted view that widows were not meant to be seen or heard, she took to travelling, singing and dancing in praise of Krishna -- the *sadhu sant sangati* of the Mira bhajans. This in fact constituted yet another challenge, for implicit in this *sangati* is the idea of association with lower, or at least non-Rajput, castes. Mira herself was well aware of the ramifications of her challenge, which manifested itself in her frequent references to *kul marjaada* and to *Mira baanwari*. If, for every person, "there is an appropriate mode of conduct (*svadharma*) defined by his or her caste, gender, age and temperament"[15], then Mira comes through as clearly deviant, and not just different. She was placed outside the family/community, because she refused to follow the norms of 'acceptable' behaviour. This aspect is very clear in the charges of *kul nasi* that are levelled against her[16].

In their different ways, all these women did pose a challenge to established patriarchal norms. For one thing, all rejected marriage, and implicitly, the identity expressed within the family. They were all, in that sense, deviant. This deviation was carried further in their individual ways; in Auvaiyyar it expressed itself in isolation from the community of worship, in Akkamahadevi (most obviously) in her nakedness, and in Mirabai, in the association with people outside the family/social organization. They did fight for personal space, through personal rebellion, and they did achieve it. This was done in full view of society, for *bhakti* was expressed both in isolation and before an audience. For the latter, it was necessary to establish a dialogue with the audience. The audience had to share, albeit vicariously, in the experiences of the *bhakta*, which meant that these experiences had to be emphasized and exaggerated, to ensure the involvement of the audience. This was done through the use of the *viraha* form of poetry which emphasized suffering. This poetry is replete with the imagery of longing for, and the pain caused by separation from the object of devotion, and looks forward to unity with that object. Within this framework, individual expressions are, of course, different. So, as pointed out earlier, Auvaiyyar's God is the virile hero, who, by his strength, induces people to follow him; Akkamahadevi's poetry uses sexual metaphors, while Mirabai's is a sensuous exploration.

To what extent, if at all, did this personal rebellion translate into social space? One could argue that social space was automatically created, by the presence of the audience. But the audience's involvement was with the words, and the feelings expressed in them, and not with the experiences of the *bhakta* that went into the poetry. And the words used were quite often, those shaped by that patriarchal society which they were challenging. Lacking a different vocabulary, no space could be made for a different discourse. This had crucial implications for identity formation.

Earlier, the levels of identity formation were defined as comprising individual, family, community and society. The above mentioned women saints may have rejected the families into which they were born, but not the *idea* of family. One of Akkamahadevi's poems talks of mother-in-law, father-in-law, and brothers and sisters-in-law[17]. Other poems refer to the *Linga* as husband and to devotees as parents[18]. One of the most famous of the Auvaiyyar stories has Muruka as a small boy and Auvaiyyar as a mother. Mirabai's bhajans are full of references to both her natal and her marital families. But here again, there is a visible difference -- while for Auvaiyyar and Akkamahadevi, the families are metaphors, for Mirabai, it is a real family. In this, therefore, her rebellion was much more a reality.

But could Mira really reject the typically submissive female language? Was there an alternative vocabulary, which could provide the basics of a different discourse? The answer is necessarily in the negative. Submissive language reflected the submission of women in reality as well as the submission of the devotee to God. So, Mira is never just Mira, but Mira *dasi*, Krishna's slave. The devotee is eternally and humbly waiting for the grace of God to fall upon her. The God is, of course, male, and so, the idea of passive, submissive womanhood is reiterated. This is further underlined by the fact that many male poets also refer to themselves as females in their relationship with God, in order to emphasize the idea of weakness. Basaveshwara talks of himself as a married woman[19]; Kabir calls himself "Hari's little wife"[20]. The devotee is ever a bride of God, willing to give up life in the service of that God – in other words, to become a *sati*. Kabir perhaps best expresses this idea, when he says "How could the *sati* fear death/when she has taken the vermilion-box in her hand?"[21]

Other recurring themes in medieval *Bhakti* poetry include *Maya* and prostitutes, all of which are 'of' women. *Maya* is always a female; so, Basava, in one poem, talks of the different ways that *Maya* has "to worry and trouble" him. Another says, "One must not trust the woman -- thief of men".[22] Akkamahadevi, too, talks of "*Maya* for mother-in-law". Some four centuries later, Kabir says "she [*Maya*] lives forever/to destroy and ruin all families"[23]. The metaphor of prostitution is also a recurring one, ranging from Basava's poem about a "whore with a child" not being able to give all of herself to either her customer or to her child[24], to Kabir, asking "If she cherishes another in her heart/how can she find grace with her Lord?"[25]

These images are a constant reiteration of patriarchal ideas. Women are submissive and passive, but fickle and untrustworthy. They must always be controlled, and this control has to be exercised through a male authority figure. God is then the ultimate symbol of this male authority, for he symbolizes father, brother, husband, or any another version of patriarchal authority. This is clear in both the North and the South Indian traditions. In both, the emphasis is on family, as though to say that *nirvana*, too, is better achieved on a group rather than an individual basis! In the North, it is noticeable that Krishna *bhakti* is centered on his worship as Gopala, the cowherd, and not as the King of Dwaraka, or as the giver of the *Gita*. As with Mira's *sadhu sangati*, so also with Gopala, there is a subtle indication of lower caste association, and therefore, of being outside *Brahmanical*/patriarchal norms. The Krishna cult then permits a great many more female associations, notably, the idea of the 'other woman'. Mira (or any other *bhakta*) is seen as competing with Radha for Krishna's attention; the underlying idea of a male having sexual freedom is clear, as also the right to polygamy. This is in contrast to the ideas of devotion to one male God expressed by the female *bhaktas*. In Surdas, the *murali* is seen as female, and as immoral and casteless[26]. In societal terms, this can easily be passed on to women, i.e., women are immoral, and can become casteless (or can affect the purity of the caste), if permitted too much freedom ('too much', of course, being defined in patriarchal terms).

Bhakti in medieval India is usually seen as a radical, transforming movement. It is studied as a movement that challenged caste, and through caste, the very foundations of society. While it is true that many of the medieval *bhaktas* did challenge caste, can one really say that they affected the caste system in any significant way? *Bhakti*, it may be argued, rather permitted certain sections of society to be redefined, and, for those sections, provided a form of legitimacy through the identity of the sect. But here again, other than for the leaders, there is an assertion of a group identity, that of the sect, or the community of *bhaktas*. By the 16th century, this identity could be placed within the framework of the Mughal empire (so that the state becomes the ultimate patriarchy). In this context, Dadu Dayal's language, linking *bhakti* with sovereignty, becomes not just understandable, but inevitable[27]. Feminine identity was then merged with the broader one of *bhakti*, so that the personal rebellion of a few saints remained just that. Within the traditions of *bhakti*, these women were then glorified, but dehumanised. Certain elements were identified for all – for example, the degree of *bhakti* had to be proved through adversity. Common adversities included persecution (by priests or upper castes) followed by proof of scholarship through a philosophical debate with the persecutors, and finally, a miraculous 'absorption' into the object of worship (these are, incidentally, common to both male and female saints). The last then qualifies them for sainthood. As saints, they themselves become objects of worship, but not examples to be followed. They become 'different', not deviant, and the difference lies in their being singled out for sainthood by God. Clearly, the 'difference' was being appropriated within the value system. In other words, personal rebellion is of no use, without the grace of God. Divorced from everyday life, these saints, female or male, become symbols, not of rebellion, but of the very systems that they challenged, for rebellion itself is appropriated within the system. The *Bhakti* movement, emerging from dissent, became one that could confer legitimacy and identity on its members, and thus dominated the social sphere. Dissent expressed in the language of devotion, negated the idea of dissent itself. It thus was subsumed within the traditional structures, just as these women saints were absorbed within the broader framework of *bhakti*. The process by which personal rebellion was transformed into a metaphor of submissive worship, and which further delineated patriarchal systems, was thus completed.

Notes

1. E. Durkheim, *The Elementary Forms of the Religious Life* (1915), quoted in T.N. Madan (ed.), *Religion in India* (OUP, 1992): "If religion has given birth to all that is essential to society, it is because the idea of society is the soul of religion."
2. T. N. Madan, *Religion in India*, op cit., p. 17.

3. Meena Kelkar, "Man-Woman Relationship in Indian Philosophy", in *Indian Philosophical Quarterly*, January 1999, pp. 71-87.

4. D.D. Kosambi, *Myth and Reality* (Popular Prakashan, Reprint, 1991), p.1.

5. The literature of classical Tamil is called Sangam literature. Tradition holds that there were three Sangams, but none of the works of the first Sangam exist. Of the second, only the *Tolkappiyam*, a work on grammar, still exists, as do some of the poems of the third Sangam. Akam poems were concerned with love, while puram poems dealt with kings, wars, etc. See George Hart, *Songs of the Ancient Tamils* (OUP, 1997) for a discussion on these aspects.

6. Susie Tharu and K. Lalita (eds.), *Women Writing in India 600 BC to the Present* (2 Vols., OUP. 1991), Vol. 1, p. 58.

7. A.K. Ramanujam (tr. and ed.), *Poems of Love and War*, (OUP, 1996), pp. 129-30.

8. For the idea of a community of worship, see R. Champaklakshmi, "From Devotion and Dissent to Dominance – The Bhakti of the Tamil Alvars and Nayanars", in R. Champaklakshmi and S. Gopal (ed) *Tradition Dissent and Ideology -- Essays in Honour of Romila Thapar* (OUP, 1996), pp. 135-163.

9. The idea here being that anything emanating from the pure cannot be impure.

10. The discussion on Virasaivism is based on Vijaya Ramaswamy, *Divinity and Deviance: Women in Virasaivism* (OUP, 1996).

11. See, for example, Ibid., pp. 40, 60-61.

12. Ibid., p. 41.

13. For details see Ibid., p.66.

14. Parita Mukta, *Upholding the Common Life: The Community of Mirabai* (OUP, 1997), p.1.

15. T.N. Madan, *Religion in India*, op cit. p. 17.

16. Parita Mukta, *Upholding the Common Life*, op. cit., p. 60. Mira is deified only outside Rajasthan -- it is noticeable that Tod's *Annals and Antiquities of Rajasthan* has no references at all to her.

17. A.K. Ramanujam: *Speaking of Siva* (Penguin, 1973) p. 141.

18. Vijaya Ramaswamy:, p. 35.

19. Ibid.
20. Charlotte Vaudeville, *A Weaver Named Kabir*, OUP, 1993 p. 182.
21. Ibid., p. 183.
22. Vijaya Ramaswamy, pp. 10-11.
23. Ibid., p. 158.
24. Vijaya Ramaswamy, *Divinity and Deviance: Women in Virasaivism*, op. cit, p. 13.
25. Vaudeville – (OUP, 1993).
26. Kumkum Sangari, "Mirabai and the Spiritual Economy of Bhakti", in *Economic and Political Weekly*, July14, 1990, p. 1538.
27. For a detailed study, see Harbans Mukhia's article on Dadu Dayal in Harbans Mukhia, *Perspectives in Medieval Indian History* (Vikas, 1996).

11

Man-Woman Relations in the Writings of the Saint Poetesses

Vidyut Bhagwat

Till very recently Indian women were treated as a silent lot in Indian history. No one had expected them to possess a voice of their own. The motion of recording their alternative conceptions of culture and power simply did not exist. Nor was there any idea of studying Indian women's successive critiques of ideology for the purposes of the present. Almost overnight we are experiencing a sea-change. Anyone who wishes to study Indian women is talking not only about their evergreen creativity but also about the vigour and quality of their expression. We have gone even further. Instead of talking about one monolithic tradition of Indian women's protest and creativity, we acknowledge the immense variety of their projects and voices. We are demanding new research on these differences with the hope that comparisons with other regions and languages may in due course of time yield a coherent and meaningful body of knowledge.

I too was part of this process of growth. I also took an inordinately long time to realize that I was a part of a tradition which I could bank upon; a rich tradition, which opened for me, when in need, new cultural vistas and made available fresh

Extracted from: Vidyut Bhagwat, "Man-Woman Relationship in the Writings of Saint Poetesses", *New Quest*, July-August, 1990 and "Marathi Literature as a Source for Contemporary Feminism", *EPW*: April 29, 1995.

conceptual frameworks in dealing with the problems of the present. Now I think I know something about this tradition in Maharashtra, as available through Marathi literature. I, therefore, need to tell you how I made this kind of a theoretical journey. My observations will obviously be rooted in my background and be limited by it. But hopefully they may make some progress in a new direction in women's studies.

I was born and brought up in an urban middle class family in Bombay. My parental family shared more or less the same values which pervaded families of similar social status. It was neither an orthodox nor a progressive household. The needs and priorities of the male members, namely, of my father and two brothers, always took precedence over the interests and aspirations of my mother and myself. But this was taken almost as a natural state of affairs by us all. It wasn't that I did not realize the secondary importance, which was given to me in comparison with my brothers. I did express some resentment about it. But no senior woman relative of mine, including my mother, nor anyone in the large circle of my schoolmate girls ever thought it fit or worthwhile to discuss similar experiences of their own. In the final years of my school life, when I was 12-16 years old, I came under the influence of two remarkable teachers -- a man and a woman – who introduced me for the first time in my life to the larger universe of social and political thought and practice. I began to take animated and uninhibited interest in all social and political events, which impinged upon my existence. Still no one, even in this new circle, paid any attention to women's problems, predicaments and perspectives. The ill-treatment experienced by women was no doubt noted and talked about. But it was believed that the emancipation of the society as a whole could eventually put an end to all women's problems.

When I left my schooldays behind and entered the realm of collegiate education, I still did not experience much of a change in terms of my experiences as a woman. As a teenager and then as a young woman, I had to take some extra precautions to

avoid eve-teasing and occasional male harassment. The need for
these additional disciplinary controls was routinely absorbed by
me. Again no one in my domestic or public circles made me see
these additional burdens as a problem. At the university level, I
specialized in Marathi language and literature. My teachers and
fellow-students owing loyalties to competing ideologies and
political programmes often used to utilize the entire body of
Marathi literature to seek support for their positions. The
radicals used to unearth and analyze protests against the
traditional social order and/or the orthodox literary canons.
Interestingly, the differentiations and the specificities related to
the case or class of these texts and authors were thoroughly
discussed. In this whole game, it was common practice to draw
upon relevant material from women writers – ancient and
modern. Yet no one took note of the voices of women as
women. In sharp contrast to the attention paid to the caste or
class dimensions, the gender dimension of the whole literary
and social history was not mentioned. In a nutshell, my formal
education left me sex-blind in tackling problems of culture and
power.

   After the first three to five years of my married life, I once
again began to participate in contemporary radical movements
around me. Both within India and outside, radicalism was in
ascendancy. The students, the youth, the blacks, the women
and oppressed minorities of all kinds had taken the path of
revolt. In India various kinds of grass roots organizations and
movements were coming up in a big way. A major and a very
welcome and creative change was taking place. The young
radicals from all quarters were throwing off the shackles of
dogmatic versions of Marxism, democratic socialism, and for
that matter even liberalism. They were adopting new
conceptual frameworks and experimenting with new strategies
of action. Problems of the various oppressed sections of the
Indian society – the tribals, cultural and religious minorities,
slum-dwellers, landless labourers, the non-organized sections of
the toiling masses, etc. – were highlighted and discussed in

depth. In most cases a conscious attempt was made at the theoretical and practical levels to reappropriate in a dynamic manner the emancipatory content of traditional texts and of the tradition itself within which they are embedded. A creative release of the essential core of tradition into a new context was sought. The Marxists as well as the liberals endeavoured to utilize the revolutionary potential in tradition to justify their new strategies and concerns.

The contemporary feminist movement in Maharashtra also arose in the wake of this development. A number of dedicated women's groups with different ideological perspectives emerged – first in Bombay, then in Pune and soon in other urban centres and finally even in the countryside. Women's studies programmes were also inaugurated. Yet the feminist movement in Maharashtra differed from other radical movements in one crucial area. The non-feminist radical movements were increasingly refusing to treat tradition as a deadweight opposed to modernity and emancipation. They were trying to develop a critique of tradition which would lay bare its essential emancipatory core. For a long time feminists ignored their own tradition of a succession of women saints and other women writers who had inverted and occasionally even subverted the classic ideals of womanhood embodied in the hegemonic texts. The movement paid a price for this failure. It appeared to be based on dry, upstart ideas lacking roots in the soil. It is only recently, when the movement lost some of its momentum, that I began to worry about this lacuna. In my restlessness and also as a part of my other commitments and interests, I turned to literature for comfort and, honestly, even some kind of an escape from the harsh realities of social life. Suddenly I discovered the tremendous potential of the Marathi tradition which asserted women's right to lead a life of their own. This realization not only provided me with new sources of energy and ideas but opened my eyes to whole areas where women's studies can achieve remarkable progress and tradition.

Accordingly, in this paper, I have tried to probe into the lives and writings of the saint poetesses of Maharashtra in the context of man-woman relations. It is possible that some critics will dub this search as pointless. They will probably say that women like Mahadaisa, Janabai and Muktabai had already transcended the physiological division of humans into 'man' and 'woman'; that their search for salvation went beyond the limitations of the human body. Freedom meant to them only freedom of the spirit. Men and women craving for spiritual salvation have a total disregard for earthly happiness or unhappiness. They are involved in the broader and deeper problem of determining the relations between humans and the divinity. The joys and sorrows, torments and exultations – all the emotions of such persons have a significance which is unique. It could thus be argued that it is wholly wrong to apply to the writings of these saints – men and women – the contemporary criterion of inequality between men and women.

If this argument is taken to be sound, it leads to another question. If the saintly women like Janabai and Muktabai were *Mahayoginis*, had acquired the eight *sidhdhis*, conquered the five bodily senses and reached their ultimate goal of spiritual bliss – if all this were true, would it not be pertinent to ask as to how far the greatness of these women saints has gained recognition? Is it adequately and readily acknowledged?

Take the men saints of Maharashtra. There have been controversies as to whether there was one Dnyaneshwar or two. The organizational brilliance of Namdeo and Ramdas has come in for high praise. The spiritual message of Tukaram's *abhangas* has been the subject of many scholarly studies. Then, how is it that the achievement of the women saints has not received any such applauding attention? All these women poetesses are invariably referred in relation to their male mentors. For instance, it is always Mahadaisa of Chakradhar, Jani of Namya, little Muktai of Dnyaneshwar, Bahenabai of Tukaram, Venabai of Ramdas and so on. Why does social history have always to mention these women only in male-oriented terms?

Many literary and social scholars feel that the achievements of these women must have been far greater than their literary works, which have come down to us throughout centuries. Why is it then the case that their other accomplishments have been forgotten all these years? Why have these other merits of these noble women suffered non-recognition and oblivion?

There are many similar questions, which can be posed. It is generally accepted that these saintly women having transcended the body, followed the teachings of ancient sages and achieved ultimate bliss. However, their writings are often interspersed with references -- direct or indirect -- which reveal extremely bitter experiences that must have been their lot, due entirely to their femininity. It is true that all saints, men and women alike, have had to suffer the tribulations of worldly problems. The writings of the women saints, however, reveal to a far greater extent the mental tortures and physical sufferings which they had to bear, just because of their being women.

While a few of these women were gifted with the art of expressing their feelings and sufferings by way of oral or written words, one can only imagine the extent to which innumerable women of those days -- girls, married women, widows -- leading traditional, routine domestic and social life must have silently suffered, merely in consequence of their being females.

How is it that history does not record the torment of myriads of these utterly helpless, faceless women? In fact, even the male saints who have vividly described various human experiences in every walk of life with the minutest details, have not touched upon, with the same fervour, the sufferings of these women, which was part of the world in which they lived.

Marriage at a very early age, then the annual ritual of delivering a child, the back-breaking daily household chores and the obligation to bear this miserable lot in silence, without a word of pretest -- that was the fate ordained for women in the past. Saint poetesses represented the contemporary woman in the fullest measure and you can reach this woman, we feel, only through the writings of the women poets of the *Bhakti* period.

In anatomical terms, one may say that the saint movement was connected to the social reality around by an umbilical cord. To put it in Gramsci's words, saints were the organic leaders of the society. It is pertinent to note that no saint considered himself or herself as a person superior to the common people, but associated fully with them. In the compositions of the women saints, particularly, we vividly experience the link which binds us to them.

Janabai belonged to the *Shudra* caste. She was a maidservant of Saint Namdeo. But what a giant leap she took! She challenged the elite leaders of the society, the whole community, even God, all alike with pointed questions. She dared to move about in the open market taking off her *sari pallav* from the head down to her shoulder, a thing never done by a woman before. Was this not a trumpet call to all women to defy the shackles of meaningless customs and to assert their freedom?

The godliness of God can have its roots only in your belief in Him. Janabai had this perspective, this belief. Does this not have a message for women of today who regard their husbands and other elders as gods?

Muktabai, let us agree, gave up all thoughts of her mortal body and attained eternal bliss. But do we have to forget the torment she had to suffer before she could achieve her goal? Bereft in infancy of parents and destined to lead a life in wilderness with her divinely gifted brethren, Muktabai, a genius herself, could not only have enthralling experiences but could express them in words of infinite beauty:

The little ant took a leap to the sky and swallowed the sun itself.

What a gracious heritage for the women's movement of our times!

Mahadaisa (13th Century) and the *Mahanubhava* Panth

The first burst of notable women's protest in the Marathi language took place under the auspices of the heretic *Mahanubhava* sect, which emerged in the second half of the 13th century. A great line of women poetesses and prose-writers including women like Mahadamba, Kamalaisa, Hiraisa, Nagaisa have left for posterity a rich store of authentic protest literature. *Mahanubhava* was a sect of *Sanyasis* which had no place for ordinary laymen. Chakradhara was the founder of this sect and was looked upon as the latest incarnation of God. There were no rituals and no worship of concrete objects. From women's point of view, it should be noted that Chakradhara's radical measures included lifting of the ban on the participation of menstruating women in rituals, a common feature of *Brahmanism*.

One can, therefore, imagine the emancipatory space which the Mahanubhava women were able to carve out to shape a life of their own nursing, their own forms of life and expressions.

Mahadaisa, for instance, became a widow at an early age. As a matter of conscious choice, she became a *Sanyasini*, a priestess and a poetess of the *Mahanubhava* sect. Her writings as well as life tell us how the heretic sect *Mahanubhava* generated a possibility of transcendence for them.

The *Mahanubhava* cult along with *Leela Charitra* is an important part of the history and culture of Maharashtra.

> A woman is a cluster of intoxicating brews; all brews excite you only when they are sipped but the mere sight of a woman is enough to excite... Do not even look at the picture of a woman.

Chakradhar Swami, the founder of this cult said these words, which are clearly derogatory to women. They put a taboo even on looking at the picture of a woman, for fear that it will disrupt the tranquility of a man. These words might lead us to consider Chakradhar as a male chauvinist, a misogynist. The *Leela Charitra* calls upon men to observe strict celibacy; but as far as one can gather, the book does not advocate with the same insistence celibacy for women!

Irrespective of this, the picture of woman and her femininity that one can see in the *Leela Charitra* is full of compassion and intense love for women. Such a viewpoint was rare in those times; it is almost extinct now.

Chakradhar says to Sarangdhar, "In the matter of religion, why can't women be associated? Are they not human beings just like you? Your life may be important; but is a woman's life trivial?"

Chakradhar has also said that there is much that is 'good and fair' in a woman; but since a woman is of service to a man in other ways, he does not care to bring out the 'good and fair' in her. Chakradhar was aware that women, much more than men, possess the capacity to develop true friendship. He had a large number of women disciples. But he never took the stance of the "I command and I demand obedience" type. That certainly was not his attitude with them.

One can find several instances of Chakradhar having protested against indignities meted out to women. One anecdote in *Leela Charitra* goes like this: A *Brahman* had five daughters, all of whom were widows. Neighbours used to refer to them as *randas* (widows referred to in a derogatory sense). But Chakradhar, when he met the *Brahman*, enquired about the *panchagangas* (five sacred rivers). One can imagine the happiness of the father and daughters at someone speaking about them in kind words.

Chakradhar lived in the 13th century. It is perhaps, not surprising that this liberal-minded preceptor had among his disciples equally liberal-minded persons. What is astonishing is the fact that even today, we find in our society a number of persons who when showering abuses on others deign to utter words and idioms vulgarly referring to the female body. The reference is often to the opponent's mother or sister. What is still more surprising is that no one has the sensitivity or courage to decry such abusive language. The ever-growing instances of eve-teasing and molestation of women too is indicative of a filthy attitude. The writings of Chakradhar and Mahadaisa clearly suggest that if man-woman relations are to develop on a healthy and equal footing, a fundamental change is essential in all respects, even in our day-to-day speech.

An instance of how the women saints have not received the recognition due to them solely on their own merit may be cited here. Chakradhar is known to have defiantly sunk idols of worship in the Gomati river. This is one of the counts on which he is recognised as a great thinker, as a heroic founder of a new reformist cult. Ausa, his equally courageous female disciple does not receive such praise when she declared, "I am the daughter, I am the son too" (when she offered *pinda* to her departed father.)

Pinda-Dan is the ritual offering of food to the soul of the dead; the *shastras* lay down that this is the duty of the son or some other male in the family. Ausa thus defied tradition and in a sense stressed man-woman equality. Why should she not be acknowledged as heroic on her own merit on this count alone? Why is she known as 'just a disciple of a great reformer'?

Chakradhar himself had this broad outlook. The husband of Gauraisa forbade her from participating in the meetings of the cult, on the plea that she had to look after the household chores. When Chakradhar knew of this, he chastised the husband by saying that, "It is wrong for a person who seeks salvation to put his wife in shackles."

It is disconcerting to note that in the Mahanubhava sect itself, founded by a man of such catholicity of mind, women, to this day, do not seem to have gained any prominent place of honour. Even followers of the sect as also the scholars delving into its history have glorified only the male saints, paying scant attention to the role of Mahadaisa and other women, whose qualities and achievements are not a bit inferior to those of the males. Chakradhar, the founder, himself expressed the following sentiment:

> Women trapped in the household are just like cows tied to a post. The more they try to get free, the more are they stifled.

Even in our times, men appear to take fright at the sight of a female's unclad body and its movements. Even men who boast of their 'conquests' when it comes to watching in public the movements of an exposed female body are often embarrassed and appear ashamed, as if with a guilty conscience. Even those men who do not mind to some extent the easy, natural movements and even partial exposure of a woman's body 'in private', are strangely enough shocked at this spectacle in public.

Chakradhar has stated in so many words that a woman has no need to be ashamed when she has to bare her breast to feed her infant nor should she be embarrassed if while bathing her child her legs are exposed upto the thighs. *Leela Charitra* mentions Baisa who used to complete her exercise of two hundred and fifty prostrate *namaskars*, unmindful of the men who might be gazing at parts of her body. It was quite a blow to the misconceived notion that a woman must always be alert and must never expose her body to the stares of men.

Mahadaisa, however, though she was enamoured by Chakradhar's handsome features and impressive personality, does not immediately agree to his suggestion that she be his disciple. The noble child-widow replies:

> No sir, please no. My home will be at sixes and sevens without me. It is for me to do all the household chores. When there is a knock at the door, it is for me to open the door. No sir, please no. I cannot stay here.

In those days, it was considered as most improper to forsake one's first *Guru* and to accept another. That may perhaps explain why Mahadaisa took quite some time before she could decide to leave Dadosa, her first *Guru* and go over to accept

Chakradhar as her preceptor. To say that she merely respected the conventions of the times does not seem to be quite fair either to her own greatness or even her new *Guru*.

It has generally been observed and emphasised that saintly men and reformers like Goraknath, Chakradhar, Tukaram, Ramdas were totally unmindful of the physical charms of their female disciples. They were put to rigorous tests to assess their sense of spiritual vocation and staying power and only those who stood those tests were accepted in the sect. If this quality of the male saints to look beyond the mere physical looks entitle these worthy saints to a place of reverence, then Mahadaisa too must receive the same place of pride. She too displayed the same calibre when she was unaffected by the charms of Chakradhar's personality, while choosing a new *Guru*.

Mahadaisa, while she held serious discourses on philosophical subjects, was ever aware of the limitations imposed on her by her being a woman, i.e., a soul embodied in a female body. It seems that she had resolved to challenge the male monopoly in the matter of conquest of the senses. She takes to *sanyasasrama* and leads an austere life. It is clear that Chakradhar and Mahadaisa must have taken an active part in developing and shaping the area of life which she shared with Chakradhar which was marked by extreme discipline, and yet was free from tedium. Tradition gives the credit for all this to Chakradhar. In justice, it must be said that Mahadaisa deserves it in an equal measure. Here too, the *Mahanubhavas* appear to be niggardly in the recognition they have accorded to the contribution, which an outstanding woman has made to the achievement which she shared with a man of acknowledged greatness.

Muktabai (1201-1219)

It is not the *Mahanubhava* but the *Varkari* sect which caught the imagination of the Maharashtrian women of the pre-colonial period. As Deleury, a French Jesuit scholar, has pointed out the

Varkari movement is not a church but a movement and ".. there is no centralised organization, no hierarchy, no general councils, no credo, no sacraments" (Deleury 1960: 2). The line of *Varkari* women writers began with Janabai, a member of the great *Varkari* saint Namdev's household, and Muktabai, the younger and the only sister of perhaps the greatest *Varkari* saint thinker Dnyandev. Women writers of note like Gonai, Rajai, Ladai, Kanhopatra and Bahenabai further enriched the tradition. Another medieval religious-cultural movement viz. the *Ramadasi* sect also produced women poetesses of the stature of Venabai and Bayabai in the 17th century A.D. Very little account is available of Muktabai. Her compositions too seem to be very few. Yet her writings are generally held in something akin to almost awe. That she had great spiritual authority is accepted. This high tribute she undoubtedly merits. But it must be noted her *Riddle Abhangas* and *Abhangas of the Closed Door* have not been quite fully studied in depth. It is thus rather difficult to come to any firm conclusions about the details of her life. One can only make surmises.

Right from birth, Muktabai was confronted by the social boycott that was the lot of her family. It is possible that it was due to these hardships that she decided to accomplish *sthitaprajnata* or complete tranquility or balance of mind.

Is there a streak of a feeling of superiority in Muktabai? Her thinking appears to be somewhat on these lines: "My brothers and myself, we are persons of great authority. Others in the society cannot aspire to reach our heights." That is why she could comment on subjects like Sublimity of Chanting God's Name, Path of Salvation, Self-Realization, subjects which transcended the mundane problems which the business of living posed before her. That was her way to overcome the thorny world around her.

Like Dnyaneshwar, his little sister too does not record any personal matters regarding herself. Perhaps she felt that it would be lowering her spiritual stature to stoop down to put into words her own felt torments. Determined to solve the riddle of the universe, she is also resolute in defence of herself in extremely hostile surroundings. This supreme self-confidence leads her to say:

> Do you desire self-realization? Then do not blindly follow others. Search for the truth in your own self. There lies wisdom.

That is her completely self-assured way of thinking. At the same time, she is modest and broad-minded, for she does not treat the truth and experiences she achieved as the ultimate truth:

> How can I find faults with others?
> I see duality and controversies everywhere.

Muktabai has shown a very simple way for women and men to follow:

> Put yourself to test when you want to verify your experiences.

She herself followed her percept. Her belief in this philosophy is so firm that her self-confidence cannot be dismissed as vanity or false pride.

Bhakti Vijay describes an episode regarding Muktabai and Changdeo. As Muktabai was having a bath in the nude, Changdeo inadvertently approached, but on seeing her, he turned his head back in shame. Addressing him as *Nigura* (one who has no *Guru*) she chastised him:

> If you had been blessed by a *Guru*, you would not have let mean thoughts enter your mind.

> One is not ashamed to stare at the niches in the wall. Do the cows grazing in the fields have any clothes? I too am like the cows. Why are you embarrassed at my sight?

These are very mature words coming as they do from a girl orphaned when she was an infant.

Tradition regards Muktabai as *Maha Yogini, Adi Maya, Vishwa Mata*. It is not by being the sister of Dnyaneshwar that she earns these tributes. She has paid a very high price for it in her very short life. She had purposefully turned her back on the earthly life; yet she was fully conscious of the inherent strength of a human being. It has been observed: "In this process, Muktabai had lost all natural attributes of her body. They were stunted. We do not see even a single sign of her being a woman. In short, she strikes us, in a sense, as merely a male person." I do not quite agree with these comments. It is also said that while Muktabai's thinking was not totally unconcerned with society, her quest for self-realisation on an entirely spiritual plane led her to be enmeshed in a passionless inward nook. I venture to disagree with this comment too. As we have already noted, Muktabai has emphatically said that one must put everything to the ordeal of a test; one must verify every notion before accepting it. If we interpret her thoughts in the historical and contemporaneous context, is it not possible to discover in them a path eminently suitable to the women's liberation movement of our days?

Janabai (1270-1350)

Janabai, born in a *Shudra* family was brought up in the village Gangakhed on the banks of the Godavari river in the present day Parbhani district of Marathwada. Her parents were the followers of the *Varkari* sect. When she was just five years old, her aged parents handed her over, for reasons not clear, to the family of Damaji, the father of the *Varkari* Sant Namdev.

Like many other households belonging to the artisan castes, Damaji's family (tailor community) was also full of the *Varkari* ethos. Janabai's status in the new family was that of a *dasi*, i.e., that of a bonded domestic servant. She has invariably referred to herself as *Namayachi Dasi* – Namdev's maid-servant:

I am known to the world as merely Nama's maid-servant. I am not learned. I have not listened to discourses, nor have I contemplated. I do not understand proprieties or improprieties of this world.

These are the words of a very modest yet revolutionary soul. The message her words give seems to have gone into oblivion in the course of all these years. The stamp *Namayachi Dasi* has however stuck firmly to this day.

She may call herself by a very humble name, but it is nonetheless true that she had an independent mind. She had firmly resolved to stand up as an independent person. She has in explicit words expressed her anguish at the sufferings of a maid-servant and that too of a *Shudra* caste:

Rajai and Gonai (women in Namdev's household) are constantly at your (God's) feet; I am low-born and am kept outside.

It is always said that in the gatherings of the *Vaishnavas*, there is no caste or class distinction, that there is complete equality; no one is superior and none inferior. It is a mere myth, as Janabai's words clearly show. The privileges that Nara, Gonda, Mahada, Vitha – all members of Namdev's family – enjoyed were denied to the maid. She appears to have faced insurmountable hardships.

It is significant here to note that Janabai compares herself with Vidura, himself the son of a maid, but a man of infinite wisdom. Janabai does not beg alms from any human, rich or saintly. She seeks direct dialogue with God – Viththal. She asserts that Chokhamela, the *Shudra* saint was the only true *Vaishnava*.

Namdev's family was quite well-to-do. But the life that Jana had to lead there was far from comfortable. Her *abhangas* are full of references to household work, the numerous chores with which women of those times were burdened. There must have been thousands of such miserable women. Janabai's uniqueness was that she made Viththal himself come down to earth to help her in her chores.

Her belief was that God derives his godliness from the
devotion of the devotee. That is why she is bold enough to
say:

> O Lord, what is the point of your getting angry?
> After all, we are the source of your strength.

On the other hand, her own righteous indignation knows
no limit. She even pours abuse on Him in choicest words, even
threatening Him:

> Vithya, you brat of Adimaya
> You begetter of umpteen kids
> How do you dare forsake me?
> Wages of adultery are burdens of responsibility
> As to myself, I have none else to look up to.

What leads her to this fury? Her hard life has convinced her
that she is connected directly to Viththal by an umbilical cord.
No matter if people around her do not realise this. But Viththal
himself whom she fondly sees in various intimate forms -- as
mother, father, brother -- why should He too desert her? That
is her anguish.

Janabai has said on several occasions that Viththal shares
her bed. He agrees to take food with her, so that she could sleep
contentedly:

> I eat Him, I drink Him;
> He shares my bed, I sleep by Him.

She experiences this state of ecstasy. On one occasion, she
even says that Viththal embraced her in the presence of
Namdev.

What are we to do with all these allusions? Is it possible to
explain it in terms of union of God with a finite soul? Janabai
has emphatically said that she was a *Shudra*, yet God himself
came down for the sheer joy of touching her.

A woman who declines to lead the humdrum life of hundreds of others, has of necessity to face ignominy even in these days. It must have been infinitely worse, centuries ago. Yet Janabai, in no uncertain words says that she will not respect the unjust rules which determine virtue and sin. In justification of what she says, she describes her physical experiences in vivid details. A woman in those days who gave up all domestic ties and craved for God must have been subjected to vile abusive words from others. But, she sustains her morale and never gives up courage. She vowed to move about in the marketplace with the *pallav* of her sari moved from the head down to her shoulder. Others may have called her a prostitute but she didn't care.

There is a lot of difference between a male saint referring to his body and a woman saint alluding to hers. To regard God as superman is certainly a big stride in the feminine thinking. Men are not inclined to treat women with fidelity and respect. Very well. We will identify the real *Purush* of our concept with God himself. We will be happy in constant contemplation of Him. Is that the road to ultimate bliss that the women saints want to follow?

Janabai says, "I am completely relaxed. I am exulted, happy in all respects. I am indifferent to distinctions of sex or body."

Bahenabai (1550-1622)

It is said that in traditional India a sense of individuality was absent. Yet traditional India did produce at least one autobiography and that too was written by Bahenabai – a woman saint. Bahenabai's life falls into an important tumultuous period in the history of Maharashtra. Bahenabai was born in the village Devgav in the northern part of Maharashtra. She wrote profusely and quite a lot is known of her life. Her life and writings are researched and studied in various aspects. Yet she merits even further research. Most women will feel a sense of intimacy and affinity with her. Her life may at first glance appear to be just like many others'; yet it is very different. When she wanted to get out of a rigid framework, she bent the frame, expanded it and in a sense even broke it.

Bahenabai's parents were poor. At the age of three, she was married to a thirty year old Vedic pandit of the *Shakta* cult. The family wandered from place to place -- Siddhanath, Mahadevaban, Neera Narsinhapur, Pandhari, Shikar Shinganapur, Rahimatpur. Even in this hectic rush, she could find solace in *katha-kirtans*.

But Bahenabai's mind did not rest with the solace she received by listening to others' *kirtans*. She met Jayaram Swamy and pursued the devotional path. Then followed a craving to meet Tukaram, the famous saint. One can imagine what a courageous step it must have been in those days for a *Brahman* woman to seek a *Shudra Guru*. Bahenabai's husband was furious; she was subjected to daily beatings. She endured it all, resolved as she was to secure her goal. It must be noted that this was not an emotional outburst.

Bahenabai translated a Sanskrit book *Vajra-Suchi*, a book which attacked *Brahmanic* privileges derived solely through the accident of being born a *Brahman*. She did this with a critical yet balanced mind. We find her fighting against *Brahmanism* that had lost its *Brahmatva*. She also protested against the disparagement of womanhood.

In the third month of her pregnancy, the husband threatened to leave her in the wilderness -- the fate of many a woman. Bahenabai was, however, different from others. On the one hand, she pacified the husband with these words: "The husband is the God, the ultimate for the wife." But then, she also succeeded in persuading him to take to the path of devotion. This was not a cosmetic change that she brought about. It was no superficial bringing together of the worldly and the spiritual ways of thinking. The husband who previously had nothing but derision for Tukaram turned into an ardent disciple. And while she achieved this amazing feat, what were her thoughts? She says, "The changes that have taken place were only inevitable and unavoidable."

It is only with this full awareness that she revolts and succeeds. She expresses her anguish saying, "A woman's body is totally dependent on others. The *Vedas* and the *Puranas* have ordained that a woman can bring no good to anyone."

It is significant to note that Bahenabai had transcended the body -- the feminine body which tradition had decried as a vicious share. Bahenabai did bear children. But as she was suffering the pangs of delivering the children, she was also experiencing the blissful total conquest of the concepts of life and death.

She gave new dimensions to the concept of *pativratadharma* -- the duties of a true wife. She did say, "You cannot approach God if you do not love your husband." But then she also stressed, "A true wife is she who is aware of her own self. Being married, she has to fulfil her family duties but she must have the craving for spiritual salvation too. It is possible that the husband, children and others may not approve, but she must not give up her true path." Bahenabai has put all this in a very ingenious way.

In one *abhanga* she has said that all women as also men who live their worldly lives with a sense of *Nijananda Ghana* or supreme self-realization, are all true wives. The path of a true wife is as healthy for a man as it is for a woman.

Who is a *Brahman* and who is not? Bahenabai says that the body, *varna*, caste, community, *Karma* or *Dharma* -- none of these can lead to *Brahmanhood*. The rituals of *Yajna* or sacrificial rituals, charity, asceticism -- these also are not the true attributes of a *Brahman*. Here, she appears to take a bold thrust at the caste system itself.

It is a matter of controversy whether Bahenabai wrote the *abhangas* describing her twelve previous lives. It is immaterial whether we deny their authorship to her or interpret them in their proper perspective. If these *abhangas* are indeed written by her, it would follow that they must have a much deeper meaning. A woman who spent her entire life in serving the cause of the *Varkari* cult (the *Bhakti* movement) and who missed no occasion to point out the seamy side of the caste system -- such a woman is unlikely to indulge in reminiscences of her past lives, as if she was narrating some fanciful tales.

In all these lives she was a woman. In one, she says she was a *Vaishya*, in another a *Gavali* (milkman caste) and so on. In the initial lives she was so involved with devotion to God that like Muktabai she was either not interested in getting married or like Meerabai she was indifferent to married life. In the later lives, however, she was born a *Brahman* and was married. Then while she was always a faithful wife, she also followed the cult of devotion and every time found ultimate salvation.

To me the best way to interpret these *abhangas* seems to be: A woman seeking spiritual emancipation and yet desiring to retain her love for humanity cannot attain significant progress by living a life without the companionship of a man. Since she is born a woman, she has to accept the earthly framework of a family, a household and children. Yet she can certainly make adjustments to this framework. She can bend the frame, or expand its dimensions. If she is resolute enough she can even persuade and lead the man to the path she herself has chosen. As a woman has a nose, eyes, hands and feet so is she endowed with a husband, household and children. She need not be wholly occupied with all this. But there is no reason why she should totally reject it either.

In the *Parmarthik Fugadi* (parlour game of *Fugadi* in relation to spiritual salvation) Bahenabai says, "If a woman craves for ultimate bliss, she must be prepared to face popular censure. She must defy this censure and must also give up being vainglorious about material possessions like wealth, erudition and children."

It is possible to cite Bahenabai's example and to suggest that it is best for a woman to somehow achieve a compromise between day-to-day life and the spiritual quest. The suggestion would be deceitful. Ramdas fled from the marriage *pandal* when he heard the *Shubha Mangala Savadhan Mantra* and saw a warning in it. For this gesture, he is glorified. Equal praise is due to Bahenabai who had so many precious and revealing thoughts to express about *Samsara* or worldliness.

Venabai (1627-1678)

Venabai was the pet student of *Samartha* Ramdas. She had successfully observed hard and fast rules of Ramdasi *Matha* and gained her name. She has written three long *Katha Kavyas* viz. *Venaswami*, *Ramayana* and *Seeta Swayamvar*.

Very little information is available about her personal life. She was born in Kolhapur (South Maharashtra) in a *Brahman* family, Gopajipanta Deshpande being her father. She was a childwidow. She was advised to read *Bhakti* literature for her remaining life by her parents. But, fortunately she met *Samartha* Ramdas, asked him some twenty-five pertinent questions and became his disciple. She said, "My body, my soul/everything is taken away by my *Guruji*."

She had to face great opposition, but she declared:

Some praise, some malign,
I don't wait for them.
I have held *Guru's* feet to heart,
I will not leave them till my death.

When her parents discovered her infatuation with her *Guru*, they poisoned her. She lay unconscious. The poison had turned her skin to a deep dark colour. Ramdas touched her and she recovered. He accepted the girl as his disciple. He said to her, "The path to eternal happiness is not easy. You have to tread the jungles. You have to suffer rigorous heat and cold. It is not for the tender ones to follow this path. Rama himself has put a blue body-armour on you."

This episode is significant. Ramdas gave her succour and guided her on the spiritual path. This speaks for the greatness and courage of Ramdas. But Venabai could be a great *Sadhak* only after, and perhaps because, she was poisoned and had lost her looks. Otherwise she would have been forever a victim of social censure and boycott. This sort of thing only goes to expose the evils of an unbalanced male-dominated tradition.

Gorakhnath was a handsome person. The charm of his body and features in no way affected, for better or worse, his image as an extraordinary *yogi*. If anythings, his looks may have contributed only slightly to his eminence. Chakradhar too was very handsome. Irrespective of his charming looks, he achieved eminence as a distinguished seer. His looks had nothing to do with either enhancing or diminishing his image.

In our tradition there are many other saints who were fortunate to be so endowed. But Venabai happened to be a woman. She had to pay the high price of losing her looks before she could be in a position to pursue her spiritual path.

Why is it that this question was never posed before, or is not being posed even now?

While studying the lives and writings of the saint poetesses, one must not ignore the context of the times in which they were born, lived and wrote. The spiritual aspect of their achievements certainly deserves to be studied. Yet tribute must also be paid to them for the extraordinary courage which they displayed when they rebelled against several evil traditions and social taboos and misconceptions. To deny them this credit is likely to further corrode our historical and cultural heritage, and secular practices within religion.

References

Deleury, G.A., *The Cult of Vithoba*, Deccan College Postgraduate and Research Institute, Pune, 1960.

Javdekar, Shalini (ed.), *Sant Bahenabaicha Gatha*, Continental Prakashan, Pune, 1979.

Joshi, K.V. (ed.), *Sakal Sant Gatha*, R.S. Avate, Pune, 1967.

Kolte, V.B. (ed.), Leela Charitra, Maharashtra Rajya Sahitya Sanskriti Mandal, Mumbai, 1982.

Sant Janabai, *Sant Janabaichi Gatha*, Jagadishwar Book Depot: Mumbai, 11th Edition, 1983.

Sant Muktabai, *Tatiche Abhanga*, Anmol Prakashan, Pune, 1978.

Shevade, Indumati, *Sant Kavayitri: Stree Muktichya Maharashtratil Paulkhuna*, Popular Prakashan, Mumbai, 1989.

12

Self-Respect Movement: An Alternate Gender Discourse from Below

Shantishree D.N.B. Pandit

Indian society and polity has been influenced by the dominant gender discourse, which has been western in its origin and moorings. But its very founding mother, Germane Greer, has challenged this discourse and the reverse position has been taking shape in the US and the West[1]. Patriarchy is universal as a structure in its ideology and function. Has it been that no Indian social reformer or thinker has ever thought of this issue? This has been one of the issues, which greatly worried E.V. Ramaswamy Naicker, popularly called "Periyar". Periyar essentially linked patriarchy as a structure to the rise of *Brahmanical* Hinduism and builds in the ideology through the many sacred texts written by this class and used it functionally to oppress the women as well as the other castes. So Periyar believed that it is this masochistic interpretation where the valour of the male and the masculine myth has been perpetuated and celebrated. Though Dravidian society has been different but this has over a long period of time influenced it.

This influence can be clearly noticed in the writings of Illango Adigal, especially his celebrated work, *Cillapadikaram*[1]. The only paradigm shift that was attempted was a part of the Dravidian movement initiated by the great rationalist leader Periyar during the years 1928-29. The feminine myth that was created could be clearly seen through the works of Illango. Even today these two major categories into which women have been structured is being followed judiciously. It is Periyar who through his writings in the paper *Kudi Arasu*[2] has deconstructed this feminine myth. Several women self-respecters had also written in the journals run by Periyar. This paper hopes to look at these contributions as a discourse that contested two hegemonic discourses of Indian society, caste and gender.

One of the two major constructions of the female identity was women as symbols of chastity, where whatever her husband and lord may do, she is steadfast in her resolve and loyalty to him. Even if he strays outside the straight and narrow path, she will practise monogamy and accept him and serve him like a loyal servant. This is the famous depiction of the character of Kannagi, who was well known in Madurai for her chastity and loyalty to her errant husband Illango who strayed from monogamy. This is the patriarchal construction where the woman's sexuality has to be protected and this is only for women. All morality is brought down to the sexual morality of a woman. The freedom to stray is the prerequisite of men alone, as though to be born a man, endows him with certain special qualities. Periyar contested this construction of the male as the superior and advised women to break these rules constructed by the men to protect themselves, as they were really the weaker sex. It was this insecurity of inferiority that made them construct patriarchy as a structure to oppress women and maintain their hegemony.

The story goes that Kannagi was unhappy about her husband's vagrant ways, especially his relationship with a courtesan Madhavi. But when he was killed for the theft of an anklet thought to belong to the queen, by the orders of the Pandya king, it is Kannagi who challenges the king's verdict, saying that her husband had taken her anklet and not the queen's, by breaking the other anklet in the imperial court. Kannagi is a chaste wife of an errant husband and it is her chastity that is able to avenge the death of her husband. The king regrets his mistake but Kannagi has the power to burn Madurai not fighting for honesty but because of her chastity. This sets a benchmark for an ethical order in the Dravidian society that in constructing the identity of a woman, the most important factor was chastity. All good women were chaste like one's mother, sister, wife and daughter. All women violating this code were bad. What is forgotten is that to violate this code it needed a man and woman, but the code was only for the woman. One sees the recurrence of this identity in several Tamil films, that for a true Tamilian, all women except one are like one's mothers and sisters. It is the bounden duty of the tamilian male to protect all the 'Thaikulum' [community of motherhood].

The other conception was that of woman as an object of desire. The depiction of Madhavi, the beautiful learned courtesan who attracts Illango and makes him desert his chaste wife Kannagi, is the other pole where the construction of a woman is made. The fact that Madhavi was learned and beautiful does not matter but the fact that she had relationships outside marriage was most obnoxious. Her whole character is judged from the structure of sexual ethics created by patriarchy. It also places women like Madhavi as objects of desire, something to be possessed and cherished for male enjoyment. This fits with the dominant interpretation of patriarchal society where women were seen for their physical attributes; intellectual qualities were secondary. This is in keeping with the dominant paradigm in all societies of seeing women as subordinate to male desires and asserting that to satisfy the male desires is the primary female duty.

It is from these two interpretations that Periyar made a drastic shift not only at the level of theory but also at the level of praxis. He has given an effective non-western framework to gender identity through the self-respect movement. This was done as early as the 1930s where the shift in the identity was contested and Periyar through his men and women followers constructed an identity of women being equals with their male counterparts. It is this discourse which contested and intervened effectively not only into the dominant western discourse but also against the hegemonic *Brahmanical* discourse. Hence it is a unique and an effective intervention. It was an attempt to construct a civil society in South India on the principles of self-respect both in status and gender categories. He is one of the few 20th century thinkers who was ready to hit the nail on the head and saw the degradation in Indian society based on the *chaturvarna* and the rise of the *Brahmanical* class.

Identities constructed on the basis of caste system and patriarchy were contested by Periyar. Periyar felt that the *Brahmanical* classes used the toll of access to education and traditional knowledge as a weapon to oppress the lower castes and women. Traditional political scientists have seen education and policies as something that belongs to two different worlds. But this has been a myth. In ancient times it was the exclusive access to this that endowed a particular caste with the power of knowledge. This exclusiveness created structures of oppression in gender and caste categories and according to Periyar this had political and social consequences. The structure of power influences the shape of educational systems. Here the decisions that have been taken by the powers have proved beyond doubt that educational institutions were political institutions.

Patterns of control over the educational system vary, of course, from one society to another. A study of these patterns can do much to clarify the ways in which education, political power and social structure are interrelated. The main impediment to the rationalization has been the social reform movements against the highly hierarchical structure of the Indian society. There is a mobilization of bias in a given institutional structure, which reflects the power of some groups over others. In many ways the problem of power in education is similar to that of Max Weber, who held that the educational ideals and practices of a particular society should be viewed in terms of its structure of domination. Where Weber focuses on the way in which cultural ideals of the dominant stratum penetrate the content of education, it is also important to emphasize their effects on the structure of the educational system.

The idea that knowledge is power dates back to the scientific revolution. Now it is not simply that knowledge is power, but that technological training is the key to personal success. Tensions have arisen between the egalitarian principle that the state should treat all citizens equally, and the meritocracy notion that equality meant status allocated by achievement. The inequalities among individuals and classes are still perpetuated to a considerable degree in the social inheritance. In the state of Tamil Nadu where the self-respect movement of Periyar was very vocal on women's rights saw that boys are given preference when it comes to higher education. Hence, it is through education that Periyar wanted to challenge the categories of caste and gender as well as the stereotypes of identity constructed by them.

Self-respect entered into the discourse of Dravidian society at a time when *Brahmanism* was being challenged in whose name hierarchy was constructed based on superiority and inferiority. Periyar contested all these institutions as well as family, marriage and the identity of woman. He decided to criticize the dominant paradigm and thereby constructed an alternate paradigm. It is from 1928 that Periyar and his followers had a coherent conception of gender where the space was provided to redefine, accommodate and advance women's concerns from an egalitarian perspective. It also fractures the myths created and nurtured by patriarchal society, of chastity and desire as the defining categories of women. This redefinition was for both the private and the public spheres. This was a radical shift that has to be acknowledged in any gender debate.

Periyar was a radical reformer whose reform was not halfhearted or only in one aspect but in all aspects, rather in a holistic approach. He condemned all types of oppression that were perpetrated in the name of superiority based on archaic and unscientific systems. The movement led by Periyar always highlighted social reform concerns. He believed that the pursuit of political power by the lower castes should also bring about break-up of the age-old social system of stratification and its basis of power. He believed that both should go hand in hand. Though one sees the reversal in the South Indian society where the Dravidian non-*Brahman* groups have appropriated political power, this has not brought about the social revolutionary agenda of Periyar. This agenda seems to have been abandoned after they attained political power. There is fragmentation among the Dravidian groups and some of them only pay lip service to the name of Periyar. Hence it is all the more important to analyze where this fracture took place that marginalized a vital societal intervention, nay a social revolution.

The reason why Periyar linked the caste system with any radical shift in the gender-feminist paradigm has been clearly stated in his writings as late as 1971, just two years before he passed away[3]. He observed: "Though I have endeavoured all along to abolish caste, as far as this country is concerned, this has meant I carry out propaganda for the abolition of God, religion, the *shastras* and *Brahmans*. For caste will disappear only when these four disappear. Even if one of these were to remain, caste has been constructed out of these four... Only after one had been made a slave and a fool would caste have thus been imposed on society. One cannot abolish caste without instilling a taste of freedom and knowledge [in the people]. God, religion, the *shastras* and *Brahmans* make for its growth as they have a vested interest in the perpetuation and spread of slavery and folly which will strengthen the existence of caste."

2222 *Shantishree D.N.B. Pandit*

Identity is not a monolith and Periyar was well aware of this. But to him in Indian society the defining factor of identity was the caste system and its social stratification. He believes that the *Brahmans*, who saw to it by means fair and foul that the other non-*Brahman* castes do not have access to knowledge, imposed this. They kept it as their singular monopoly and even devised methods not to write it. For writing would have meant its availability and whatever was later written was written in a language that the masses never understood. There were punishments as well. He always quoted the example of Ekalavya who despite all odds learnt the art of archery and venerated a *Brahman* guru, Dronacharya. What the guru gave him in return was that he asked for his thumb so that he would never challenge Arjuna. Periyar felt that this was justice. Identity cannot be defined unless the individual was liberated internally and externally. Internally in the mind the structures of domination are built by knowledge, especially sacred that has been interpolated and changed to benefit a particular caste. This led to subjugating the masses and Periyar sees Manu as the most vulgarised mind. He is notorious for defining the position of women. Hence, in most of his campaigns, Periyar asked for the burning of the *Manusmriti* which he did as well. This ideology of subjugation of the mind defined identity internally as well as defined one's identity externally.

Periyar saw the whole problem of identity defined by a class that claimed special powers not by merit but by birth and held autocratic and frightening powers to subjugate other castes. He dismissed the idea of the *Brahmans* as the twice born and the genome theory of superiority. He said that *Brahmans* did not have any special powers, only the exclusive access to the structures of knowledge and constructed God, religion, and the caste system to support the same. He saw them as man-made, rather *Brahman*-made structures to define not only their identity as superior, but the identities of the other as inferior, which was pernicious.[4]

For Periyar, caste was not simply a form of social stratification, which in its benign form was a division of labour but rather a hegemonic system of oppression and ideology of dominant perception. It comprised of complex hierarchical social relations as well as those percepts and principles that informed, sustained and justified this oppression. The oppression and subjugation of women was a part of the caste framework for women were placed with *Athi-shudras*. Their identity was defined only in relation to the male. Hence, Periyar felt that any change in this interpretation couldn't be taken in a piecemeal way but holistically which logically led to the linkage of all the elements that sustained caste.

In 1928 the *Kudi Arasu* paper carried articles of a woman by the name of Penn-ina-nallar. The discussion on women's education, Tamil culture, marriage and widowhood and *Brahmanism* continued for the entire year. This was a statement of ideology of the Dravidian movement. This was a critical discourse on the status of women and culture and customs that sustained such an oppressive system. It stated explicitly that all morals were one-sided and it was the women who were blamed, degraded and abandoned though men were equally guilty but were allowed to go scot-free.[5] This destroyed the self-respect and self-dignity of women. It led to the degradation of the feminine and developed the superiority of the masculine myth. The idea was to reconstruct gender on egalitarian values.

The alternative was suggested in the same article in the second part. The marriage should be of individuals and not between families or a business deal or an act of male convenience. It should be based on love and comradeship and nothing else. Mutual respect and affection should strengthen this relationship. The importance of education was stressed in giving women economic independence. Marriage of girls before the age of consent should be avoided at all costs for the girls to develop the physical and the psychological maturity to handle a relationship. These writers praised Periyar for his courage of conviction to fight a conservative caste-ridden society. Though some articles did appear in 1926 on women's education but a sustained campaign began in 1928-29. This is a turning point in reconstructing gender from a Dravidian perspective.

The self-respect movement that received substantial support from women changed the way the marriage ceremony was conducted. The traditional Hindu ceremony totally degraded the woman in the ceremony of *Kanyadaan*. Women were liabilities to be got rid of. One would gift cows and with them women were included. In most marriages the girl's consent was never asked for. Most of the time the family, especially the men, took decisions. Periyar felt that any marriage should be a ceremony of self-respect for both the bride and the bridegroom. He argued that their consent was more important, rather central to a self-respect marriage. The services of the priest (who was himself unsure of the meaning of the *mantras*) were dispensed with.[6] Periyar gave a lot of importance to the bride's wishes that so much so that in one case where two inseparable friends Nagammal and Rathintyammal wanted to marry one person Arangaswamy as they were inseparable as friends he allowed it.[7] This did not mean that Periyar propagated bigamy but his respect for the wishes of the human being, especially in this case the brides concerned, was evident. He refused to force anything and respected the individual wishes.

It was not only rituals that the self-respect movement discarded but it also helped inter-caste marriage though this was vehemently opposed by the affected caste groups. As long as the bride and bridegroom were ready, Periyar was ready to invite the wrath of caste groups. For he believed that when one human being was marrying another, such artificial divisions like caste which were unscientific, should not come in the way. The self-respect vow was unique for it required both the bride and the bridegroom to abide by each other's views, needs and concerns:

Today our conjugal life that is based on love begins. From today I accept you my dear and beloved comrade as my spouse, so that I may consecrate my love and cooperation for the cause of social progress in such a manner as would not contradict your desires.[8]

This respected the individual's right to choose, whether male or female. Periyar did not differentiate and taught these self-respecters that most of the morality was sexually based and to the disadvantage of women. There was a lot opposition[9] to Periyar's marriage ceremonies, which opposed all accepted norms and proved them to be unscientific. He also stressed that a woman is not an object of desire but a human being who also has desires like the male counterpart. For him chastity was a two-way process for it has to be applied to both, the male and the female. It is not that Periyar and his followers were unaware of this opposition but they deliberately wanted to debunk time-honoured ideals of femininity, such as modesty, chastity, rectitude and courtesy.

The redefinition of marriage challenged patriarchy and gave women the freedom to construct their relationship as equals, failing which they were free to discontinue the relationship. There was nothing sacroscant about it but it was just a social and individual contract of two people to live together. This challenged the integrity and sanctity of caste and thereby the *Brahmanical* tradition as well. "To control their women, Aryans devised a system which would characterize their enemies as untouchable and which would ensure that the women do not even touch these other men".[10] He brought in the thesis that the origins of untouchability as an ideology and actual control related to the control over women. "..... Because our forebears held women as property, they were automatically constituted as objects of suspicions and paranoia."[11]

The world suddenly opened to the women who were attracted to the Dravidian movement especially the self-respect movement that gave them freedom as well as opened a world of knowledge. This movement made women more mobile and increased their visibility in the public sphere. It also increased their space in their homes and the private domain. Periyar was one of the first to destroy the myth of masculinity. One sees such writings much later in the West. This was done in 1928-29. He denounced as false and deceptive the ideal of manhood or masculinity. It is important to analyze the essay of Periyar on *Karpu* chastity. Periyar defended a woman's right to desire and openly refuted the myth of chastity that had been woven around female sexuality.

He argued that originally the word *Karpu* stood for the qualities of firmness, steadfastness and honesty etymologically read. Early in history *Karpu* was a universal quality; it was only after the entry of Aryan Hinduism that the word was used for a narrower meaning. The idea of *pativrata* from Sanskrit denoted subjugation, surrender and control whereas the Tamil equivalents of *manavi* and *nayaki* were connatively equal, atleast in the realm of love and desire. Periyar was also critical of the Tamil poetry and literature that just was not gender sensitive. He did not spare even Tiruvalluvar, whom he thought was otherwise egalitarian but not with respect to chastity as a feminine quality. Periyar said that his insensitivity was because of the fact that he could not understand women. Periyar compared women with the depressed classes, for both were denied access to the means of knowledge, were prevented from learning and thereby oppressed and consigned to servitude.

Periyar vociferously argued that the gender distinction did not endow different intellectual qualities; that the dominant groups and part of the institution of patriarchal ideology constructed them all. He remarked, "Though women get pregnant and carry children in their wombs for nine months this does not make them different from men. With respect to qualities such as courage, anger, the power to command and the will to violence, women are like men....... On the other hand just because men do not bear children it cannot be said that they differ from women in respect of love, peace and the ability to nurture."[12]

His critique of masculinity was original and in an article titled "Masculinity must be destroyed", he observed that the very word masculine degraded women. He thought that until and unless this norm was destroyed, women would never be respected. At the same time the other norm femininity also should be destroyed for this kept women in a golden cage and in a mental frame of subservience. Periyar realized that women depended on men and required their help and support and during childbirth completely negotiated their autonomy and freedom. He radically advocated that unless women shrug off the burden of reproduction, their emancipation cannot take place. This is their Achilles heel, their point of vulnerability.[13]

He refused to accept male privilege in the realm of sexuality and the partisan use of the ideal of chastity. He also felt that the ideal of motherhood was an important part of patriarchy as it robbed women of their right to desire and their right over their bodies. He argued that the Aryans wanted to enslave women through injunctions to them to observe, chastity and decorum. It only enjoined on women to do these things. Periyar observed that chastity and promiscuity are interlinked concepts which put limitations on one gender while giving the other unlimited freedom in the area of desire and sexual autonomy.

The period from 1928 to 1937 saw the liberation of women and the paradigm shift in Dravidian society with regard to women. This decade through the sustained campaign in the press and with the public regarding the self-respect movement regained for women their self-respect. Both men and women began to write and debate these issues and reconceptualize new constructions of the other. In the marriage of one Nagammal, Guruswamy suggested that men should also wear a *mangalsutra*, so that they realize the power and authority of restrictive symbols.[14] The movement greatly sensitized the men to imagine themselves as women so that they could understand the disgrace they meted out magnanimously. The horror of their misdeeds could be brought to the notice in such a way that in one such self-respect wedding, the groom agreed to wear the *mangalsutra*. This decade indeed was one that brought out remarkably, the possibility that an attempt to take a conscious gender-turn in a social movement could take place at the level of the masses.[15]

The battle that Periyar began was not an easy one, for on the one hand he had to disentangle the whole ideology of patriarchy that was very deep-rooted in society and on the other hand he and the self-respecters had to reconstruct the sex-gender system with all its complexities. The vested interests that withstood and contested this reconstruction also had to be dealt with, at the level of theory as well as praxis, which led to an emancipation of women. The vested interests had different agendas to oppose the gender reconstruction by the Dravidian movement. They were those who resisted all and any attempt at reforming marriage customs and the status of women, those who resisted the creed of Periyar and those who saw women's reform from a different perspective.

Those who opposed reforms totally came from the Congress and the upper castes. They were those who resisted any changes in the marriage practices, the Age of Consent Bill and the Child Marriage Abolition Act. One Congress leader, M.K. Acharya, a Tamil *Brahman* while speaking in the Central legislature felt that "unless girls were married off before puberty, their chastity could not be ensured, that morality in marriage would suffer and conjugal life would invariably become corrupt."[16] Another Congress member T.R. Ramachandra Iyer remarked, "Once girls attained puberty, they developed sexual desires, to regulate which they needed to be married early."[17]

Periyar was extremely caustic in reply to this opposition. He opined that if the *Brahmanical* scriptures could give elaborate structures for containing female desire and the sexuality of widows, its modern day successors could be no less behind. Hence they wanted to control girls who were more easier to manage and manipulate to serve their interests. Periyar was shocked that such learned men used the scriptures to legitimize their oppression of women. He was for stringent action both at the social and the political levels so that a new egalitarian order could be built based on equality.

Periyar opposed the *devadasi* system. When Muthulakshmi Reddi proposed an amendment to the existing Hindu Religious Endowment Act, which would strike at the economic basis of the *devadasi* system, in the Madras Legislative Council in 1927, leading Congressmen opposed the bill.[18] Periyar and his followers saw the *devadasi* system as a form of exploitation that dedicated entire families of women to "the pleasure of Gods", which he thought was really for the pleasure of the priestly class. A *devadasi*, Ramamrithammal wrote a novel, which was semi-autobiographical in nature and opposed the system of exploitation and oppression in the name of Gods by the priestly class and asked all *devadasi* women to reflect on their condition. She left the vocation, married a music teacher and joined Periyar's self-respect movement.[19]

To Periyar, chastity [*Karpu*] and debauchery were two different constituents of the same sexual ethic, which he refused to accept as a given moral category. For him the two terms gave degrees of male ownership over female sexuality and desire. The idea of chastity insisted that only one man could possess a woman while that of debauchery sought to make women objects of sexual pleasure. This was within the earlier construction of woman as a symbol of chastity or an object of desire.

Periyar felt that the theorization and construction of the other within the *Brahman* patriarchy and the values and ideology this systems produced were reprehensible. The chastity attribute was closely linked with reproductive capacities of the woman, hence she should be kept physically chaste to be fertile and able to reproduce male progeny for propagation of the clan of the male. The woman became just an instrument in the maintenance and the propagation of patriarchy. Periyar rejected this construction. For him, there were no differences, "To make strength, anger and ruling-ability solely male attributes and calmness, patience and the ability to nurture life female ones is to say that bravery, strength and ruling prowess are characteristic of the tiger while the ability to care characterizes the lamb."[20]

Periyar thought that these stereotypes were myths created to perpetuate patriarchy and these were arbitrary with no scientific basis. He added, "We maintain that while it is the case that women possess the attribute of bearing a child in the womb for nine months and eventually giving birth to it, this, in itself, does not make them different from men with respect to qualities such as anger, ruling prowess and strength. Likewise we think that though men do not possess the biological means to get pregnant, it cannot be said that they possess qualities different from women in respect of love, calmness and the power to nurture. If we are to value true equality – if there exists true love between man and woman – it is certain that all responsibilities except that of bearing a child should be considered common to both."[21]

He made parenthood the decisive factor of nurture, thereby giving both the male and female equal emphasis. He also liberated the woman from the perpetual and the lifelong burden of motherhood, thus making her body an instrument of propagation of the race and perpetuation of patriarchy. He went further and gave her control over her body, the control to decide whether she wants to have a child or not. For, the ethic of motherhood totally suffocated her and made her lose all control over body. He even refused to take the argument that women had only physical attributes and no mental and intellectual qualities. He thought that culture and literature tried to socialize women into the stereotypes and prepare them only for marriage and not for a career.

"We allow girl children to play about from their infancy and prance from infancy to childhood, shower them with kisses, nurture them without the least hint of discrimination on our part. But when such creatures attain maturity and intelligence we worry about them in an unnatural fashion, distinguish them from the rest of humanity and finally constitute them as useless dolls and come to consider them as a burden to parents; women become a matter of concern to themselves and others and having thus made them objects of worry we then strive to protect them, satisfy their every whim, decorate them so that they become inert, lifeless dolls which need to be pampered and praised."[22]

The construction of motherhood as a female virtue owes its origin to the coming into existence of private property. It was this that brought the necessity of knowing the father's name, started the concept of woman being brought into the family to safeguard the private property and produce heirs to do so. Later the woman was degraded by being considered as a part of man's property. So in this oppression it was the capacity of reproduction that was important and therefore the elevation of all the fertility rituals in a woman's life. He placed the logic of all this as a part of the caste system which was presided over by the priestly class. "After it had become the norm for people to want children to safeguard property, *Brahmans* who had invented fictions of heaven and hell to keep the poor from stealing from the wealthy and to secure some of that wealth for themselves now sought to argue that ...... man must have a male child who would keep alive his name after death and perform his obsequies."[23]

Periyar laid domesticity itself as a feminine virtue for public scrutiny. He advocated the option of divorce as a way out of an unhappy marriage. If the right to divorce is not granted, polygamy and polyandry should become norms. To bear in silence and patience the travails of an unhappy marriage is a slur on one's humanity, self-respect and clear folly.[24] The paradigm shift in the reconstruction of marriage by the self-respecters under Periyar's leadership was that it defined women as human beings rather than wives and potential mothers. He devalued the importance given to motherhood and made women equal partners by calling for equal rights to property. He wanted women to practice birth control, so that they are liberated from publicly determined role stereotypes and also as a health safeguard so that they are not totally drained off. The decision should be a woman's. He always felt that if men were to bear children they would have practiced birth control from time immemorial. To empower women he believed that she should have information and knowledge of her self and her body.

Through this reconstruction of gender, the Dravidian movement influenced civil society as well as tried to appropriate politics. The whole paradigm shift was not only in an anti-imperialistic realm but also in anti-caste and anti-*Brahmanical* realms. The woman who wrote profusely in the papers run by Periyar echoed several of his ideas. "It is often asked how women who have been born to housework may be called workers. It is said that women have nothing to do with work and they are fit to perform only certain tasks such as child-bearing, i.e., housework is reduced to child-bearing. It is also said that women may not aspire to be considered a part of the labour force as men. Those who say these things refer to the oft-repeated maxim 'work is the mark of a man'. But no rationalist can accept this, that there is something about work that it could thus be considered essentially male. From dawn to night..... women labour with their bodies..... They have been condemned to household tasks and in reality ought to be known as kitchen workers. Women labour thus through the year without respite.... One cannot claim they are not labourers on the argument that cooking is not work."[25]

Periyar's intervention in reconstruction of the feminine both in the private and public spheres was important. It constituted a paradigm shift as well as a community of equals. It is a useful framework for situating the women's movement in India. His intervention was radical as well as realistic both at the level of civil society and the political realm. His dream is still one as his followers and women are looking to the West for inspiration. His followers who chant his name have been able to successfully appropriate political power but the social revolution has been incomplete. It is the women's question, which he reconstructed in the thirties and the forties that is still relevant to the civil society in India as well as the whole world.

Notes

1. This is a Tamil classic literary work during the *Sangam* period.
2. Periyar's complete and collected works is published by Emerald Publishers, Madras.
3. *Periyar, Ninety-third Birthday Souvenir*, 17/9/1971. Anaimuthu 1974.
4. M.B. Gopalakrishnan, *Periyar: Father of the Tamil Race*, Madras, Emerald Publishers, 1991.
5. 'Women's Depressed Status' *Kudi Arasu* dated 29/4/1928.
6. *Kudi Arasu* dated 3/6/1928.
7. Ibid.
8. Natalie, Pickering, *Recasting the Indian Nation: Dravidian Nationalism Replies to the Women's Question.* Thatched Patio: International Centre for Ethnic Studies, May-June 1993. Colombo. See also, Samy, Sitambaranar, who is biographer of Periyar. In his marriage to a widow Sivagami this oath was first taken. This is mentioned in his biography of Periyar in Tamil, *Thamizhar Talaivar Periyar E Ve Ra Vazhakai Varalaru* [The life of the leader of the Tamils, EVR] Trichy: Periyar Self-Respect Propaganda Institute, 1971.

9. See issues of *Deshbandhu* in 1929. This paper alleged that Periyar by making women demand these marriages was making them into witches.

10. S. Ramanathan in *Kudi Arasu*, dated 12/4/1931.

11. *Kudi Arasu*, dated 12/4/1931.

12. *Kudi Arasu*, dated 12/2/1928.

13. Anaimuthu, V., ed. *Thoughts of Periyar*, 3 vols. In Tamil: *Sinthanaiyalar Pathippagam*, 1974.

14. *Kudi Arasu*, dated 12/5/1929.

15. One witnesses the outpowerings of these women, their anger, desire, talent, intelligence and sensitivity.

16. *Kudi Arasu*, dated 23/9/1928.

17. *Kudi Arasu*, dated 25/11/1928.

18. They were S. Sayamurti and Swami Venkatachalam Chetty.

19. Ramamrithammal, Dasigalin Mosavalai, 1936.

20. Anaimuthu, 121.

21. Ibid.

22. *Kudi Arasu*, dated 21/4/1946.

23. Viduthalai, 11/10/1948.

24. Anaimuthu, 148

25. Puratchi, 29/4/1934.

References

Anonymous, *Periyar E.V. Ramaswamy: A Pen Portrait*, Madras: The Periyar Self-Respect Propaganda Institution, 1992.

Appadurai, Arjun. *Worship and Conflict under Colonial Rule: A South Indian Case*, Cambridge, Cambridge University Press, 1981.

Arnold, David. *The Congress in Tamil Nadu: Nationalist Politics in South India: 1919-1937*, Delhi, Manohar, 1977

Baker, Christopher, John. *The Politics of South India: 1920-1937*, Bombay, Vikas, 1976.

Baker, C.J. and David Washbrook. *South India: Political Institutions and Social Change*, Delhi, Vikas, 1975.

Chandrababu, B.S. *Social Protest in Tamil Nadu*, Madras, Emerald, 1993.

Diehl, Anita. *Periyar E.V. Ramaswamy: A Study of the Influence of Personality in Contemporary India*, Delhi, BI, 1978.

Gopalkrishnan, M.B. *Periyar: The Father of the Tamil Race*, Madras, Emerald, 1991.

Irschick, Eugene. *Politics and Social Conflict in South India: The Non-Brahmin Movement and Tamil Separatism, 1916-1929*. Berkeley, University of California Press, 1969.

—, *Tamil Revivalism in 1930s*. Madras, Cre-A, 1986.

Nambi, Arooran. *Tamil Renaissance and Dravidian Nationalism: 1905-1944*. Madhurai, Koodal Publishers, 1980.

Saraswati, S. *Towards Self-Respect: Periyar on a New World*. Madras, Institute of South Indian Studies, 1994.

Sivathamby, K. *Understanding the Dravidian Movement: Problems and Perspectives*. Madras, New Century Book House, 1995.

Thavamani, *Periyar on Women*. Madras, Emerald Publishers, 1993.

Veeramani, K. *The History of Struggle for Social Justice in Tamil Nadu*. Madras, Dravida Kazhagam Publications, 1992.

Vellore Senthamizhkko, Periyar in History. Vellore: Periyar – Gora – Kovoor Atheist Centre, 1987.

Vishwanathan, E.Sa.. *The Political Career of E.V. Ramaswamy Naicker: A Study in the Politics of Tamil Nadu, 1929-1949*. Madras, Ravi & Vasnath publishers, 1983.

Washbrook, David. *The Emergence of Provincial Politics*, Delhi, Vikas, 1976.

13

Devis, Kumaris, Balas and Extras: The Grand Reduction Sale

Shyamala Vanarase

When a medium arrives in a culture, its properties and interactions with the hardware technology as well as the software styles generate a transitional force. Film came to India when the agricultural dominance in the culture was strong and the industrial patterns were just emerging in a few urban centres. Film with its rapidly developing technology offered a transition to the ways of creating audio-visual images. It also provided a clear articulation of the way composition works to express certain themes and meanings. It brought in a new device of storytelling that was attractive and engaging because of the very nature of the medium itself.

Its dominant 'tense' was the present, the here and now of it. Its capacity to be anywhere and everywhere could place the stories anywhere, anytime. The life-like quality of the image created the 'real' in its exact audio-visual replica. This makes fiction and documentation look very similar. The initial response of the audiences, particularly in India, was that of the 'eyewitness' account. If the story was placed in a period, in a society, at a particular place, its content was almost treated as evidence.

These basic elements have to be kept in view when one looks at social issues or portrayals in films. In Indian cinema, the portrayals of women within the framework of commercial cinema were the only available material, as the art of the cinema, the experimental work or genre development were not taken up by the film-makers. The development of the film industry had very different motivations, the upper hand of the financier always affecting the kind of image that would be brought in the market. The image of woman in Indian films is a creation of the ideas of selling and the considerations that went into making the image saleable.

Let us look at the reality of women over the period 1900 to 1950. This was a period of great transition in women's lives, their self concept and the way they were regarded by society. Because of the modern education the lives of the young men were changing. The women were, largely, either illiterate or just literate. The drive for women's education was slowly gathering strength at least in the urban centres. Emancipation of women was on the agenda of social reformists. By 1950, a century of effort for women's education, political independence and the economic influence of the two World Wars, had offered considerable freedom to the upper and middle section of society. With adult franchise, there was an opening for political participation. During the political struggle, women had been exposed to the rethinking about tradition, the need to change and the redefinition of womanhood in particular and humanity in general. A few women, as they received education got into teaching and other professions. From the completely controlled life of the daughter, the wife and the mother of the household, women had grown into a greater sense of individuality, greater control over their lives and better contribution to social life. None of this was free. The struggle was a part of growing as a person and asserting one's will.

The story of the lower-middle and lower classes was different in some respects, as the majority was custom-bound, inarticulate and locked within narrow limits. The socio-religious pattern was under stress and it had its own

charm with the song and dance and craft built into it around the
rituals at the family level as well as at the social level. The
celebrations and religious observances spread over the calendar
and something or the other was 'happening' round the year.
Putting the total womenfolk together, they did share some
norms of good behaviour, emphasis on decency, politeness as a
lady's virtue (non-assertive is perhaps a better word), and values
of womanhood being vested in motherhood, particularly,
bearing a son.

When one starts looking at the film portrayals, the general
response to films has to be kept in mind. The examples of the
western films brought the sociality and sexuality in
man-woman relations from a different society to the Indian
audiences in the concrete audio-visual form. The mode of
dressing and the freedom in sexually loaded or directly sexual
gestures in the films were promptly declared as vulgar. It was
another story for the film-makers. The convention of male
actors playing the female roles operated in theatre because there
was a kind of taboo on the public appearance of women. The
first film on the Indian screen had to use the same convention.
In his early efforts, Dadasaheb Phalke persuaded the ladies of
the family to appear in front of the camera, playing the
mythological roles. The story of Krishna killing Kaliya the
cobra king, featured his daughter Mandakini in the role of Bal
Krishna. Later on some women from the All-Women Theatre
groups appeared on screen in his later film, Bhasmasur –
Mohini. The early portrayals were largely the mythological
figures of devoted wives, sacrificing daughters or suffering
women who bring good fortune to the family etc. Here one
finds the answer to the problem of respectability of cinema
itself. The films from the west were not good or 'virtuous', but
if it were an Indian mythological film, it was acceptable.

But cinema, with its verisimilitude, created another
problem. Goddess or vamp, the cinema presented the woman
on the screen to be looked at. This was not acceptable for a

respectable woman. It was bad manners for a man to be staring at women. It was bad manners for women to invite their gaze. Anyone who belonged to this social milieu, shared this norm, irrespective of class, caste or creed. There was no midway for this. If a woman wished to act, it meant that she was stepping out of the norms of respectability. For women on stage, the conventions of theatre called for ways of not meeting the eye, not getting intimate etc. It is quite clear that in real life all norms are not perfectly followed, but the guiding principle remains as prescribed by the norm. But, the social conditions based on austerity changed; due to the economic and political factors mentioned above, several norms and almost ritualistic patterns of behaviour had to change. Women had to sort out the issues of home-making and man-woman relationships in different ways in different contexts. The women as actresses or as characters were subject to two different frames of considerations. As actresses, they had to step out, think of careers, and get into the man's world. As characters however, they had to portray within the frames of stories. The story would have to make sellable images. These images were a part of the beginning of the Grand Reduction Sale of the surface of the great Indian culture. With the basic qualities of the medium, the imagined heaven, celestial beings like *Apsaras*, the gods, and the goddesses had to be visualized into concrete shapes and costumes. India has a long tradition of sculpture and iconography. Trying to dress up women to look like a sculpture coming alive resulted in the kind of goddesses of the screen.

If one starts looking for the types of images, one comes across the stereotype of the highly worshipped virtues of womanhood. She is a Goddess. The adulation and devotion for the Goddess was conditioned to the virtues of womanhood, and any mortal with those, was regarded as Devi, the Goddess. The absolutely self-sacrificing, suffering, non-assertive pattern is repeated ad-infinitum. The romantic overtones are somehow

brought to the framework of the acceptable norm. The
dialogues would always have odes to these virtues of
womanhood. The one on the pedestal, the Devi, is of course the
ideal. But in real life, everyone knows that there is no bridge
over the gap between the ideal and the real. If the question
"How do you regard the woman?" is to be answered with "As
Devis", then the stories have to have such superhuman
characters. The problems of portrayals are, however, hidden in
the audio-visual language of cinema. What would the Devi look
like? The answers in the visual qualities in painting introduced
by Raja Ravi-Varma were in terms of literal and realistic
conversion of the verbal images. For instance, the Goddess
Laxmi would be drawn literally standing in the centre of a lotus
flower, complete with the rippling water and swans around.
The icons changed from sculpted ones to the framed
reproductions from the litho press. Cinema brought in the
walking and talking Devi. Visually she defined the contours of
the womanly body, the clean, elaborately decorated and
well-nourished person. She had the virtues of ultimate
self-sacrifice and in a mythological film, would be the
benevolent, forgiving and omnipotent Mother. The
mythologicals would portray the characters of Goddesses as
cohorts of Gods, in terms of the husband worship, joys of
bearing a son, penance and trials by various tortures for
ultimate release from this world and attainment of bliss.
Heroines of this kind were enacted by famous actresses like
Shobhana Samarth, Sulochana, Durga Khote and others.

Within the story of a Devi type, there would be the vicious
one. In a 'social' story, the educated, modern woman will be
cast into a vicious selfish mind-set. The earthly woman who
was trying to be a Devi would have her worldly failings. She
could not escape the sexuality that moved her from within. The
concept of the female as the complete and equal complement of
the male had moved to that of the willing, submissive husband
worshipper. For her, virginity was sacrosanct and the biggest

calamity of life would be to get pregnant before marriage. Her persecution when found with the evidence of sin was a popular theme. But the major chunk of romantic stories made her a combination of a Devi and a westernized 'darling' ready for social dancing etc. Being the virgin was portrayed as being an innocent, beautiful, and sexually attractive girl. The contradiction here is obvious, but Indian audiences accepted the blatant contradictions as long as the visual pleasures were intact. From the spirituality of the first type, the romantic ambience of the second type brings her closer to the earthly woman. The contradictions of being a *Sati Savitri* in slacks helped the wish fulfilment of the Indian male, who was attracted to the free and frolicking young girl and yet was weighed down by the norms of the *Ramayana* expecting him not to look her in the eye.

Even as the taboo lifts bit by bit through the new challenge of rational thinking and economic compulsions, the friendship of the opposite sexes was always at the center of gossip. As women moved out of the sanctum of the domestic limits, they were getting too close for comfort. The professional life changed for educated men and women. The real challenge was to create a mode of interaction with the members of opposite sex, which did not have sexuality as the central point. The films never ever addressed this issue. The stories called for images, which were pleasing to the eye and as such had no problems in presenting suitably decorated doll-like images, film after film. The mythological, the historical, the social, the crime and horror, the stunt and the devotional, all had created the woman's image either as the Devi type or as the virgin type. The dramatic opposite would always be in terms of the modern, the educated and the freedom lover.

The heroines entered the film careers as young girls wanting to earn a living, or move from careers on stage to the screen, or through some male relative or acquaintance looking for a suitable cast. In theatre, the convention allows a thirty year old to 'act' the sixteen year old. The camera does not allow that. As the films presented heroines and the romantic content, they moved from young adulthood to late adolescence and to early adolescence too. Younger girls appeared on the screen and through the story awareness of sexual identity got underlined from an earlier age. The Bala or the young girl too had to have precocious gender awareness and, on occasion, the coquetry. The vulnerability of the virgin and the precocity of the girl child kept on attacking the innocence of the young. It happened to both, the boys and the girls. Shelley's words "One word is too often profaned for me to profane it" came true through the popular film; the word was fully profaned. From the spiritual to the platonic, from the platonic to the romantic, from the romantic to the physical ......the images moved visually, making the body of the woman more and more an object of male desire.

Once this happens, the object tended to lose its specificity, its uniqueness or its privacy as a human being. It moved to woman, any woman. The use of the word 'extras' expresses fully, all the characteristics. They used to be in the groups. The groups appear around the bride, around the grieving character, in bazaars, at community gatherings and so on. In the song and dance formula of Indian popular cinema, they came in as material to be choreographed. As the pop and rock stars of the western screen and stage were copied in India, the culture of gesture changed, irrespective of its relevance to the contexts of characters. The costumes changed slowly. This movement of the image has continuously functioned to nudge the norms of decency and this too, has moved from nudging to jostling, from jostling to elbowing and ultimately to pushing out. If we take a simple boy-meets-girl situation, the event moves from a benign 'chance' meeting to a calculated cornering of the girl. The interactions in these situations move from the coy and the shy to the aggressive and the abrasive. Instead of winning the girl's mind, it gets more and more directed at her body.

With the mass character of the medium, anything shown in the film reaches the eyes of an indefinitely large audience. The visual seems to be quite common, and stealthily, acceptable. The loosening of norm initiated by modern thought was a very different and responsible process, which did not move to a normless situation. Indian society has an intricate system of norms for maintaining the dignity of the individual even in its highly coercive hierarchy. Simple acts of respect, kindness and tenderness were deeply woven into behaviours of women. As mothers, they were in charge of this cultural transmission. The job of modernizing the woman was not easy and demanded very rigorous self-criticism and a careful establishment of a new way. The first step in this direction was the movement for women's education. The educated woman had to prove that she was, by the strength of her education, a better homemaker. Her bringing up of her own daughters was fraught with the tensions of establishing the new boundaries while taking the new liberty that education offered.

In popular belief however, education was neither necessary nor good for women. The films supported the belief. An educated wife would be portrayed as a threat to the male ego. Her assertions would be labelled as blatant attacks on the norms of modesty and decency, believed to be the natural virtues of womanhood. She was not supposed to have an opinion of her own; even if she had, she was not supposed to express it, particularly in front of the elders, the in-laws and strangers.

The details of the images and their import may be examined at the sensory-perceptual level, at the conceptual level and also at the value level. The reduction of the image from the Goddess to the extra is also a foreclosure of identity issues.

At the audio-visual level, the hair, the facial make-up, the quality of cloth used as dress material (this particular detail is complicated by the large majority wearing unstitched dress), the look of the body, the postures regarded as 'proper', the walk, the manner of speech, the textures and colour combinations are all involved in expressing the content. But, these can also be treated as 'pleasing' in themselves. So, rather than making it expressive, it could be made just attractive. This is yet another aspect of the woman's image, whereby the need to individualize is dispensed with, and all that she has to do, is to look good and be 'easy-on-the-eyes' as Hollywood slang would have it. The whole range of covering and uncovering of the body has also been treated in a similar fashion. From loose to tight fit, from thick to thin and from thin to thinner materials, the function of attracting the eye has proceeded to sell, sell at all cultural costs. Sellers sell and buyers buy. Along with every pleasure of the eye, they buy a norm of the way of looking at a woman. That way has been decided by the technical decision regarding camera placement. If these technical acts have been looking at women to emphasize their sexuality, to get them to cover without modesty and reveal without abandon, what the audiences have been offered subliminally is the vulgar way of looking at women as such. Whatever the portrayal, whatever the situation, whatever the sentiment, the technical decisions remain focused on the same purpose. It has to please the eye.

As mentioned earlier, there were norms linked to these details. The composition and the technical decisions were not only creating the visual aesthetics of cinema, but were also nudging the norms. A single example that would suffice to make the point is the handling of the breast cover. Be it the end of the sari in whatever style, be it the *dupatta/odhani* in certain regional variations, the norm was to keep it in place. As a woman grew up, she learned to handle it as part of her training in modesty and socially acceptable behaviour. In films, it became slowly and surely a method of covering without modesty. It was also used as a gesture to attract rather than to avert gaze.

At the conceptual level, women as characters get stereotyped, reduced in richness and variety. If the issues of identity are addressed, they are against the massively forceful foreclosures offered by the cultural past. The typical feminine image of the tender, sentimental, sweet and beautiful person was repeated film after film. So, the stories would be built around how she suffers when she steps out or, is made to step out by evildoers. The message was quite clear, the woman should never ever step out. What should she look like? There were already norms in place, based upon seeking male approval. The films underlined them and in the process, taught her how to attract attention. The subtle difference between the two is wiped out. Over the years, brides have started looking more and more like some film heroine or the other. The individuality was drowned earlier in the common conformity norms, now it was drowned in the tinsel of the visual effect. Her motherhood was, similarly turned into another narrow band, reduced to binary options of the self-punishing kind or the controlling autocratic kind. The concepts of honour, love, harmony, emotional security were all treated by a version of all-or-none principle. The black and white of it was always heavily loaded in favor of the static, custom-bound pattern.

At the value level, the place of the Adimaya -- the Mother Goddess who was worshipped in temples and through several ritual observances -- as the female principle in its fulfilment was lost to the virgin in peril because of the impending 'danger' of motherhood. The celebration of life and of sexual union as an aspect of the positive force of life, gave way to sensation seeking, aggressive, irresponsible animal drive. The place of sexuality in Indian thinking was not as a source of sin, but as a step in this worldly fulfilment, as a man's and a woman's way of seeking the togetherness and the communion that yields and ensures biological and cultural transmission of the wisdom of the community. This large composite of living under the guidance of truth, beauty and goodness was made into an audio-visual shell, drained off of the original thoughtful substance.

These reductions work on the three levels of the synthesized experience that cinema offers. The viewing public has a very confusing situation around in the early days of cinema. The medium is new. Its language sounds attractive and instantly pleasant. Before one has a chance to check with real life variety, the time and money spent on viewing the film becomes almost a surrogate experience. The women spectators had no method of checking whether people behave the way they show in the films, as even the act of viewing the film was under heavy supervision. It continued to be low on respectability of the form of entertainment for a generation, became a matter of lenient regard, subsequently a method of social enjoyment, a peer group 'in thing', and eventually a routine aspect of life. Women spectators gradually became a target audience for family dramas, tragedies and mythologicals.

Initially however, women had to withstand censure for visiting cinema houses. Their getting out of the homes was a digression from the norm of modesty. When considered as audiences, Indian women are a heterogeneous lot. Even today, there are at least four layers. The sophisticated cine-goer who has access to world cinema and is equipped with the critical apparatus, the educated cine-goer who has grown with films and maybe, fallen out of the habit, the teenagers and finally, the deprived group that takes every chance to see a film because the opportunities are so few and far between. With the arrival of television and the cable network, the very mode of film viewing has changed. Bad quality images, commercial breaks and interference of day-to-day happenings do make it 'cold'. In pre-television era, cinema functioned as many things rolled in one. What should a woman look like? What are the clothes in fashionable circles? How do the rich live? What are the manners and mannerisms that are exciting? What happens when boy meets girl? What is the wedding night like? How to react to advances? and so on and on. In the post-independence years, cinema kept on giving a sense of freedom from norms, and at the same time, giving a stereotyped understanding of various issues related to women. While the spectators enjoy the play of the lovers, the stereotype was that adult approval was absolutely necessary for entering into wedlock. While new fashions of dress, hairstyles, and ornaments were seen on the big screen for visual enjoyment, the stereotype was that the 'traditionally approved' look was appropriate for the young girl. In moments of appreciation for good behaviour, she would always be in tune with the traditionally correct attire. The different generations responded differently. New disapprovals were built, and the separation of taste became sharper.

At the emotional level, the frustrations and tensions of living in a restrictive society and dreaming about the free and normless pursuit of wish fulfilment were put together by film stories in a heady concoction which caught the fancy of the women spectators with its simple, easy to grasp formulations of the problems of living. In reality, life was getting more and more complicated and solutions were hard to find. But the films would take you to the Grand Reduction Sale of the dream world, in which you staked nothing and received the best of both the worlds. You could enjoy the raw sexuality with high-flown rhetoric about virtue. This, as one can see, acts as an anesthetic for development of a rational view. The trouble is, however, that films are always referred to as trivial, known to be fictional, not to be taken seriously. The deeper influence shows through the way the commercial circuits spread the 'filmi' ideas. Ideas of decorating the house, the designs of even ritual icons and other visual materials are made in the copy of the film. In many instances of visual considerations, a shift occurred that regarded visual effect as sufficient as long as it gave the impression of being something intended. For women, the 'look' of the precious metal, gold, was enough. For ornaments, swift movement from precious metals to tinsel and plastic was seen. There was a double advantage. It looked good and it was cheap, so you could have more of it. Ideas of 'matching' clothes, ornaments, footwear, and facial make-up were clearly influenced by film, and the markets were full of the cheap and the tinsel with a 'top' look. A whole vocabulary and jargon exists in Indian languages, of words from the English language taken up only with a specific meaning.

Emotional response to films is a complex phenomenon. There is a difference between the audience which has real life experiences of the atmosphere, the lifestyles portrayed in the films; and the audience which does not have such an experience. The later takes viewing a film as a substitute of real life experience in the absence of even a possibility of ever having a chance. The emotional trip has the added advantage and strength of letting them assume that they 'know' the places, events and people, which they have not actually seen. As the spectator receives the visual prepared by the director's decision of the camera placement, the spectator in turn, in terms of the director's compositions puts the scenes of the story together. The position of greatest significance is given to the spectator. In Indian society, even conceptually, women do not have an opportunity to take such a position. They are on the sidelines, behind the curtains or watching from a distance. The intimate scenes participated in the very manner of 'making' them, is a very different kind of experience that liberates the emotional response. It can be free from the usual controls and at the same time it can be very private, not available for scrutiny by any authority. Relating with a life-like image without the critical equipment tends to create a real emotional bond with a pseudo being. Different versions of the images being sold in this manner people the psychological world of the spectator. Under the deprivations of daily needs and impossibility of changing their lot in any substantial manner, the women find a wonderful escape from the harsh realities into a land of promise and wish fulfilment.

These emotional trips let the shallow ideas sink in. Acceptance of the system seeps in even as the heroine offers the vicarious joys. Ideas of destiny and fate persist. One's own sense of identity gets hitched to the husband's or the family's 'given' foreclosures. The educated, the modern, the earning woman having access to money and the power to take a decision about its use goes with the villainy of the characters portrayed in the typical story. Thus a complex set of ideas that keep the entertainment market going is formed. This did not exist in the Indian context, as the category of buying entertainment was new to the society as a whole which had its own norms and forms of theatre, devotional and secular song and dance and many more. The women were leading lives in which the song dance and poetry came in without having to be bought. The set of ideas that was woven in it had the framework of tradition along with a space to ask questions and express dissent. In acceptance of the tradition, there was a deeper understanding of the assumed character of norms and restrictions. Such cultural reading was neither necessary nor initiated by cinema. It was something you paid for and received. It did have a take it or leave it attitude. The audience took it, hardly noticing the consequences and sweetly encapsulating itself in the private world of escape, though there was always something decent to talk about, which was built in the story itself.

The story of Devis, Kumaris, Balas and extras does not end here. The self-regard implied in each of these settles with the repeated message of the marketplace. From the status of the Mother goddess (which was ritually bestowed on some occasions) to the status of an object of desire meant for satisfaction of the male, the passage has been parallel to the increasing strife for social recognition of women's rights and increasing violence against women. It is not a matter of blaming it on cinema. It is a matter of recognizing what accompanies the years of buying the images of a retrograde kind.

Contributors

Meena Kelkar is former Reader, Department of Philosophy, University of Pune.

Deepti Gangavane is Lecturer, Department of Philosophy, University of Pune.

Sucheta Paranjape is Lecturer, Department of Sanskrit, Tilak Maharashtra Vidyapeeth, Pune.

Nirmala Kulkarni is Research Scientist, Centre for Advanced Studies in Sanskrit, University of Pune.

Mangala Athalye is a Lecturer, Department of Philosophy, Abasaheb Garware College of Arts, Science and Commerce, Pune.

Lata Chhatre is Reader, Department of Philosophy, University of Pune.

Vaijayanti Belsare is Lecturer, Department of Philosophy, S.P. College, Pune.

Radhika Sheshan is Lecturer, Department of History, University of Pune.

Vidyut Bhagwat is Reader in Sociology and Director, Women Study Centre, University of Pune.

Shantishree Pandit is Reader, Department of Political Science and Public Administration and Director, International Centre, University of Pune.

Shyamala Vanarase is a Pune-based consulting psychologist, art critic and visiting faculty to National Film Archives, Pune.

Index